cut pour

965 3605

RESEARCH REPORT SERIES, INSTITUTE FOR SOCIAL RESEARCH

The Subjective Well-Being of Young Adults

Trends and Relationships

Willard L. Rodgers
Jerald G. Bachman

Survey Research Center
Institute for Social Research
The University of Michigan

1988

The Research Report Series of the Institute for Social Research is composed of significant reports published at the completion of a research project. These reports are generally prepared by the principal research investigators and are directed to selected users of this information. Research Reports are intended as technical documents which provide rapid dissemination of new knowledge resulting from ISR research.

Library of Congress Cataloging-in-Publication Data:

Rodgers, Willard L.
    The subjective well-being of young adults: trends and
relationships / by Willard L. Rodgers and Jerald G. Bachman.
        p.   cm. -- (Research report series / Institute for Social
Research, University of Michigan)
    Bibliography: p.
    ISBN 0-87944-323-5
    1. Young adults--United States--Attitudes. 2. Quality of life--
United States--Psychological aspects. 3. Married people--United
States--Attitudes. 4. Single people--United States--Attitudes.
5. Quality of life--United States--Statistical methods.
I. Bachman, Jerald G. II. Title. III. Series: Research report
series (University of Michigan. Institute for Social Research)

HQ799.7.R63 1988
305.2'35--dc19   88-9455
                                                              CIP

ISR Code Number 9027

Published in 1988 by:
Institute for Social Research
The University of Michigan, Ann Arbor, Michigan

6 5 4 3 2 1

Manufactured in the United States of America

PREFACE

We have two objectives in this monograph. On the one hand is a substantive focus: the description of the subjective quality of life of young people, and the estimation of the effects of major life transitions on the quality of life. On the other hand is a methodological focus: what procedures are most appropriately applied to panel data in order to estimate causal models? These objectives have been closely intertwined in our thinking throughout the analysis and we have found it difficult to divorce them in our writing.

We recognize that many, perhaps most, readers will not share our interest in both of these objectives. Some will be looking for answers to substantive questions about the subjective quality of life, or will have a general interest in psychological development during the late adolescent and early adult segment of the life span. At the end of Chapter 1 we provide an outline of the remaining chapters, along with a preview of the major findings, and hope that this will facilitate readers in finding their way to the particular chapters most central to their interests.

For the reader who is primarily interested in the methodological issue involved in choosing between alternative approaches to the estimation of causal models using panel data, it may be helpful to note that Chapter 6 provides the statistical framework for these alternatives, while Chapters 7 through 10 document a case study in which these methods have been applied to a particular substantive area.

ACKNOWLEDGEMENTS

The research described in this report was funded by a grant from the National Science Foundation. The data that we analyzed were originally collected under grants from the Russell Sage Foundation (1971 Quality of American Life study), the National Science Foundation (1978 Quality of American Life study), and the National Institute on Drug Abuse (Monitoring the Future study). We are grateful for the research support provided by Dawn Bare in data management and data analysis. We also want to thank our colleagues Greg Duncan and Frank Andrews for their careful reading of this report. The responsibility for the analyses and for our interpretations of those analyses rests, of course, entirely with us.

CONTENTS

SECTION II: CAUSAL ANALYSIS

TABLES

FIGURES

CHAPTER 1

INTRODUCTION

An overriding concern in our society since its very inception has been with the quality of life of the citizenry. Government agencies are devoted to keeping track of a host of indicators of how well we are doing with respect to such dimensions as income, unemployment, crime, and health. The bulk of such measures are what we call "objective" indicators of the quality of life because they refer to units that are more-or-less clearly defined and that can be enumerated without taking into account evaluations of any qualitative aspects that might distinguish one unit from another. While this objectivity makes it relatively easy to produce counts and to compare groups and years, it also means that dimensions that most of us would consider crucial are underrepresented in most descriptions of the quality of life: namely, those having to do with its subjective qualities. Dollars are countable, but they can mean something quite different according to how they are gained and who gets them, and how they are spent and who spends them. Indeed, subjectivity is implicit in the very term, "quality": any assessment of quality, whether with respect to beauty or to any other dimension, lies in the eye of the beholder.

It is because of such truisms that increasing emphasis has been placed on the *subjective* quality of life: how individuals evaluate their own lives and their various components. Such subjective evaluations are apparently only weakly explained in terms of the traditional social indicators that focus on economic and other objective conditions. The examination of differences and trends in these subjective measures, and the identification of what factors influence them, has been the focus of considerable research in the last two decades or so (Cantril, 1965; Bradburn, 1969; Campbell, Converse, and Rodgers, 1976; Andrews and Withey, 1976). Almost all of this research, however, has been concerned with the *adult* population. The study that we describe in this report is one attempt to correct this deficiency by exploiting a large volume of data that has been collected since 1975 concerning the subjective quality of life of high school seniors and recent graduates from high school.

There are substantial reasons for interest in the quality of life of adolescents and young adults, not only because of its intrinsic importance, but also for the additional insights such research could provide with respect to the interpretation of data from adults. Levels of satisfaction with life as a whole and with specific domains of life have been found to differ across age/cohort groups (Campbell *et al.*, 1976). Several explanations for this phenomenon have been offered, and support for some of these have been found in data analyses, but these explanations have not proved sufficient to explain completely the age relationship (Herzog and Rodgers, 1981, 1986).

1

Extension of the data base to younger age levels and to new cohorts may offer insights into the generality and explanations of the phenomenon.

Another characteristic of most research on the subjective quality of life is that it is restricted to data collected from cross-sectional designs. The paucity of longitudinal data means that we have little understanding of the dynamic aspects of individual well-being. A series of cross-sectional data sets allow aggregate trends to be detected, but tells us nothing about how stable are the feelings of individuals or about the extent to which events and transitions that characterize their lives are reflected in their evaluations of their situations. We can know from a cross-sectional study how much variation there is in such evaluations, and how strongly those evaluations are related to characteristics that differ across individuals such as their age or their income, but we learn very little from such a study about how individuals came to develop their evaluations. Panel data offer the opportunity to examine such changes. The late adolescent and early adult years are a particularly rich source of information, since they are characterized by major and frequent changes in living arrangements, marital status, schooling, and employment. The study of how subjective evaluations of their lives made by young persons change across these years offers the opportunity to gain valuable insights into the process by which such evaluations develop and change.

Panel data not only offer the opportunity to describe change and developmental processes, but even more important are the advantages they offer with respect to the estimation of causal models. The relationships observed in cross-sectional data are open to numerous interpretations with respect to causal mechanisms. Panel data are not the perfect answer to resolve such ambiguities, but they are a major advance over cross-sectional data. In particular, they allow greater certainty about temporal sequencing of events, and temporal priority is taken as a necessary condition for the inference of causality.

Techniques appropriate for the analysis of panel data are not as familiar to most social scientists as are those for the analysis of cross-sectional data. There is a smaller literature in which alternative techniques have been applied, and therefore there is less confidence in the soundness of statistical assumptions which underlie their use. In addition to its substantive focus, a second major objective of this monograph is to explicate and exemplify alternative approaches to the estimation of causal models from panel data.

Significance of the Research

The well-being of the populace is a primary objective of government and other institutions, and individual well-being is a primary objective of most people. Various approaches to the assessment of well-being have been proposed and developed. One such approach is the direct one of simply asking individuals to evaluate the quality of their lives. Questions can be raised about the validity and usefulness of such assessments, and there is reason to suspect the usefulness of subjective measures of this type as in-

2

dicators of *changes* in the quality of life or of *differences* in the quality of life of individuals or groups (Wilcox, 1978; Rodgers, 1981). There are apparently strong forces toward equilibrium levels of satisfaction, and although the mechanisms involved are not entirely clear, they likely include self-selection into social and physical environments that meet the needs of the individuals, adjustment of standards of comparison as conditions improve or deteriorate, and a tendency to deny the presence of unsatisfactory conditions. The simple fact is, however, that our knowledge about such processes remains limited, and there is a need for research concerning change, and factors that influence change, in measures of the subjective quality of life. The research described in this report is one step toward fulfilling that need.

The need for the type of analysis that we report here is cited in a review of studies of achievement:

> While virtually all of this review has been directed toward adolescent and early adult orientations and roles, two other phenomena, ongoing through the remainder of the life-cycle, merit comment. Each represents an area meriting much greater investigation in the future. *First, the generic life satisfactions and aspirations, held and readjusted throughout the adult years . . .* , are not well understood. How are these "achievement orientations" (basically noneconomic) related to those of adolescence and the early career? In what measure do they both reflect prior role experience and direct future undertakings?
> Second, adult roles (particularly one's job and occupation) act as socializing contexts, in part replacing the family and other aspects of social origins. The literature on job satisfaction has been the major source of studies in this area. . . *But the effects of work roles on other aspects of psychological functioning or on orientation to future roles* (rather than affective orientations to present or past roles) have been less extensively investigated. (Spenner and Featherman, 1978, pp. 408–9; emphasis added.)

Both of the areas cited by these reviewers as "meriting greater investigation" are addressed in this monograph. Moreover, a concern of a Presidential advisory committee on youth, as expressed in the final paragraph of its report, is also directly addressed in this report:

> Discussions of the desirability of various alternative environments for youth are very much hampered by the lack of appropriate instruments to measure the impact of social institutions on those within them. Often, measurement is limited to measures of academic success (graduation and test scores) and economic success (income and occupation). These measures do not capture all important aspects of an institution's impact. *More research is needed on non-cognitive measures of personal development and on more direct measures of social well being.* The fact that we can neither measure nor agree on a definition of what constitutes a good life should not deter us from trying to improve the measures we have and to develop new ones.

3

(Report of the Panel on Youth of the President's Science Advisory Committee, 1974, p. 175; emphasis added.)

Data Sets

The analyses presented in this report draw on two major lines of research that have been conducted at the Institute for Social Research: several studies of the subjective quality of life that have involved personal interviews with national samples of the adult (age 18 and older, for the most part) American population; and the Monitoring the Future project, which since 1975 has administered questionnaires annually to large-scale, nationally representative samples of high school seniors, with longitudinal follow-ups of each of these cohorts.

The Monitoring the Future Project

This section provides a brief description of the Monitoring the Future project. More detailed descriptions, including the sampling and field procedures and the characteristics of the respondents, are available in other publications (Bachman and Johnston, 1978; Johnston, Bachman, and O'Malley, 1985; plus others cited below). The project was launched by an initial five-year grant from the White House Special Action Office for Drug Abuse Prevention in 1974, and then taken over by the National Institute on Drug Abuse in 1975. The primary objective of the project is to monitor drug use, along with a wide range of potentially related dimensions, among American youth in their late teens and early twenties, and a considerable amount has been published on this subject (e.g., Johnston, O'Malley, and Bachman, 1984, 1985; Bachman, O'Malley, and Johnston, 1984; O'Malley, Bachman, and Johnston, 1983, 1984; and Bachman, Johnston, and O'Malley, 1981).

At the heart of the monitoring system is a series of annual, nationwide questionnaire surveys of 16,000 to 17,000 seniors in high schools, beginning with the class of 1975. Approximately 130 schools participate in the study in any given year. The senior year data collection procedures consist of questionnaire administrations of one class period in duration. Professional ISR interviewers conduct the administrations. Because of the limited time available in a class period, the very extensive instrument content has been distributed across five different questionnaire forms. A core section of demographic items and questions about drug use is common to all forms.

Another feature of the design, and one that is crucial to the analyses reported here, is that it includes a longitudinal component. Follow-up questionnaires are mailed annually to a specially selected subset of each senior class cohort. In order to monitor changes, the follow-up questionnaires contain many of the same questions as are used in the senior year, but they also include a number of new questions about experiences and behaviors after high school.

4

The data from this project have a limitation with respect to some of the types of questions that we have analyzed. Since the domain satisfaction questions were asked in only one of the five forms, and since other items that we might have wished to examine in relationship to those domain questionnaires were included only on one of the remaining four forms, such relationships could not be examined. This is not a problem for most of the objectives of the present study, since our primary concern is with the levels of satisfaction, their interrelationships, and how they are related to demographic characteristics of the respondents, all of which are included on the same form.

A summary of the base-year and follow-up data sets that we have used in our analyses is provided in Table 1–1. Note that the data span the years from 1976 through 1984, and cover an age range from approximately 18 through 24.

The Quality of American Life studies

The 1971 Quality of American Life study involved personal interviews with a national sample of adults age 18 and older. A geographic frame was used to select housing units with known, equal probabilities; an individual respondent within each selected household was designated using a procedure that gives each adult an equal chance. The overall response rate was 80 percent. Personal interviews, lasting an average of one hour, were conducted with 2,164 respondents; those interviews asked about perceptions and evaluations of environmental characteristics, and levels of satisfaction with various domains of experience. The findings from this study, which was funded by a grant from the Russell Sage Foundation, are reported most extensively in a monograph by Campbell *et al.* (1976).

For the 1978 Quality of American Life study, interviews were sought with one or two individuals at the same housing units as those from which interviews were obtained in 1971: (1) with a randomly selected adult from each household, and (2) also with the same individual who was interviewed in 1971 if that person was still living there. Additional housing units were selected to obtain a proper cross-sectional sample of all housing units existing in 1978. A total of 3,692 interviews were obtained in 1978, of which 691 were with individuals who also participated in 1971. The 1978 interview included many of the same questions that were asked in 1971, plus additional questions including a series on major events that had occurred to the respondent in the previous five years.

Preview of Chapter Contents

A preview of the contents of the remaining chapters of this book may prove helpful to the reader, especially for one with particular substantive or methodological interests who wants to get to the chapters most relevant to those specific topics. The remainder of this report is divided into two sections. The first of these sections is primarily descriptive, examining a

5

Table 1-1

Overview of Data sets from the Monitoring the Future Study Used in Analyses Described in This Report

High School Senior Class	Year of Data Collection								
	1976	1977	1978	1979	1980	1981	1982	1983	1984
1976	Age 18	Age 19	Age 20	Age 21	Age 22	Age 23	Age 24		
1977		Age 18	Age 19	Age 20	Age 21	Age 22	Age 23	Age 24	
1978			Age 18	Age 19	Age 20	Age 21	Age 22	Age 23	Age 24
1979				Age 18	Age 19	Age 20	Age 21	Age 22	Age 23
1980					Age 18	Age 19	Age 20	Age 21	Age 22

NOTES: The table entries indicate the modal ages of respondents; actual ages ranged from one year younger to one year older, and a very few lying outside that range. "Age 18" refers to the base-year, when the respondents were high school seniors. There were about 17,000 respondents in each such base-year sample.

The follow-up sample for each cohort was divided into two subsamples each with about 1,200 selections, who were mailed questionnaires in alternate years as shown.

variety of measures of the subjective quality of life, trends that may exist over time in their average levels, and their relationship to several characteristics of the respondents. The focus of the second section is on possible explanations of some of the relationships observed in the first section, and in particular on that between marital status and subjective well-being. A brief preview of each chapter in these two sections follows.

Chapter 2 provides descriptive data about age patterns and time trends in a variety of measures relevant to the subjective quality of life. Data are examined both for the full adult age range available from the 1971 and 1978 Quality of Life surveys, and specifically for the late adolescent and early adult years available from the Monitoring the Future cross-sectional and panel components. The dominant picture to emerge from our examination of these data is one of stability rather than change. While there are statistically significant age and secular trends on some variables and for some subgroups, these are generally small in magnitude.

The concern of Chapter 3 is with the quality of the measures of subjective well-being. Using data from three waves of panel data from several cohorts of young people included in the Monitoring the Future study, we assess the reliability and stability of several satisfaction measures. Our conclusion from this analysis is that level of satisfaction is moderately stable during the years following high school, though not so stable as to preclude the possibility of finding changes consequent to major life transitions. The reliabilities of the measures of satisfaction, however, are quite low, indicating that these variables include considerable measurement error.

Chapter 4 describes the relationship between marital status and subjective well-being measures. Four marital status categories are distinguished for adults: single, married, divorced or separated, and widowed. The most satisfied are those who are married and living with their spouses, while the least satisfied are those who are divorced or separated. Among young adults the number of divorced, separated, and widowed respondents is too small to permit useful analysis, but we find it useful to distinguish among single respondents according to whether they say that they are engaged to be married: the latter are about as well off as those who are already married. We also present data about levels of satisfaction reported retrospectively by adults who have been in a marital status category for varying lengths of time, as a first step toward examining the causal path. More useful in this respect are panel data from young adults. Patterns of changes in level of well-being are examined for respondents who have made various transitions in their marital status. It appears that life satisfaction tends to increase when a person makes a commitment to marriage but that it declines in the year or two following marriage. There is also evidence that those who are more satisfied with their lives are more likely to marry in the next year or so, suggesting a reciprocal relationship may exist between marital status and subjective well-being.

The relationships of other characteristics and transitions to subjective life quality are described in Chapter 5. Specifically, we examine differences between young adults who are students and those in various employment categories, and patterns of change which accompany changes in student and work status. Similarly we examine living arrangements of unmarried respondents, parenthood, and several other characteristics which often undergo major changes during the early adult years. Our findings indicate that, relative to these other factors, marital status is an important (but not overwhelming) predictor of subjective well-being.

Chapter 6 opens the second section of this report, and our focus shifts from the descriptive level of the first section to causal analysis of observed relationships. In Chapter 6 we describe various approaches that have been taken to the causal analysis of survey data. We focus our attention on two types of causal models, and consider two strategies for estimating the parameters of each of those types.

The first type of model is concerned with static relationships. In the context of this report, such a model might focus on explaining an observed relationship between a characteristic of individuals and the quality of their lives. This is the only type of model that can ordinarily be estimated from cross-sectional data. Panel data, however, offer distinct advantages over cross-sectional data even with respect to such static models. The more traditional approach in using panel data to estimate static models analyzes differences in the level on the dependent variable at a particular time, but includes prior level on that variable as a predictor of current level. An alternative is to analyze *changes* in the dependent variable. This approach has fallen into general disfavor; but we explore the reasons for this disfavor, and for the adoption of the first approach, and find them less than compelling on *a priori* grounds.

The second type of model that we describe in Chapter 6 is concerned not so much with the level of a dependent variable, but with *change* in that variable, and more specifically how various characteristics of individuals influence the rate of change. Panel data offer important advantages over cross-sectional data for the estimation of such dynamic models. More waves of data than are available for the analyses described in this report would be useful, but useful analyses are possible even with two or three waves of data. As with the estimation of static models, two approaches to the estimation of dynamic models are considered: one in which the dependent variable is level at a later data collection, and levels at earlier data collections are included as predictors; the second in which the dependent variable is change from one data collection to the next.

Chapters 7 and 8 are concerned with the estimation of static models. The focus of Chapter 7 is on the relationship between marital status and the subjective quality of life, and describes a series of analyses intended to test several hypotheses about causal pathways that might account for the observed relationship between these variables. We begin by examining three specific possibilities that would explain the observed relationship as spurious. Using data from the national Quality of Life surveys, we first examine the extent to which differences in demographic composition can explain the relationship between marital status and life satisfaction. We find that age differences may account for part (but not all) of the observed marital status differences in well-being. We repeat this question with respect to differences on a personality characteristic, level of personal competence, and find that this also may account for some of the marital status differences, but that most of these differences remain unexplained by the compositional and personality characteristics for which we have measures. Finally we ask whether differences in the ways respondents use the satisfaction scales might explain the marital status differences, and find that while there are indeed rather strong method effects on the satisfaction items, these apparently suppress, rather than explain, the underlying differences in satisfaction across marital statuses.

In the latter half of Chapter 7 we report a series of multiple regression analyses using data from the Monitoring the Future study in which we include marital status along with several other characteristics as predictors of subjective well-being. We use both of the approaches described in Chapter 6 to estimate the effects of marital status on subjective well-being; that is, we do parallel sets of regression analyses, in one set using level of satisfaction as the dependent variable, in the other set using change in satisfaction as the dependent variable. We find that the estimates of marital status effects based on change scores are generally smaller than, but in the same direction as, those based on static scores. We also find that the change score estimates are considerable more robust than the static score estimates, in that introducing other variables into the causal model has only slight effects on the former, but often substantial effects on the latter, estimates.

In Chapter 8 we return to the relationships between well-being and the characteristics described in Chapter 5. Based on the regression analyses described in Chapter 7, we estimate each of these relationships after controlling on the other variables. Again we compare the estimates of these relationships based on the two approaches described in Chapter 6. Analysis of both static and change scores indicate that marital status is one of the most important of the set of characteristics, whether the set of characteristics is considered singly or in a multiple regression analysis. Both types of analysis also indicate the importance of social relationships, as measured by dating frequency. For other characteristics, however, the static score estimates tend to indicate effects that are not detected with change scores. In particular, those living with parents appear to have lower subjective quality of life than other young adults, based on static scores, but no such effect is found from change scores; and the change score estimate of the effects of unemployment is not statistically significant and considerably smaller in magnitude than the static score estimate. While we cannot demonstrate that the change score estimates are more accurate than the static score estimates, on *a priori* grounds we expect the former to be less biased than the latter. Moreover, the standard errors of the change score estimates are only about ten percent larger than those of the static score estimates.

Chapter 9 illustrates the two approaches to the estimation of *dynamic* models that were described in Chapter 6, with the focus on changes in well-being that follow commitment to a marriage (either actual marriage or engagement). Only a simple bivariate model is considered, but it suffices to show that there can be important differences in the estimates from the two procedures. Both procedures agree in confirming that marriage, or the commitment to marriage, is associated with higher subjective well-being, but the analysis of change scores indicates, more clearly than does the analysis of static scores, that those who remain married decline in their level of well-being.

Chapter 10 is parallel to much of Chapters 7 and 8 in that it describes analyses intended to estimate the effects of transitions and changes with respect to the characteristics considered in those chapters on change in the subjective quality of life. We begin by estimating the effects of getting married, and changing living arrangements, on change in well-being. First, bivariate regression analyses are reported; then a series of multivariate analyses in which the changes with respect to the other characteristics are included as predictors. These multivariate analyses confirm the findings reported in earlier chapters that marriage has a positive effect on the subjective well-being of young people, and shows more clearly than have any analyses of static scores (including those using initial well-being scores as a predictor of later scores) that the initial elevation in well-being is followed by a decline. These findings persist after controlling on a set of additional characteristics. We then go on to estimate the effects of changes on these other characteristics. Using both change and static scores, we find that becoming a parent has relatively little effect on subjective well-being. Well-being tends to decline when a young person moves out of the student role, but the transition to full-time employment has relatively little effect, although becoming unemployed has a negative effect. With respect to some characteristics, we find some important differences between estimates based on static scores and those based on change scores: change scores fail to confirm a positive effect of change toward a more conservative political orientation or of an increase in frequency of attending religious services. Both approaches, however, indicate that the quality of life increases if frequency of dating increases, and it is plausible to suppose that some of the positive effects of dating (such as meaningful social relationships) are similar to the positive effects of engagement and marriage.

SECTION I DESCRIPTIVE DATA

CHAPTER 2

TIME AND AGE TRENDS IN
QUALITY OF LIFE MEASURES

The data described in this monograph were collected during the 1970s and early 1980s. If anecdotal and media evidence are to be believed, this period in American history was marked by economic upheaval; by changes in the political climate as well as changes in the holders of political offices; and by countless other changes in the educational system, in family life, in standards of morality, and so on. Did such turbulence lead to any substantial change in overall quality of life? The data that were collected in the 1971 and 1978 Quality of Life surveys, and in the nine waves of the Monitoring the Future from 1976 through 1984, permit us to address such questions. In this chapter, our focus will be on the question of whether there have been shifts in reported levels of satisfaction and happiness among older adolescents and young adults over the eight year period from 1976 through 1984; but to give more meaning to whatever change (or lack of change) is detected for this age group we will examine older age groups along with the focal younger age group.

Not only might we expect period trends, there are also compelling reasons to expect differences in the quality of life of persons of different ages, and in particular across the ages of late adolescence and early adulthood on which we focus our attention. It is at this stage in life that major decisions are made about educational goals, career ambitions, where to live, and with whom. A large proportion of young people experience such major transitions as leaving school, entering the labor force, leaving the parental home, and marriage. It is reasonable to suppose that such decisions and transitions have important influences on the quality of life experienced by individuals. If this is true, we could expect differences in the average quality of life reported across the young adult years as increasing proportions of the respondents have experienced these various events.

In this chapter our focus is on change at the aggregate rather than the individual level. In other words, we will examine changes in the average levels of reported satisfaction and will be ignoring most of the change that occurs at the individual level. Indeed, most of the data we will consider in this chapter were collected from different individuals in different years. The analysis of Monitoring the Future data will utilize successive cohorts of high school seniors, and most of the respondents in the two Quality of Life surveys were from non-overlapping samples. This chapter, with its focus on changes in average levels, is intended to serve as a backdrop to the remaining chapters of this monograph in which the focus will be on changes at the individual level.

It should also be noted that this chapter is meant to be descriptive rather than analytic, in the sense that we have not at this point specified any sort of causal model with respect to the relationships among the time and satisfaction variables. In particular, the differences observed between years of measurement and years of age of the respondents are not interpreted as indications of effects linked to period or age. Such issues will be considered in subsequent chapters; but at this point it is important to note that, depending on the specific data being analyzed, observed differences between years and age levels could equally well be interpreted as differences between birth cohorts. For example, data from successive cross-sections of high school seniors from the Monitoring the Future study were, on the one hand, collected in successive years and so could differ because the economic, political, and other contextual conditions differ between those years; and on the other hand, these data were collected from samples of persons born (predominantly) in successive years and so could differ because people born in different years differ in the values and standards against which they judge their current conditions in reaching a decision about how satisfied they are with their lives. On *a priori* grounds, we find period- and age-related explanations generally more compelling than cohort-related explanations. Therefore, we will generally simplify our descriptions in this chapter by speaking of period and age differences. It should be kept in mind, however, that such differences could also reflect cohort-related effects, or the interactive effects of some combination of age-, period-, and cohort-related factors.

Monitoring the Future Data

The trends in satisfaction with each of thirteen domains of life, and also the trends in overall life satisfaction and happiness, are summarized in Table 2-1. (The wording of each item and the yearly averages are shown in detail in Tables 2-A1 — 2-A16, included in an appendix to this chapter.) The correlations of each of these items with year are shown in the first data column in Table 2-1, and reveal that none of them shows a strong or even a monotonic trend over this eight-year period, although the large samples mean that even small correlation coefficients for linear time trends are statistically significant. There is a faint positive tendency in these time trends: twelve of the fifteen items have positive correlation coefficients, eight of which are statistically significant ($p < .05$), but *none* of which is as large as 0.05 in magnitude. In order of decreasing strength, the domains with significantly positive trends are:

(1) "Yourself" ($r = .045$);

(2) "Your educational experiences" ($r = .037$);

(3) "The way our government is operating" ($r = .037$);

(4) "The safety of things you own. . ." ($r = .028$);

(5) "The amount of time you have for doing things you want to do" ($r = .023$);

(6) "The way you spend your leisure time. . ." (r = .018);

(7) "Your friends and other people you spend time with" (r = .016); and

(8) "Your personal safety" (r = .014).

Analyses of variance were also done with each of the fifteen evaluative measures in turn taken as the dependent variable and with year as the control variable. Shown in the second column of Table 2–1 are the eta coefficients derived from these analyses of variance; these coefficients are useful because, unlike the correlation coefficients, they capture non-linear as well as linear trends across the years.[1] The eta coefficients are generally a bit larger than the correlation coefficients, but for only one variable is the difference substantial. This is the reported level of satisfaction with "The way our national government is operating," for which the eta coefficient is .150 — substantially larger than the etas for all of the remaining satisfaction measures. The pattern of mean satisfaction scores across years for this variable, as shown in Table 2-A13, is more readily interpreted in terms of presidential popularity than as a manifestation of any long-term historical pattern.

For the other fourteen items, the analyses of variance showed that although year of measurement had a statistically significant (p < .01) effect on all but three domains, the variance explained was only a small fraction of one percent of the total variance of each item (the eta coefficients, adjusted for degrees of freedom, were in the range of from 0.0 to 0.055). Comparison of the amount of variance explained by a linear trend to the total variance explained by year of measurement shows that the linear component is responsible for less than half of the total explained variance for all except two domains. These exceptions are with respect to satisfaction with "yourself" and with "your educational experience," for which the trends, while weak in absolute terms, are not only stronger than for any other satisfaction score, but are also largely linear (see Tables 2-A5 and 2-A8). Inspection of the actual mean values across years for these two items reveals little compelling evidence for a true secular trend, and this is even more true for the remaining items. It is our conclusion that the observed differences in satisfaction between years are better interpreted in terms of short-term factors rather than as long-term trends toward increasing satisfaction. Such short-term factors cannot be identified from these data, although one could speculate on the possible importance of national economic variables, international events, and so on.

The last two items listed in Table 2–1 are broader in scope than the others. The first of these is measured on the same satisfaction scale as those concerning specific domains, asking the respondents to describe "your life as a whole these days" (see Table 2-A12). There is no evidence of any

---

[1]It should be noted that the eta coefficients are adjusted for degrees of freedom; thus it is possible for eta to be lower than r (and this occurred in two instances).

13

Table 2–1
Summary of Time Trends on Satisfaction Items
(Monitoring the Future Base-Year Data, 1976–1984)

ITEM	Linear r	Analysis of Variance		
		eta	F	Prob.
SPECIFIC DOMAINS:				
Present Job	0.007	0.000	0.833	0.574
Neighborhood	0.010	0.026	3.669	0.000
Personal Safety	0.014	0.028	3.953	0.000
Safety of Property	0.028	0.040	7.084	0.000
Educational Experience	0.037	0.046	8.943	0.000
Friends	0.016	0.027	3.721	0.000
Relationship to Parents	0.008	0.024	3.215	0.001
Yourself	0.045	0.055	12.570	0.000
Standard of Living	−0.015	0.030	4.358	0.000
Time for Doing Things	0.023	0.040	7.246	0.000
Leisure Time Activities	0.018	0.032	4.905	0.000
How Government Operates	0.037	0.150	89.567	0.000
Fun You Are Having	−0.001	0.000	0.736	0.661
OVERALL LIFE:				
Life as a Whole	0.001	0.014	1.771	0.077
Happiness	−0.007	0.038	6.438	0.000

NOTE: The wordings of these items are given in Tables 2-A1
through 2-A15.

trend in the answers to this item ($r = .001$), or indeed of any differences across years (eta = 0.014, F = 1.771). The second item which seems to encompass an equally broad scope asks about happiness: "Taking all things together, how would you say things are these days—would you say you're very happy, pretty happy, or not too happy these days?" The answers to this item also do not show any monotonic trend across years ($r = -.007$). This is consistent with a finding reported elsewhere (Rodgers, 1982) for an earlier period: during the 1970s, no significant trend in happiness was detected among those under age 65, although there was a decline in happiness among those age 21 to 34 across the years from 1957 to 1971.

Differences in Satisfaction and Time Trends for Subgroups of Respondents

Perhaps the reason for the absence of any important trends in the levels of satisfaction reported across these years is that we have taken too broad a picture of young people. It is possible that there are trends and countertrends, depending on which group of people we consider. We could examine the trends among any number of groups, but in this report we focus on just three characteristics: race, sex, and plans of these high school seniors to attend college. To detect differences in the trends between groups defined by these dimensions, analyses of covariance were done for each of the satisfaction items and the happiness question.

The analyses for black and white differences are summarized in Table 2-2. In columns 2 and 3 are shown the mean values for white and black respondents, respectively, averaging across all nine years, and with the standard errors of these means shown in parentheses. Column 5 gives the difference in the mean values for the two racial groups. Similarly, columns 6 and 7 give the regression coefficients when each variable in turn is predicted by year, for whites and blacks respectively. These can be interpreted approximately as the average change per year. The last column shows the difference in the regression coefficients for whites and blacks, and again the standard errors are shown in parentheses.

Black respondents expressed significantly ($p < .05$) less happiness than did white respondents, and less satisfaction with life as a whole and with ten of the thirteen specific domains. Blacks reported significantly more satisfaction with just two domains: "yourself" and "the way you get along with your parents." The "satisfaction with yourself" item may be interpreted as an abbreviated measure of self-esteem, and from this perspective the relatively high satisfaction of black high school seniors is consistent with previous research showing that black young men have higher levels of self-esteem than do whites (Drury, 1980). The interpretation of the present finding, as well as those from previous studies, is called into question by Bachman and O'Malley (1984), who reanalyzed data from several large national samples of young people and found that the black-white difference in self-esteem disappears if a different scoring method is used: that is, if levels of positive or negative responses are ignored, thereby eliminating what may be a confounding factor, the tendency of black respondents to use extreme response categories to a greater extent than white respondents. Indeed, these differences in the use of the response scale complicate the interpretation of any observed difference in mean satisfaction levels between blacks and whites.

The trends in the responses of black respondents across time differs at a statistically significant level ($p < .05$) from the trend for whites for two of the fifteen items. As shown in Table 2–2, white students show a slight (and significantly) positive trend in their responses to the question about satisfaction with time for doing things they want to do; the regression coefficient is 0.023 on the seven-point scale. For blacks, the trend is negative ($-.016$, which is *not* significantly different from zero but which *is* significantly different from the value for whites). The other domain for which blacks show a trend that is significantly different from that for whites is with respect to "the way our national government is operating." The trend for blacks on this item is negative (regression coefficient $= -.060$), while for whites the trend is positive (.040). Inspection of the yearly means, however, reminds us of the peculiar historical pattern for this item, and suggests that the present finding is of more interest with respect to what it says about political and economic changes over this period than with respect to quality of life concerns. Specifically, the difference between blacks and whites is primarily a difference in the timing of an upturn in satisfaction with government operations; for whites, an upturn is observed beginning with the 1981 data, whereas for blacks the upturn is not observed until the 1983 data.

Those high school seniors who expected to complete four years of college were significantly more satisfied than other seniors in assessing their life as a whole and nine of the thirteen domains about which they were asked (Table 2–3). College-bound students were significantly less satisfied with their friendships, and there were not significant differences in satisfaction with their present jobs (among those who were working as high school seniors), with the ways in which they spent their leisure time, or with the fun they were having; but for all other satisfaction questions the college-bound students were more satisfied than those who had no plans for college. We suspect that these differences reflect mostly the socio-economic differences between students who do plan to go to college and those who do not, rather than being direct results of differences in plans for further education. In addition, past educational success, which correlates strongly with college plans, probably contributes heavily to satisfaction with educational experiences and perhaps also to positive relationships with parents.

For four of the satisfaction items, college-bound students show more favorable trends across time than their non-college-bound classmates: their "neighborhood," "safety of things you own," their "educational experience," and "the way the national government is operating." There is also a very small, but statistically significant, decline in happiness among non-college bound students, but no change for those planning on college. Such trends suggest that the differences in the levels of satisfaction among these two groups of students has broadened over the last decade. Again, however, it should be emphasized that none of these trends is large in absolute terms.

Female respondents were significantly less satisfied than males with six of the domains, and significantly more satisfied with one. As shown in Table 2–4, girls reported more satisfaction with their "friends and other people [they] spend time with." The girls expressed somewhat more happiness than the boys, but boys report greater satisfaction with their lives as a whole. As noted in O'Malley and Bachman (1979), the boys were, on the average, more satisfied with "yourself." Boys also reported more satisfaction with their "neighborhood," "personal safety," "the way you get along with your parents," "the amount of time for doing things you want to do," and "the way you spend your leisure time."

There are significant differences between males and females in the trends on answers to two of these satisfaction items: (1) boys show a trend toward more satisfaction with the safety of their property (regression coefficient = .032), while girls show no time trend (b = .008)); and (2) boys show a trend toward more satisfaction with the way the government is operating (b = .043), while girls show no overall trend (b = .007). Again, the peculiar time pattern observed for the latter item dominates the weak linear trend, even for females; inspection of the mean values for each sex and for each year shows that females were somewhat less satisfied with the national government in 1976 through 1980, but that this pattern reversed in 1982 and 1984.

Age Trends

There is very little variation in the ages of respondents in the base year of the Monitoring the Future study, so this is not a useful source of data for exploring age patterns in responses to satisfaction measures. Subsets of these respondents, however, participated in follow-up data collections conducted between one and six years after their senior years in high school, and data from these follow-ups along with the base year data provide information about differences in satisfaction levels among persons in their late adolescence and early adult years.

Age patterns were examined for two global assessments of the quality of life: "satisfaction with life as a whole," and "happiness." We restrict ourselves to these global measures because they were asked of all or most of the respondents, whereas the more specific domain satisfaction questions shown along with these global items in the previous section were asked only of respondents on one of five questionnaire forms used in the Monitoring the Future study. Since we are necessarily restricted to the subset of respondents who were asked to, and did, participate in at least one follow-up data collection, the number who completed that particular form is rather small, producing substantial sampling variability in the estimates of the mean domain satisfaction levels at each age.

As explained in Chapter 1, subsamples of the participants in the base-year data collections with high school seniors were asked to participate in follow-up data collections in subsequent years: half of those selected were mailed questionnaires one year, the other half two years, after high school. Those in both subsamples have been mailed further follow-up questionnaires at two-year intervals — eventually this will extend to at least ten years after high school, although data for the present analysis cover only the first six years post high school. The base-year data are from the years 1976

Table 2-2
Differences in Time Trends on Satisfaction Items
White and Black Respondents
(Monitoring the Future Base-Year Data, 1976-1984)

ITEM	Mean			Trend		
	Whites	Blacks	Diff.	Whites	Blacks	Diff.
SPECIFIC DOMAINS:						
Present Job	4.868 (0.017)	4.513 (0.055)	0.355* (0.058)	0.011 (0.007)	-0.007 (0.021)	0.018 (0.022)
Neighborhood	5.300 (0.014)	4.770 (0.042)	0.530* (0.044)	0.009 (0.006)	0.013 (0.014)	-0.005 (0.015)
Personal Safety	5.649 (0.013)	4.817 (0.041)	0.832* (0.043)	0.013* (0.005)	0.013 (0.013)	0.001 (0.014)
Safety of Property	4.637 (0.015)	4.063 (0.044)	0.574* (0.047)	0.029 (0.021)	0.002 (0.035)	0.026 (0.016)
Educational Experience	5.006 (0.013)	4.984 (0.038)	0.022 (0.040)	0.021* (0.005)	0.035* (0.013)	-0.014 (0.014)
Friends	6.007 (0.010)	5.719 (0.032)	0.288* (0.033)	0.011* (0.004)	-0.002 (0.010)	0.013 (0.011)
Relationship to Parents	5.332 (0.014)	5.430 (0.038)	-0.098* (0.041)	0.003 (0.006)	0.011 (0.014)	-0.008 (0.015)
Yourself	5.371 (0.012)	5.852 (0.033)	-0.481* (0.035)	0.029* (0.005)	0.018 (0.012)	0.011 (0.013)

Table 2-2 (continued)
Time Trends among Blacks and Whites

ITEM	Mean			Trend		
	Whites	Blacks	Diff.	Whites	Blacks	Diff.
Standard of Living	5.612 (0.012)	5.114 (0.039)	0.498* (0.040)	-0.007 (0.005)	0.005 (0.012)	-0.012 (0.013)
Time for Activities	4.370 (0.015)	4.237 (0.043)	0.133* (0.046)	0.023* (0.006)	-0.016 (0.015)	0.039* (0.016)
Leisure Time Activities	5.259 (0.013)	4.997 (0.041)	0.262* (0.043)	0.017* (0.005)	0.013 (0.013)	0.004 (0.015)
How Gov't Operates	3.248 (0.012)	2.818 (0.035)	0.429* (0.037)	0.040* (0.005)	-0.060* (0.012)	0.100* (0.013)
Fun You Are Having	5.260 (0.012)	4.911 (0.038)	0.349* (0.040)	0.000 (0.005)	0.004 (0.013)	-0.004 (0.013)
OVERALL LIFE:						
Life as a Whole	5.198 (0.012)	4.910 (0.036)	0.288* (0.038)	0.006 (0.005)	0.005 (0.012)	0.000 (0.013)
Happiness	2.082 (0.0C4)	1.872 (0.012)	0.211* (0.013)	0.000 (0.002)	-0.001 (0.004)	0.000 (0.005)

NOTES: The wordings of these items are given in Tables 2-A1 through 2-A15.

The entries in the "Trend" columns for whites and blacks are unstandardized regression coefficients.

The parenthesized entries are standard errors of the estimated means, trends, and differences.

Asterisks indicate trends that are statistically significant ($p < .05$).

Table 2-3
Differences in Time Trends on Satisfaction Items
Respondents With and Without Plans to Attend College
(Monitoring the Future Base-Year Data, 1976-1984)

ITEM	Mean			Trend		
	College	Non-coll.	Diff.	College	Non-coll.	Diff.
SPECIFIC DOMAINS:						
Present Job	4.846 (0.021)	4.809 (0.025)	0.037 (0.033)	-0.002 (0.009)	0.001 (0.010)	-0.003 (0.013)
Neighborhood	5.267 (0.017)	5.162 (0.021)	0.105* (0.027)	0.016* (0.007)	-0.005 (0.008)	0.021* (0.011)
Personal Safety	5.588 (0.016)	5.421 (0.019)	0.167* (0.025)	0.008 (0.007)	-0.001 (0.007)	0.009 (0.010)
Safety of Property	4.586 (0.019)	4.508 (0.022)	0.078* (0.029)	0.031* (0.008)	0.000 (0.008)	0.031* (0.011)
Educational Experience	5.129 (0.016)	4.867 (0.019)	0.262* (0.025)	0.026* (0.006)	0.007 (0.007)	0.020* (0.010)
Friends	5.938 (0.013)	5.999 (0.015)	-0.061* (0.020)	0.010* (0.005)	0.004 (0.006)	0.005 (0.008)
Relationship to Parents	5.398 (0.017)	5.284 (0.020)	0.114* (0.026)	-0.002 (0.007)	0.009 (0.008)	-0.010 (0.010)
Yourself	5.446 (0.014)	5.400 (0.017)	0.046* (0.023)	0.026* (0.006)	0.027* (0.007)	-0.002 (0.009)

Table 2-3 (continued)
Time Trends among Those With and Without College Plans

ITEM	Mean			Trend		
	College	Non-coll.	Diff.	College	Non-coll.	Diff.
Standard of Living	5.624 (0.015)	5.424 (0.018)	0.200* (0.024)	-0.014* (0.006)	-0.019* (0.007)	0.005 (0.009)
Time for Activities	4.385 (0.019)	4.280 (0.023)	0.106* (0.029)	0.013 (0.008)	0.019* (0.009)	-0.006 (0.011)
Leisure Time Activities	5.217 (0.016)	5.210 (0.020)	0.007 (0.026)	0.009 (0.007)	0.014 (0.008)	-0.005 (0.010)
How Gov't Operates	3.297 (0.015)	3.060 (0.018)	0.237* (0.023)	0.039* (0.006)	-0.002 (0.007)	0.041* (0.009)
Fun You Are Having	5.217 (0.015)	5.178 (0.019)	0.039 (0.024)	0.006 (0.006)	-0.010 (0.007)	0.016 (0.009)
OVERALL LIFE:						
Life as a Whole	5.235 (0.014)	5.046 (0.017)	0.190* (0.023)	0.000 (0.006)	-0.002 (0.007)	0.002 (0.009)
Happiness	2.081 (0.006)	2.011 (0.006)	0.070* (0.008)	0.001 (0.002)	-0.008* (0.002)	0.009* (0.003)

NOTES: See Notes to Table 2-2.

Table 2-4
Differences in Time Trends on Satisfaction Items
Male and Female Respondents
(Monitoring the Future Base-Year Data, 1976-1984)

ITEM	Mean			Trend		
	Males	Females	Diff.	Males	Females	Diff.
SPECIFIC DOMAINS:						
Present Job	4.841 (0.022)	4.802 (0.023)	0.039 (0.031)	0.006 (0.009)	0.001 (0.009)	0.005 (0.013)
Neighborhood	5.266 (0.018)	5.147 (0.018)	0.119* (0.027)	0.006 (0.007)	0.007 (0.007)	-0.001 (0.010)
Personal Safety	5.717 (0.016)	5.296 (0.018)	0.422* (0.024)	0.016* (0.007)	0.001 (0.007)	0.015 (0.009)
Safety of Property	4.554 (0.020)	4.528 (0.019)	0.026 (0.028)	0.032* (0.008)	0.008 (0.008)	0.024* (0.011)
Educational Experience	4.967 (0.017)	5.014 (0.017)	-0.046 (0.024)	0.023* (0.007)	0.026* (0.006)	-0.003 (0.009)
Friends	5.906 (0.014)	6.014 (0.013)	-0.107* (0.019)	0.012* (0.005)	0.003 (0.005)	0.009 (0.008)
Relationship to Parents	5.409 (0.017)	5.281 (0.018)	0.129* (0.025)	0.008 (0.007)	0.003 (0.007)	0.005 (0.010)
Yourself	5.552 (0.015)	5.328 (0.015)	0.225* (0.022)	0.032* (0.006)	0.023* (0.006)	0.009 (0.008)

Table 2-4 (continued)
Time Trends among Males and Females

ITEM	Mean			Trend		
	Males	Females	Diff.	Males	Females	Diff.
Standard of Living	5.549 (0.016)	5.506 (0.016)	0.043 (0.023)	-0.009 (0.006)	-0.013* (0.006)	0.005 (0.009)
Time for Activities	4.424 (0.020)	4.262 (0.020)	0.162* (0.028)	0.018* (0.008)	0.015 (0.008)	0.003 (0.011)
Leisure Time Activities	5.300 (0.017)	5.128 (0.018)	0.172* (0.025)	0.010 (0.007)	0.014* (0.007)	-0.004 (0.010)
How Gov't Operates	3.178 (0.016)	3.192 (0.015)	-0.015 (0.022)	0.043* (0.006)	0.007 (0.006)	0.036* (0.009)
Fun You Are Having	5.205 (0.016)	5.190 (0.017)	0.015 (0.023)	0.007 (0.006)	-0.008 (0.006)	0.015 (0.009)
OVERALL LIFE:						
Life as a Whole	5.184 (0.015)	5.099 (0.016)	0.084* (0.022)	0.004 (0.006)	-0.001 (0.006)	0.005 (0.009)
Happiness	2.022 (0.006)	2.065 (0.006)	-0.043* (0.008)	0.000 (0.002)	-0.004 (0.002)	0.004 (0.003)

NOTES: See Notes to Table 2-2.

through 1980 only, and only respondents who participated in at least one follow-up data collection are included in the base-year means.

The mean levels of life satisfaction and happiness at the base year and at follow-ups conducted from one to six years after the base year are shown in Table 2-5, separately for males and females. If there is any relationship at all between age and these measures, it is a very weakly positive trend. The correlation between age and happiness for women is 0.045, for men 0.032; and for life satisfaction the correlations are even smaller. Examination of the proportion of respondents at each age who said that they were "very happy" confirms the positive trend indicated by the correlation coefficients: only 21 percent of the women said that they were very happy with their lives at the base-year data collection, but 29 percent or more gave this reply when asked two or more years after high school. For men, the proportion very happy increased from 17 percent in the base year to 23 percent or more after three years.

In interpreting the patterns observed in Table 2-5, weak though they appear to be, it should also be noted that period differences are confounded to some extent with the age differences. Base-year data (from respondents who were about 18 years old) were collected in 1976 through 1980, whereas data at four years after high school (approximately age 22) were collected in 1980 through 1984. However, very little change was observed on these global measures across time (cf. Table 2-1), so unless there is some unsuspected interaction of period and age it is unlikely that this possible confounding has distorted the age pattern.

National Quality of Life Data

The Quality of Life studies lack the time-series depth offered by the nine waves of the Monitoring the Future data, but do offer a much broader age range, thus permitting a comparison of age and period trends for young people with the corresponding trends for older people. Table 2-6 summarizes a large amount of data from the 1971 and 1978 studies.

In this analysis, respondents were classified into nine age groups of seven years each: 18-24, 25-31, and so on, up to a final category consisting of those age 74 and older. The coefficients shown in the first two data columns of Table 2-6 may be interpreted as the average increase or decrease in satisfaction when age increases by seven years.[1] This table replicates previously reported analyses of the relationship between age and satisfaction measures (Herzog and Rodgers, 1981): satisfaction with all but one of the specific domains increases with age, weakly but consistently, both in the 1971 and the 1978 studies. The one exception, health, is entirely reasonable, given the objective decline in health that generally accompanies

---

[1]Preliminary analyses, not reported here, showed that relationships between age and the various satisfaction measures were all close to linear; the squared correlation coefficients were similar in magnitude to Hays' omega statistic, which estimates the total – linear plus non-linear – explanatory power of the nine age categories.

24

Table 2-5

Age Differences in Measures of Life Satisfaction and Happiness, Age 18 to 24

(Monitoring the Future Panel Data)

Number of Years Beyond High School	Approximate Age	Life Satisfaction				Happiness			
		Females		Males		Females		Males	
		Mean	% Sat.	Mean	% Sat.	Mean	% Hap.	Mean	% Hap.
0	18	4.790	21.5	4.765	20.6	2.085	20.9	2.051	17.2
1	19	4.834	22.1	4.794	20.3	2.134	25.2	2.065	18.5
2	20	4.827	22.5	4.707	23.3	2.188	29.3	2.076	20.6
3	21	4.915	19.4	4.806	19.7	2.194	30.4	2.105	23.1
4	22	4.904	20.4	4.821	19.8	2.201	31.1	2.091	23.1
5	23	4.898	20.0	4.794	21.2	2.197	31.0	2.129	26.9
6	24	4.849	21.9	4.751	22.2	2.169	29.3	2.089	23.1
Eta (adj.)		0.029		0.025		0.059		0.029	
r		0.018		0.003		0.045		0.032	

NOTES: The question wordings and scales for these items are given in Table 2-A12 (life satisfaction) and 2-A15 (happiness). Note, however, that the data in this table are from a different set of respondents than are those in the earlier tables: whereas those tables were from base-year data collections with high school seniors using just one of five forms (i.e., the form which included the larger set of domain satisfaction items), these data are based on data from respondents in the follow-up samples only, for those using four (satisfaction) or all five (happiness) of the forms.

"% Sat." is the percentage of respondents who said that they were "completely satisfied" with their lives.

"% Hap." is the percentage of respondents who said that they were "very happy."

Table 2-6
Age Trends in Satisfaction Measures
(1971 and 1978 Quality of Life Data)

ITEM	Age/Cohort Trend		Age/Period Trend, 1971 to 1978	
	1971	1978	Overall	Interactions
SPECIFIC DOMAINS:				
(a) Community	0.130	0.089	0.132	18-24: +.289 25-73: (+.086)
(b) Neighborhood	0.146	0.106	(0.065)	18-24: +.259 25-73: (+.017)
(c) Dwelling Unit	0.151	0.121	0.192	18-24: (+.000) 25-52: +.325 53-73: (+.065)
(d) Education	0.155	0.042	-0.244	18-38: -.190 39-45: -.697 46-73: (-.144)
(e) Health	-0.175	-0.123	-0.251	18-52: -.328 53-73: (-.041)
(f) Spare Time	0.089	0.063	-0.112	n.s.
(g) Life in U.S.	0.104	0.078	0.102	18-31: +.235 32-73: (+.039)
(h) Friendships	0.076	0.046	(0.010)	n.s.
(i) Family Life	0.067	0.087	(-.066)	18-66: -.082 67-73: (+.146)
(j) St. of Living	0.132	0.102	(-.033)	n.s.
(k) Savings	0.163	0.192	(0.018)	18-24: -.447 25-73: +.134
(l) Job	0.079	0.125	(0.042)	18-59: (+.004) 60-73: +.277

Table 2-6 (continued)
Age Trends in Satisfaction Measures

ITEM	Age/Cohort Trend		Age/Period Trend, 1971 to 1978	
	1971	1978	Overall	Interactions
(m) Housework	0.100	0.128	-0.282	18-38: -.441 39-52: (-.014) 53-73: -.262
(n) Marriage	0.050	0.056	(0.008)	18-24: -.261 25-73: (+.046)
OVERALL LIFE:				
(o) Life as a Whole	-0.040	-0.053	(0.028)	n.s.
(p) Happiness	(-.004)	(-.003)	(0.031)	n.s.

NOTES: The age/cohort trends are estimated from cross-sectional data collected in the 1971 and 1978, while the age/period trends are the changes in the average levels of satisfaction for persons age 18 to 73 in 1971 and those age 25 and older in 1978.

All the satisfaction measures used a seven-point scale ranging from (1) "Completely satisfied," to (4) "Neutral," to (7) "Completely dissatisfied." The other four points were not given verbal tags.

The specific item wordings are as follows (the variable numbers refer to the codebooks for the archived data sets -- Campbell, Converse, and Rogers, 1975; and Campbell and Converse, 1980; if there are minor wording differences between the two surveys, that from the 1978 is given):

(a) V101/V45 "Here is a card that I want you to use to tell me how satisfied you are with (CITY/TOWNSHIP/COUNTY) as a place to live. This is how we will use it. If you are completely satisfied with (CITY/TOWNSHIP/COUNTY) as a place to live you would say "one." If you are completely dissatisfied, you would say "seven." If you are neither completely satisfied nor completely dissatisfied, you would put yourself from two to six; for example, four means you are neutral, or just as satisfied as you are dissatisfied. How satisfied are you with (CITY/TOWNSHIP/COUNTY) as a place to live?"

(b) V102/V53 "And what about this particular neighborhood in (CITY/TOWNSHIP/COUNTY). All things considered, how satisfied or dissatisfied are you with this neighborhood as a place to live?"

(c) V118/V56 "Considering everything, how satisfied or dissatisfied are you with this (house/apartment/mobile home)?"

(d) V154/V111 "How satisfied are you with the amount of education you received?"

(e) V269/V121 "Of course most people get sick now and then, but overall, how satisfied are you with your own health?"

(f) V239/V198 "Overall, how satisfied are you with the ways you spend your spare time?"

(g) V131/V79 "All things considered, how satisfied are you with life in the United States today?"

(h) V279/V240 "All things considered, how satisfied are you with your friendships -- with the time you can spend with friends, the things you do together, the number of friends you can have, as well as the particular people who are your friends?"

(i) V318/V268 "All things considered, how satisfied are you with your family life -- the time you spend and the things you do with members of your family?"

(j) V275/V301 "The things people have -- housing, cars, furniture, recreation, and the like -- make up their standard of living. Some people are satisfied with their standard of living, others feel it is not as high as they would like. How satisfied are you with your standard of living?"

(k) V276/V302 "How satisfied are you with your family's situation as far as savings and investments are concerned?"

(l) V509/V624 This variable uses information from different questions asked of employed, unemployed, retired, and homemaker respondents. For those employed the question was: "All things considered, how satisfied are you with your job?"

(m) V506/V667 This variable uses information from different questions asked of working, unemployed, retired, and homemaker respondents (women only). For those employed the question was "Overall, how satisfied are you with being a homemaker -- I don't mean with your family life, but with your housework?"

(n) V300/V252 "All things considered, how satisfied are you with your marriage?"

(o) V357/V425 "We have talked about various parts of your life, now I want to ask you about your life as a whole. How satisfied are you with your life as a whole these days?"

(p) V373/V454 "Taking all things together, how would you say things are these days -- would you say you're very happy, pretty happy, or not too happy these days?"

aging. The age relationship to overall life satisfaction is also negative, although very weak; and there is virtually no relationship observed between happiness and age.

As was pointed out early in this chapter, such age differences could reflect cohort- as well as age-related effects. In a cross-sectional study, age is completely confounded with cohort. It is useful, therefore, to look at the same data from a different perspective, now taking more direct advantage of the fact that the same questions were asked on two different occasions. Since these occasions were seven years apart, we can examine differences in average satisfaction for people in the same cohort but seven years apart in age. Unfortunately, this does not eliminate the possible confounding of age-related effects with other time-related variables. Not only are the respondents from the second survey seven years older than their counterparts interviewed in the first survey, they also were interviewed in a different year, so that age-related effects are now confounded with period-effects.

The third data column in Table 2-6 shows the differences in satisfaction levels for people born in the approximate range of years, 1898 to 1953 (specifically, those who were age 18 to 73 in 1971 are compared to those age 25 and older in 1978; non-significant differences — $p < .05$ — are shown in parentheses). Some of these age-period differences are similar to the age-cohort differences shown in the second and third columns of the table, but there are also several discrepancies. Whereas the analysis of cross-sectional data indicated significant increases in satisfaction across age levels for all fourteen domains except health, the analysis of longitudinal data indicates significant increases with age for only three domains: community of residence, dwelling unit, and life in the United States. Three of the domains which show an *increase* with age in cross-sectional data show a significant *decrease* with age in these longitudinal data: educational attainment, spare time activities, and housework (asked of women only). Satisfaction with health shows a decline with age in both types of data, but the decline appears stronger in the longitudinal data. Satisfaction with the remaining seven domains, and also life satisfaction and happiness, show only small, non-significant changes with age in these longitudinal data.

If we assume that there are no cohort effects (and it must be emphasized that this is an untestable assumption) and that there are no interaction effects involving period and age (an assumption which we will soon call into question) then the difference in the age effects as estimated from longitudinal and cross-sectional data can be attributed to period effects. This would lead us to the conclusion that satisfaction with several domains decreased in the interval between 1971 and 1978. Satisfaction with educational attainment and with housework showed the biggest such declines, .3 to .4 on the seven-point satisfaction scale. A decline of about .2 was registered with respect to spare time activities, and declines of about .1 were registered with respect to health, standard of living, and savings. Despite these declines in satisfaction with several domains, and despite the absence of significant increases in satisfaction for any of the domains included in the studies, there was a significant increase in overall life satisfaction.

Given the strong assumptions that had to be made to obtain these estimates for period effects, we do not place much confidence in their accuracy. Nevertheless, they do make some sense in terms of the events and trends across this period. For example, the decline in satisfaction with standard of living could well reflect the recession of 1974–75 and the generally slow economic growth of the 1970s. The decline in satisfaction with savings could reflect these factors and also the high rate of inflation that characterized these years. Such inflation may have shaken people's values concerning the virtues of saving and their confidence in the usefulness of their accumulated savings and investments. The decline in satisfaction with education could be a reflection of the technological advances of the period and its effect on the demand in the labor market for increasing amounts of education. And the decline in satisfaction with housework might well reflect the concerns expressed in the women's movement for more equitable treatment of men and women in the labor market, questioning of the traditional housewife role, and so on.

Assuming that the observed differences do indeed reflect period-related factors, there is evidence that these effects are not uniform across age levels; that there are, in fact, age-period interactions. Statistically significant interactions are shown in the last column of Table 2–6. These patterns call into question some of our interpretations of period effects in the previous paragraph, offer supporting evidence for others of those interpretations, and in general lead to greater specificity in our interpretations of period effects. For example, the decline in satisfaction with educational attainment is considerably stronger for people born in the years 1926–32: that is, people who were in the middle of their careers in the period from 1971 through 1978 and who may have felt themselves most vulnerable to competition for advancement and entry into new jobs from those with more education. These were people whom Levinson (1978) said were most likely to experience a mid-life crisis, questioning the value of their current careers and considering alternatives — alternatives which they might well have considered constricted by their level of educational attainment. This explanation, however, does not fit the pattern with respect to satisfaction with housework, which declined significantly for all *except* those born in 1919 to 1932.

On the other hand, satisfaction with life in the U.S., which showed little or no change overall across this period, increased by about a quarter of a point on the 7-point satisfaction scale for those born in 1940–1953. These include another group familiar in best-sellers and the news media: the college students of the late 1960s and early 1970s, many of whom were active in anti-Vietnam demonstrations and who by 1978 had begun to settle into often-traditional careers and in the process became more conventional and conservative.

Satisfaction with savings, which showed an overall decline that we speculated might reflect the high inflation rate during this period, actually increased somewhat for all except the youngest cohort (those born in 1947 to 1953). Since many in this cohort left the parental home and established their own households during this period, the decline is probably attributable to change in their own financial situations rather than a reflection of a period effect. Similarly, there was a decline in marriage satisfaction for those in this cohort, but no significant change for those in previous cohorts; this decline probably reflects changes in individual circumstances, such as the birth of children and increasing responsibilities, rather than a period effect. This youngest cohort also shows an interesting pattern with respect to satisfaction with the residential environment: an increase in average satisfaction with the community and neighborhood of residence, but no change in satisfaction with dwelling unit, whereas older cohorts showed no significant change on the first two of these domains but increased satisfaction with their dwelling units. Perhaps this also reflects the fact that many in the youngest cohort were moving out of their parental homes and establishing their own households in communities and neighborhoods of their own choice, and therefore ones with which they were more satisfied; but the quality of their own housing units would often be lower than those of their parents.

At the other end of the age spectrum, satisfaction with one's job increased for those born in 1898 to 1911, whereas there was no change, on the average, for those in later cohorts. This can most readily be explained as a selection effect, in that those who are more dissatisfied with their jobs are more likely to retire at a younger age. This interpretation is not straightforward, since those who were retired were asked about their satisfaction with their previous job and their answers were combined with those of persons still working concerning their present jobs. Thus it is necessary to suppose either (a) that reported satisfaction level tends to increase after leaving a job (that is, things look better in retrospect than they do as they are experienced), or (b) that some people in their sixties quit jobs that they dislike and start jobs, perhaps on a part-time basis, that they enjoy more.

Perhaps the least expected pattern shown in Table 2–6 concerns satisfaction with health. There was a decline in satisfaction for those born after 1918, but an increase for those in earlier cohorts. Since health problems appear more frequently at older ages, we expected that satisfaction would, if anything, decline more rapidly among those in the earlier cohorts. Perhaps it is this very expectation that explains the pattern, however; since most of us expect health problems to appear in older age, many older people may be pleasantly surprised by the absence of such problems, and those who do experience problems may judge them less harshly because of their lowered expectations. On the other hand, health problems do appear at younger ages as well, and those who experience them may find them all the more troublesome because they are unexpected.

There were no significant age-period interactions with respect to either of the more global items, overall life satisfaction and happiness. This is somewhat of a contrast to trends observed with respect to happiness over the period from 1957 to 1978, with those over age 65 showing a positive trend while those in younger age groups initially showed declines, then very little change during the 1970s (Rodgers, 1982).

Summary

Across the period from 1976 to 1984, successive cohorts of high school seniors showed faintly positive trends in levels of satisfaction with most of the domains included in the Monitoring the Future study, and practically no evidence of any trend at all on global happiness or life satisfaction. Black respondents expressed somewhat lower levels of satisfaction with most of these domains than did whites, although this may be accounted for at least in part by differences in the use of the response scale rather than true differences in satisfaction; and there were few differences in trends across time for the racial groups. College-bound students expressed somewhat higher levels of satisfaction with most domains than did others, and there is some indication that the gap may have broadened to some extent over this period.

Using data from two national samples of the national population of adults, we took two approaches to the estimation of age differences in levels of satisfaction: cross-sectional comparisons of persons in different birth cohorts, and comparisons of persons in the same birth cohorts but at different times. These two approaches yielded discrepant age patterns for satisfaction with several domains, implying that these satisfaction measures are affected by period- or cohort-related factors as well as by age-related factors; our interpretation of the data is in terms of age and period. We also observe some apparent interactions, in that trends across time are stronger for some age/cohort groups than for others.

Although we have observed trends on some of the satisfaction items across both periods and age levels, the dominant picture that has emerged from our examination of these data for young people and for the full adult population is one of stability rather than of change. Moreover, while there are some differences in the trends across years for young men and women, for blacks and whites, and for those with and without plans for college, these differences are mostly small and not of great substantive importance relative to the total variances in these measures.

This is not to say, however, that there have not been changes within individuals. Our analysis in this chapter has been at the aggregate, not the individual, level; we have looked at mean levels and trends and therefore have ignored a large amount of variation across individuals. It is to variation and trends at the individual level that we will turn in subsequent chapters.

Table 2-A1
Overall Trend in Satisfaction with Present Job
(Monitoring the Future Base-Year Data, 1976–1984)

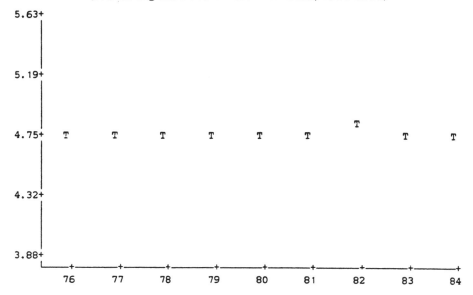

```
5.63+
     |
     |
     |
5.19+
     |
     |
     |                                                              T
4.75+   T      T      T      T      T      T             T      T
     |
     |
     |
4.32+
     |
     |
     |
3.88+
     L____+_____+_____+_____+_____+_____+_____+_____+_____+
         76     77     78     79     80     81     82     83     84
```

Total

	-76-	-77-	-78-	-79-	-80-	-81-	-82-	-83-	-84-
Mean:	4.755	4.800	4.808	4.840	4.781	4.840	4.855	4.837	4.775
SD:	1.749	1.780	1.778	1.752	1.741	1.722	1.746	1.718	1.755
Wtd N:	1857	1984	2462	2304	2213	2399	2249	2116	2001

Longitudinal Statistics

		r	Eta	F	Prob
Total	....	0.007	.0	0.833	.574

```
┌─────────────────────────────────────────────────────┐
│                                                       │
│    A006:*How satisfied are you with...                │
│                                                       │
│    A006A:Your job? (If you have no job,               │
│          leave blank)                                 │
│                                                       │
│          7. Completely satisfied                      │
│          6.                                           │
│          5.                                           │
│          4. Neutral                                   │
│          3.                                           │
│          2.                                           │
│          1. Completely dissatisfied                   │
│                                                       │
└─────────────────────────────────────────────────────┘
```

Table 2-A2
Overall Trend in Satisfaction with Neighborhood
(Monitoring the Future Base-Year Data, 1976–1984)

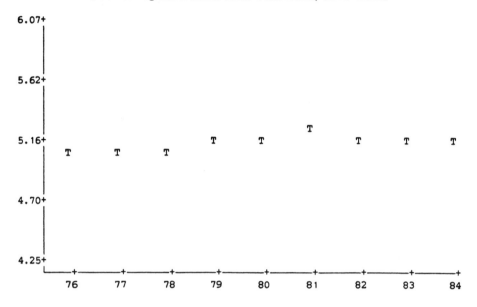

Total

	-76-	-77-	-78-	-79-	-80-	-81-	-82-	-83-	-84-
Mean:	5.160	5.135	5.096	5.219	5.250	5.286	5.185	5.190	5.164
SD:	1.828	1.787	1.857	1.833	1.764	1.767	1.812	1.821	1.800
Wtd N:	3026	3191	3778	3363	3315	3622	3666	3431	3297

Longitudinal Statistics

		r	Eta	F	Prob
Total	....	0.010	.026	3.669	.000

```
         [How satisfied are you with...]

  A006B:The neighborhood where you live?

      7. Completely satisfied
      6.
      5.
      4. Neutral
      3.
      2.
      1. Completely dissatisfied
```

34

Table 2-A3
Overall Trend in Satisfaction with Personal Safety
(Monitoring the Future Base-Year Data, 1976–1984)

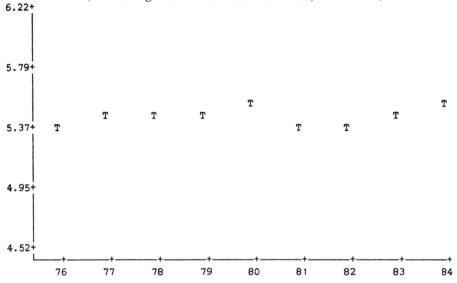

	-76-	-77-	-78-	-79-	-80-	-81-	-82-	-83-	-84-
Mean:	5.370	5.457	5.533	5.493	5.551	5.445	5.449	5.491	5.551
SD:	1.692	1.706	1.682	1.687	1.630	1.726	1.725	1.717	1.672
Wtd N:	3025	3193	3778	3358	3305	3624	3661	3427	3296

Longitudinal Statistics

		r	Eta	F	Prob
Total	....	0.014	.028	3.953	.000

[How satisfied are you with...]

A006C:Your personal safety in your
      neighborhood, on your job, and in
      your school--safety from being
      attacked and injured in some way?

7. Completely satisfied
6.
5.
4. Neutral
3.
2.
1. Completely dissatisfied

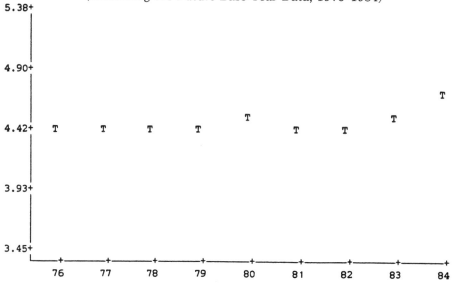

Table 2-A4
Overall Trend in Satisfaction with Safety of Property
(Monitoring the Future Base-Year Data, 1976–1984)

```
5.38+
     |
     |
     |
4.90+
     |
     |                                                                    T
     |                                       T                 T
4.42+  T     T     T     T                       T     T
     |
     |
3.93+
     |
     |
     |
3.45+
     L___+_____+_____+_____+_____+_____+_____+_____+_____+
         76    77    78    79    80    81    82    83    84
```

Total

	-76-	-77-	-78-	-79-	-80-	-81-	-82-	-83-	-84-
Mean:	4.416	4.476	4.512	4.503	4.575	4.459	4.456	4.577	4.713
SD:	1.935	1.945	1.957	1.938	1.899	1.933	1.964	1.922	1.900
Wtd N:	3012	3181	3771	3342	3294	3613	3652	3413	3288

Longitudinal Statistics

		r	Eta	F	Prob
Total	....	0.028	.040	7.084	.000

```
┌────────────────────────────────────────────────────┐
│                                                    │
│         [How satisfied are you with...]            │
│                                                    │
│    A006D:The safety of things you own              │
│          from being stolen or destroyed            │
│          in your neighborhood, on your             │
│          job, and in your school?                  │
│                                                    │
│          7. Completely satisfied                   │
│          6.                                        │
│          5.                                        │
│          4. Neutral                                │
│          3.                                        │
│          2.                                        │
│          1. Completely dissatisfied                │
│                                                    │
└────────────────────────────────────────────────────┘
```

Table 2-A5
Overall Trend in Satisfaction with Educational Experience
(Monitoring the Future Base-Year Data, 1976–1984)

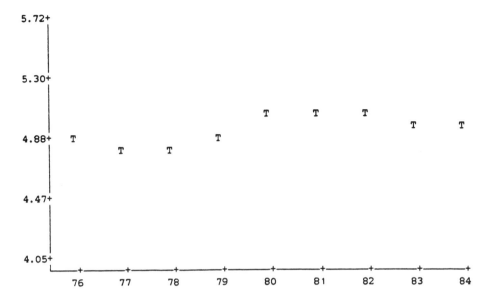

```
5.72+
     |
     |
5.30+
     |
     |                                  T         T         T
     |                                                              T         T
4.88+   T                         T
     |         T         T
4.47+
     |
     |
     |
4.05+
     L-----+---------+---------+---------+---------+---------+---------+---------+---------+
          76        77        78        79        80        81        82        83        84
```

Total

	-76-	-77-	-78-	-79-	-80-	-81-	-82-	-83-	-84-
Mean:	4.884	4.878	4.852	4.954	5.052	5.058	5.061	4.988	5.028
SD:	1.669	1.688	1.693	1.657	1.615	1.596	1.619	1.652	1.643
Wtd N:	3017	3177	3760	3345	3291	3616	3639	3402	3280

Longitudinal Statistics

		r	Eta	F	Prob
Total	....	0.037	.046	8.943	.000

[How satisfied are you with...]

A006E:Your educational experiences?

7. Completely satisfied
6.
5.
4. Neutral
3.
2.
1. Completely dissatisfied

37

Table 2-A6
Overall Trend in Satisfaction with Friends
(Monitoring the Future Base-Year Data, 1976–1984)

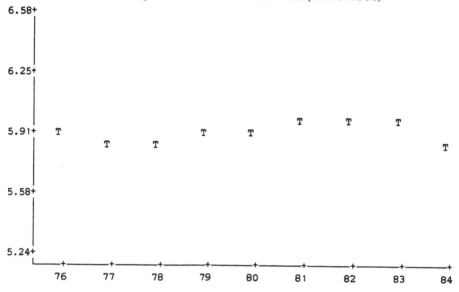

```
6.58+
     |
     |
6.25+
     |
     |
                                                      T     T     T
5.91+    T                          T     T
     |         T     T                                            T
     |
5.58+
     |
     |
5.24+
     L__+_____+_____+_____+_____+_____+_____+_____+_____+
        76    77    78    79    80    81    82    83    84
```

Total

	-76-	-77-	-78-	-79-	-80-	-81-	-82-	-83-	-84-
Mean:	5.912	5.883	5.909	5.963	5.966	5.999	5.999	5.985	5.908
SD:	1.345	1.380	1.368	1.344	1.297	1.322	1.327	1.316	1.406
Wtd N:	3021	3190	3781	3356	3302	3623	3660	3430	3294

Longitudinal Statistics

		r	Eta	F	Prob
Total	....	0.016	.027	3.721	.000

```
┌─────────────────────────────────────────────┐
│                                             │
│        [How satisfied are you with...]      │
│                                             │
│   A006F:Your friends and other people       │
│         you spend time with?                │
│                                             │
│         7. Completely satisfied             │
│         6.                                  │
│         5.                                  │
│         4. Neutral                          │
│         3.                                  │
│         2.                                  │
│         1. Completely dissatisfied          │
│                                             │
└─────────────────────────────────────────────┘
```

Table 2-A7
Overall Trend in Satisfaction with Relationship to Parents
(Monitoring the Future Base-Year Data, 1976–1984)

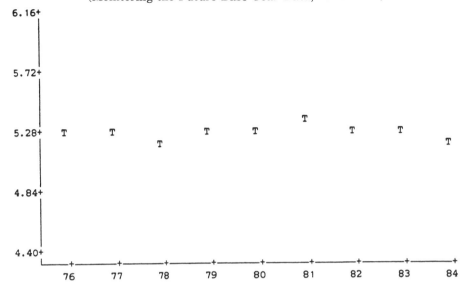

```
6.16+
     |
     |
5.72+
     |
     |
                                              T
5.28+   T       T           T       T                 T       T
     |               T                                               T
     |
4.84+
     |
     |
     |
4.40+
     L--+-------+-------+-------+-------+-------+-------+-------+-------+
        76      77      78      79      80      81      82      83      84
```

                                   Total

	-76-	-77-	-78-	-79-	-80-	-81-	-82-	-83-	-84-
Mean:	5.280	5.327	5.276	5.315	5.346	5.434	5.360	5.362	5.265
SD:	1.762	1.720	1.817	1.792	1.776	1.710	1.763	1.753	1.768
Wtd N:	3025	3190	3771	3357	3304	3616	3652	3423	3286

                          Longitudinal Statistics

		r	Eta	F	Prob
Total	....	0.008	.024	3.215	.001


```
┌─────────────────────────────────────────────────────┐
│                                                       │
│           [How satisfied are you with...]             │
│                                                       │
│    A006G:The way you get along with                   │
│          your parents?                                │
│                                                       │
│          7. Completely satisfied                      │
│          6.                                           │
│          5.                                           │
│          4. Neutral                                   │
│          3.                                           │
│          2.                                           │
│          1. Completely dissatisfied                   │
│                                                       │
└─────────────────────────────────────────────────────┘
```

39

Table 2-A8
Overall Trend in Satisfaction with Yourself
(Monitoring the Future Base-Year Data, 1976–1984)

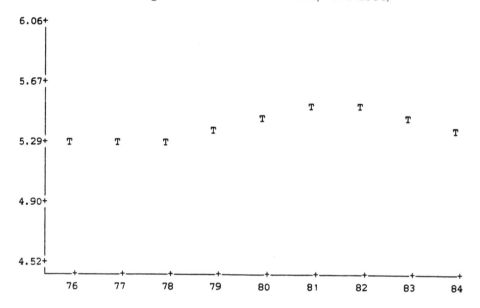

```
6.06+
      |
      |
      |
5.67+
      |                                          T       T
      |                                 T                        T
      |                          T
5.29+    T       T       T               T
      |
      |
      |
4.90+
      |
      |
      |
4.52+
      L___+_____+_____+_____+_____+_____+_____+_____+_____+
          76      77      78      79      80      81      82      83      84
```

Total

	-76-	-77-	-78-	-79-	-80-	-81-	-82-	-83-	-84-
Mean:	5.288	5.332	5.357	5.408	5.513	5.540	5.519	5.508	5.441
SD:	1.534	1.515	1.542	1.531	1.463	1.486	1.492	1.481	1.509
Wtd N:	3026	3179	3768	3335	3288	3609	3641	3409	3266

Longitudinal Statistics

		r	Eta	F	Prob
Total	....	0.045	.055	12.570	.000

```
┌─────────────────────────────────────────────────────────┐
│                                                         │
│              [How satisfied are you with...]            │
│                                                         │
│       A006H:Yourself?                                   │
│                                                         │
│              7. Completely satisfied                    │
│              6.                                         │
│              5.                                         │
│              4. Neutral                                 │
│              3.                                         │
│              2.                                         │
│              1. Completely dissatisfied                 │
│                                                         │
└─────────────────────────────────────────────────────────┘
```

Table 2-A9
Overall Trend in Satisfaction with Standard of Living
(Monitoring the Future Base-Year Data, 1976–1984)

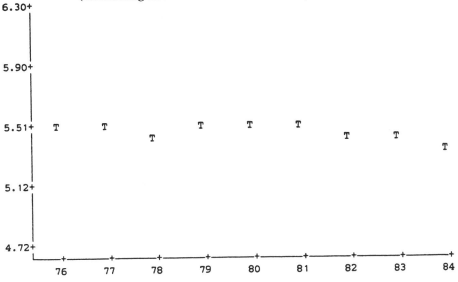

Total

	-76-	-77-	-78-	-79-	-80-	-81-	-82-	-83-	-84-
Mean:	5.510	5.559	5.485	5.515	5.582	5.585	5.507	5.452	5.415
SD:	1.580	1.571	1.635	1.588	1.549	1.571	1.600	1.604	1.652
Wtd N:	3028	3195	3782	3358	3300	3629	3666	3428	3291

Longitudinal Statistics

		r	Eta	F	Prob
Total	....	-.015	.030	4.358	.000

[How satisfied are you with....]

A006I:Your standard of living--the
things you have like housing,
car, furniture, recreation, and
the like?

7. Completely satisfied
6.
5.
4. Neutral
3.
2.
1. Completely dissatisfied

41

Table 2-A10
Overall Trend in Satisfaction with Time for Doing Things
(Monitoring the Future Base-Year Data, 1976–1984)

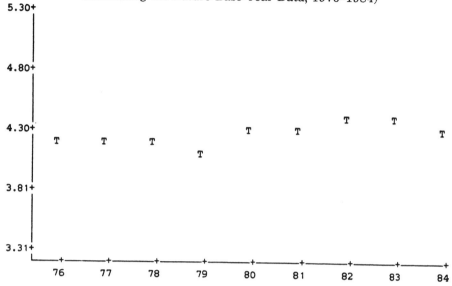

```
5.30+
     |
     |
4.80+
     |
     |
                                                      T       T
4.30+|                                         T       T               T
     |  T       T       T                 T                            
     |                          T
3.81+|
     |
     |
3.31+|
     L___+_____+_____+_____+_____+_____+_____+_____+_____+
        76      77      78      79      80      81      82      83      84
```

Total

	-76-	-77-	-78-	-79-	-80-	-81-	-82-	-83-	-84-
Mean:	4.304	4.301	4.239	4.178	4.398	4.397	4.452	4.406	4.317
SD:	1.993	1.986	1.968	1.955	1.919	1.907	1.911	1.955	1.927
Wtd N:	3026	3194	3770	3361	3308	3629	3657	3426	3292

Longitudinal Statistics

		r	Eta	F	Prob
Total	....	0.023	.040	7.246	.000

```
┌──────────────────────────────────────────────────────┐
│                                                        │
│         [How satisfied are you with...]                │
│                                                        │
│      A006J:The amount of time you have for             │
│            doing things you want to do?                │
│                                                        │
│            7. Completely satisfied                     │
│            6.                                          │
│            5.                                          │
│            4. Neutral                                  │
│            3.                                          │
│            2.                                          │
│            1. Completely dissatisfied                  │
│                                                        │
└──────────────────────────────────────────────────────┘
```

42

Table 2-A11
Overall Trend in Satisfaction with How Leisure Time Is Spent
(Monitoring the Future Base-Year Data, 1976–1984)

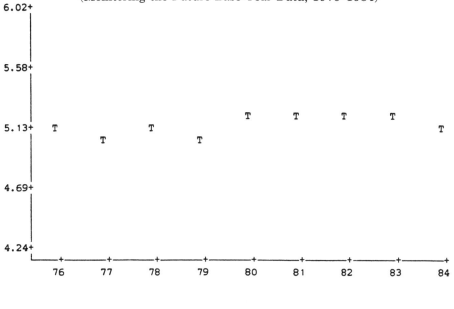

```
6.02+
     |
     |
5.58+
     |
     |
     |                                    T     T     T     T
5.13+  T                 T                                         T
     |        T                 T
     |
     |
4.69+
     |
     |
     |
4.24+
     L___+_____+_____+_____+_____+_____+_____+_____+_____+
         76    77    78    79    80    81    82    83    84
```

                                 Total

              -76-   -77-   -78-   -79-   -80-   -81-   -82-   -83-   -84-
Mean: 5.134   5.132   5.219   5.119   5.234   5.276   5.293   5.240   5.164
SD: 1.779   1.785   1.763   1.764   1.702   1.650   1.661   1.707   1.739
Wtd N: 3022   3192   3776   3362   3305   3630   3665   3433   3290

                          Longitudinal Statistics

                                       r   Eta   F   Prob
        Total   .... 0.018   .032   4.905   .000


```
┌──────────────────────────────────────────────────┐
│                                                    │
│           [How satisfied are you with...]          │
│                                                    │
│   A006K:The way you spend your leisure             │
│          time--recreation, relaxation,             │
│          and so on?                                │
│                                                    │
│          7. Completely satisfied                   │
│          6.                                        │
│          5.                                        │
│          4. Neutral                                │
│          3.                                        │
│          2.                                        │
│          1. Completely dissatisfied                │
│                                                    │
└──────────────────────────────────────────────────┘
```

Table 2-A12
Overall Trend in Satisfaction with Life as a Whole
(Monitoring the Future Base-Year Data, 1976–1984)

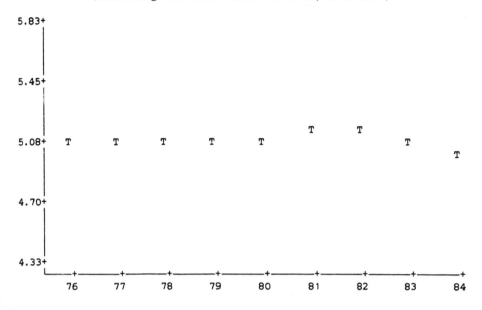

```
5.83+
     |
     |
     |
5.45+
     |
     |
     |                                              T        T
5.08+   T       T       T       T       T                            T
     |                                                                      T
     |
4.70+
     |
     |
     |
4.33+
     L___+_____+_____+_____+_____+_____+_____+_____+_____+
         76      77      78      79      80      81      82      83      84
```

Total

	-76-	-77-	-78-	-79-	-80-	-81-	-82-	-83-	-84-
Mean:	5.079	5.142	5.113	5.132	5.133	5.183	5.155	5.115	5.074
SD:	1.504	1.489	1.548	1.532	1.507	1.492	1.503	1.513	1.543
Wtd N:	3019	3188	3772	3347	3299	3621	3654	3425	3282

Longitudinal Statistics

		r	Eta	F	Prob
Total	....	0.001	.014	1.771	.077

```
+-----------------------------------------------------------+
|                                                           |
|         [How satisfied are you with...]                   |
|                                                           |
|     A006L:Your life as a whole these days?                |
|                                                           |
|         7. Completely satisfied                           |
|         6.                                                 |
|         5.                                                 |
|         4. Neutral                                        |
|         3.                                                 |
|         2.                                                 |
|         1. Completely dissatisfied                        |
|                                                           |
+-----------------------------------------------------------+
```

Table 2-A13
Overall Trend in Satisfaction with How Government Operates
(Monitoring the Future Base-Year Data, 1976–1984)

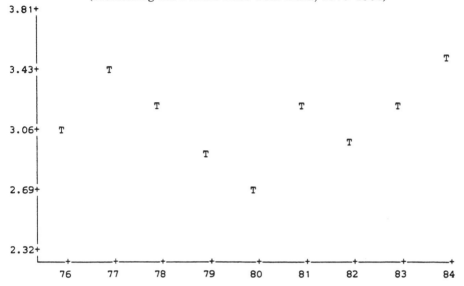

```
3.81+
     |
     |
3.43+                 T                                                          T
     |
     |                          T                         T              T
3.06+    T
     |                                                           T
     |                                  T
2.69+                                            T
     |
     |
2.32+
     L---+-------+-------+-------+-------+-------+-------+-------+-------+
         76      77      78      79      80      81      82      83      84
```

Total

	-76-	-77-	-78-	-79-	-80-	-81-	-82-	-83-	-84-
Mean:	3.063	3.453	3.235	2.982	2.739	3.229	3.054	3.264	3.580
SD:	1.486	1.514	1.482	1.516	1.494	1.545	1.605	1.558	1.567
Wtd N:	3023	3180	3773	3349	3303	3624	3659	3422	3287

Longitudinal Statistics

		r	Eta	F	Prob
Total	....	0.037	.150	89.567	.000

```
+----------------------------------------------------+
|                                                    |
|          [How satisfied are you with...]           |
|                                                    |
|   A006M:The way our national government            |
|         is operating?                              |
|                                                    |
|         7. Completely satisfied                    |
|         6.                                         |
|         5.                                         |
|         4. Neutral                                 |
|         3.                                         |
|         2.                                         |
|         1. Completely dissatisfied                 |
|                                                    |
+----------------------------------------------------+
```

45

Table 2-A14
Overall Trend in Satisfaction with Fun in Present Life
(Monitoring the Future Base-Year Data, 1976–1984)

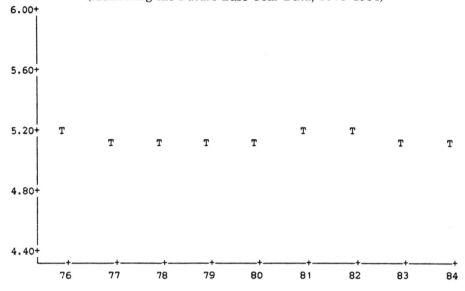

Total

	-76-	-77-	-78-	-79-	-80-	-81-	-82-	-83-	-84-
Mean:	5.200	5.154	5.185	5.181	5.198	5.213	5.206	5.192	5.141
SD:	1.595	1.631	1.648	1.618	1.581	1.587	1.582	1.630	1.644
Wtd N:	3027	3190	3782	3361	3309	3628	3668	3436	3295

Longitudinal Statistics

		r	Eta	F	Prob
Total	..................:...............	-.001	.0	0.736	.661

```
        [How satisfied are you with...]

   A006N:The amount of fun you are
         having?

         7. Completely satisfied
         6.
         5.
         4. Neutral
         3.
         2.
         1. Completely dissatisfied
```

46

Table 2-A15
Overall Trend in Happiness
(Monitoring the Future Base-Year Data, 1976–1984)

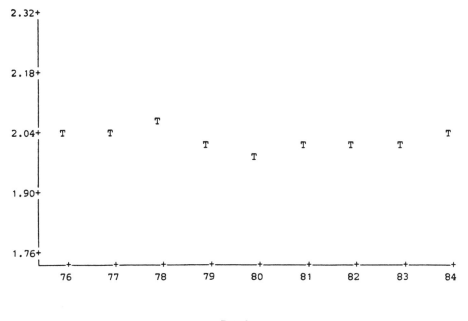

	-76-	-77-	-78-	-79-	-80-	-81-	-82-	-83-	-84-
Mean:	2.040	2.058	2.074	2.032	1.993	2.030	2.019	2.037	2.063
SD:	0.557	0.561	0.560	0.575	0.593	0.577	0.578	0.560	0.544
Wtd N:	3024	3194	3778	3360	3300	3630	3666	3434	3293

Longitudinal Statistics

		r	Eta	F	Prob
Total	....	-.007	.038	6.438	.000

A01: Taking all things together, how
would you say things are these
days--would you say you're very
happy, pretty happy, or not too
happy these days?

3. Very happy
2. Pretty happy
1. Not too happy

47

CHAPTER 3

MEASUREMENT QUALITIES OF SATISFACTION REPORTS

In Chapter 2 we observed that the average levels of satisfaction with the various domains of life have been highly stable, both across calendar years and cohorts of high school seniors over the past decade, and across years of age for young adults from their senior year in high school to five or six years following graduation. In this chapter we move from the aggregate level to the individual level and examine the question of the stability of reported satisfaction levels across several years of study. Examination of the stability of these satisfaction levels also leads us to evaluate the reliability of these reports — that is, the extent to which such reports can be replicated in the absence of any real change. Stability in reported satisfaction across time reflects both the reliability of the reports at each point in time and the amount of real change that transpires between the times at which the respondent is asked to make such evaluations. This chapter thus serves as a prelude to the remaining chapters in which we will address the primary focus of this study: the extent to which marriage and various other life events affect levels of reported satisfaction, thereby reducing the stability of such reports.

Techniques for Assessing Reliability and Stability

In terms of classical measurement theory, the relationships among parallel measures of a particular concept at a single point in time can be represented in schematic form as shown in Figure 3-1. The observations for each individual are represented by the x_is, enclosed in squares in Figure 3-1. It is assumed that there is a true score for each person, which is represented by the ζ enclosed in a circle in Figure 3-1. The influence of the true score on each observation is represented by the arrow from the ζ at time t to each x. Since the true score cannot be directly observed, its variance is arbitrary and for convenience is set to the value of 1.0. Moreover, it is conventional to standardize the observed variables. The variance of the observed scores that *cannot* be explained by variation in the true scores is attributed to sources which are assumed to be unrelated either to the true scores or to one another; these residual sources of variance are represented by the δ_is in Figure 3-1.

Given these specifications, the validity of the observations is given by the coefficient, λ_i, associated with the arrow from ζ to x_i. Given the assumption that the δ_is are independent, the reliability of each measure is simply its squared validity. When there are several parallel measures of

49

Figure 3–1
Path Diagram Representing Relationships among Multiple
Indicators of a Single Concept at One Time Point

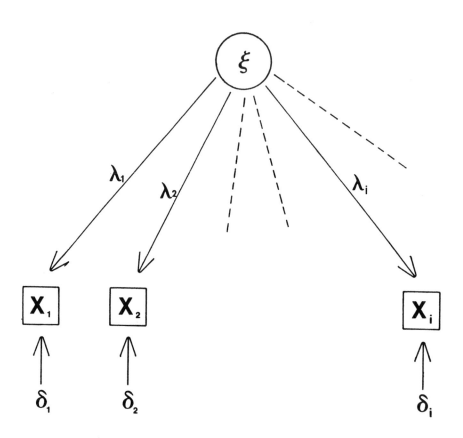

the same concept, it is possible to combine those measures into a summative index, thereby obtaining a measure of the concept which is more reliable, and presumably a more valid measure of the true scores, than are the individual items. A convenient measure of the reliability of such an index is coefficient alpha, which for parallel measures is defined as:

$$\alpha = \frac{k\bar{r}_{ij}}{1 + (k - 1)\bar{r}_{ij}} \tag{3.1}$$

where k is the number of items and $\bar{r}_{ij}$ is the mean correlation across all distinct pairs of items included in the index.

A similar representation can be made for the case where we have parallel measures of a single concept at two or more points in time. A representation of the relationships among such measures that accords with classical measurement theory is shown in schematic form in Figure 3–2. The observed score at time t is represented by x_t, and the true score at time t is represented by ξ_t. The remaining variance of the observations is again attributed to sources which are assumed to be unrelated either to the true scores or to one another; the residual variance is represented by δ_t in Figure 3–1. The λs are the same as in Figure 3–1, representing the validity coefficients of the items. The stability of the true satisfaction level from time t to time t+1 is represented by the arrow drawn between ξ_t and ξ_{t+1}; the strength of this relationship is denoted by the coefficient $\phi_{t,t+1}$. Given the absence of any other sources of correlated variation in the true score at time t+1 and the assignment of values of 1 to the variances of the true scores at both times, the phi coefficients are simply the correlations of the true scores.

Even with the stringent set of assumptions that have already been specified, it is not possible to estimate the parameters shown in Figure 3–2. There are five coefficients to estimate (two ϕs and three λs; given the standardization of the observed variables, the three δs are simply computed as residuals), but only three observed correlations (between each pair of the three observed variables). The solution that has generally been adopted in this situation is to add one more assumption: that the validities of the measures are the same at each point in time. This reduces the number of distinct parameters to be estimated to three, and the model is just identified.

The parameter estimates are obtained as follows:

$$\lambda^2 = r_{x_1 x_2} * r_{x_2 x_3} / r_{x_1 x_3} \tag{3.2}$$

Figure 3–2
Path Diagram Representing Cross-Time Relationships of an Indicator of a Single Concept at Multiple Time Points

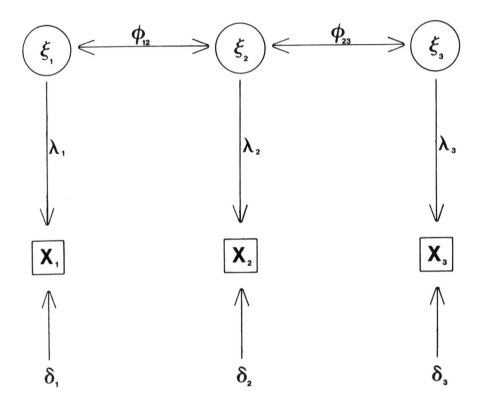

$$\phi_{1,2} = r_{x_1 x_3} / r_{x_2 x_3} \tag{3.3}$$

$$\phi_{2,3} = r_{x_1 x_3} / r_{x_1 x_2} \tag{3.4}$$

where $r_{x_t x_{t'}}$ is the observed correlation of the measures at times t and t'.
The item reliability is estimated as the square of the validity coefficient, λ.

Reliability and Stability Estimates for Satisfaction Items

The satisfaction measures in the Monitoring the Future study, as discussed in the previous chapter, were included in the base year and in each follow-up questionnaire, allowing us to make estimates of the reliability of these scores and the stability of the true satisfaction levels in the years following graduation from high school. The reliability and stability estimates are displayed in Table 3–1 for each of fourteen satisfaction measures asked in Form A of the Monitoring the Future questionnaires. Also shown are similar estimates for the single-item happiness measure, and for an index of domain satisfaction formed by taking the average score for an individual respondent across twelve of the satisfaction items (omitting "life as a whole" and "government operations"). The reliability estimates (squared lambdas) range from .33 (for satisfaction with "present job") to .56 (for satisfaction with "educational experience"). The estimates of the stabilities of the true satisfaction levels from the senior year in high school to one or two years later range from .50 (for satisfaction with "government operations") to .82 (for satisfaction with "relationship with parents"). This indicates a moderate amount of stability in satisfaction with most of these domains across time.

None of the reliability estimates is as high as might be desired; they imply that less than half of the variance in most of these reports of satisfaction is attributable to the true satisfaction level. On the other hand, for single-item measures on a self-administered questionnaire we probably should not expect to obtain much better success, especially for evaluative questions of this type.[1] More disturbing, however, is the low estimated

---

[1]Based on previous studies, however, we expected at least somewhat higher reliabilities. Andrews (1984) estimated the validity coefficients of a wide range of survey items, including but not restricted to satisfaction items of the type considered here, using LISREL to estimate measurement models for multiple concepts each measured by multiple methods. The mean validity coefficient across more than two thousand estimates was 0.81, corresponding to an average reliability of 0.66. The corresponding average across the fifteen items in Table 3–1 is 0.46, considerably smaller than that reported by Andrews. Moreover, Andrews found that reliability tended to be higher for younger than for older respondents, so we would have expected our estimates to be somewhat higher than his. It is possible that the lower reliabilities found in the present study reflect the mode of data collection (i.e., group-administered questionnaires in the base year, self-administered questionnaires in the follow-ups), but Andrews failed to detect important differences at-

Table 3-1

Estimates of Reliability of Satisfaction Items and Stability of True Satisfaction Levels
(Monitoring the Future Panel Data)

ITEM	OBSERVED CORRELATIONS:			Relia-bility	ESTIMATES OF: Stability,	
	BY-FU1	BY-FU2	FU1-FU2		BY-FU1	FU1-FU2
SPECIFIC DOMAINS:						
Present Job	.203	.142	.234	.334	.609	.700
Neighborhood	.380	.246	.341	.528	.720	.646
Personal Safety	.324	.270	.373	.448	.723	.833
Safety of Property	.337	.231	.341	.497	.677	.685
Educational Experience	.345	.234	.382	.563	.614	.679
Friends	.252	.245	.361	.372	.678	.971
Relationship to Parents	.372	.340	.413	.451	.824	.915
Yourself	.416	.328	.404	.512	.812	.790
Standard of Living	.345	.300	.395	.454	.762	.870
Time for Doing Things	.278	.217	.290	.372	.747	.780
Leisure Time Activities	.258	.181	.339	.484	.534	.701
How Government Operates	.262	.180	.365	.530	.495	.688
Fun You Are Having	.308	.282	.428	.467	.659	.916
OVERALL LIFE:						
Life as a Whole	.338	.265	.395	.503	.672	.784
Happiness	.266	.259	.376	.387	.688	.971
Domain Index	.486	.445	.535	.585	.831	.916

NOTES: The item wordings are given in Tables 2-A1 through 2-A15. The "Domain Index" is the average for each individual across twelve domain satisfaction items, omitting "how government operates."

The three data collections are noted as BY (base-year), FU1 (first follow-up), and FU2 (second follow-up).

reliability (.59) of the multi-item index of domain satisfaction. Moreover, for this index we have a separate estimate of reliability based on the cross-sectional correlations of the component items. Coefficient alpha for this index is 0.77, substantially higher than the reliability estimate based on the longitudinal correlations. How should this discrepancy be interpreted, and which estimate (if either) is likely to be more accurate?

Such questions compel us to reconsider the assumptions which underlie the two estimation procedures. Neither set of assumptions is above suspicion. With respect to the estimation of reliability of a multi-item index from the cross-sectional correlations of the components, the critical assumption is that the true score on the concept being measured is the only source of common variance across those items. This assumption is not very persuasive, especially with respect to an index such as the index of domain satisfaction which is created by combining several items that use the same response scale and are asked as a set in the same questionnaire. It is quite plausible that respondents differ in how they interpret that scale and that they tend to use it in idiosyncratic ways; for example, some respondents may be more likely to use the extreme categories while others may confine themselves to intermediate categories (Bachman and O'Malley, 1984b; Rodgers and Herzog, 1984). Such differences in the use of the response scale would constitute a methods factor that contributes to the strength of the inter-item correlations, thereby inflating the reliability as estimated by coefficient alpha.

The assumptions which underlie the estimates of reliability from panel data are also open to question. As with estimates based on cross-sectional data, it is assumed that the only source of common variance is variation on the true score. If, however, differences in how respondents use response scales persist over time, such method factors could contribute to the correlation of measures across time as well as cross-sectionally. Moreover, there are other potential sources of common variance; for example, some respondents may try to be consistent in how they answer the questions from one year to the next. Another way of saying this is that the assumption of independent error terms across waves of a panel study may not be realistic.

All of this is to say, then, that the estimates of reliability, both those based on panel data and coefficient alpha from cross-sectional data, are probably overestimates of the proportion of variance in the measures that reflect true differences on the concepts. Based on the fact that the estimate of reliability of the index of domain satisfactions derived from cross-sectional data is considerably higher than the estimate derived from panel data (.77 vs. .59), it appears that the assumption of independent error terms is violated to a greater extent in cross-sectional data than in panel data. We would not want to claim, however, that the estimates from panel data are

---

tributable to mode of data collection (face-to-face, telephone, or group-administered). Perhaps the discrepancy is explained by the method used to estimate the reliability. Andrews' analyses were based on cross-sectional data, whereas ours are based on panel data, and as

unbiased; it is more likely that the estimates from panel data are also over-estimates of the validity of these measures.

Despite these reservations about the assumptions which underlie the estimation procedures, it is probably safe to conclude that there is moderate stability in the levels of satisfaction with life and the various domains among persons across the first few years following their graduation from high school. This is in some respects rather surprising, given the changes that are taking place in the lives of so many young people in this age range. On the other hand, the stabilities of these satisfaction concepts are not so high as to preclude the possibility that some of the transitions experienced by these persons may have had an impact on their levels of satisfaction with their lives and with some of these domains of life. If we thought that the true levels of satisfaction were almost perfectly stable, then observed variation in the measures of satisfaction would reflect only measurement error and any effort to try to explain such variation in terms of major life transitions would be meaningless; so it is reassuring to find that real changes are taking place.

The estimates of the reliabilities of these measures of satisfaction, however, are distressingly low. A large proportion of the observed variation in satisfaction with life and with each domain is, we estimate, unrelated to the true level of satisfaction; and an even greater proportion of the observed *change* in satisfaction reported by an individual at different times is a reflection of nothing more than measurement error. The reliability estimates are not so low as to prevent analysis of the causes of level and change in satisfaction, but the fact that they are so low does mean that our estimates of the strengths of causal relationships will have relatively large standard errors. Some important causal paths may be overlooked, while some unimportant factors may happen to appear to be strong predictors. We will try to exercise appropriate caution in our interpretation of our findings, and we urge the reader to exercise similar caution.

---

we point out in the text we obtain a higher estimate of the reliability of an index from cross-sectional than from panel data.

CHAPTER 4

MARITAL STATUS DIFFERENCES IN THE SUBJECTIVE QUALITY OF LIFE

In previous chapters, we have examined evaluative measures included in the Monitoring the Future surveys and in the 1971 and 1978 Quality of Life surveys, and the changes (or lack of changes) observed in these measures across age levels and across periods. We have also taken note of the extent to which the survey measures appear to reflect the underlying concepts as opposed to other sources of variation, and the apparent stability of those concepts across time. In this and the following chapters, the central issue is the extent to which variations on these evaluative measures are related to differences in the situations of the respondents: their marital status, their work status, and so on. Although we begin by examining differences in satisfaction expressed by persons in different situations, our goal is to go beyond such descriptive statements and draw inferences about why the observed relationships exist.

Cross-Sectional Differences

The quickest kind of data to collect is cross-sectional; that is, information which is gathered in one fairly short period of time. Typically, interviews are conducted with a set of respondents, or individuals are asked to complete a self-administered questionnaire. Characteristics of each respondent, as measured in these interviews or questionnaires, can then be examined and descriptive statements made about such things as the proportion of respondents who are in a particular marital status, or who report a particular level of satisfaction with their lives. Furthermore, the answers to different questions can be cross-tabulated in order to describe the relationship between those variables — for example, the differences in the proportions of persons in different marital statuses who express high levels of satisfaction with their lives, or the average satisfaction reported by persons in each status. If the respondents were selected with known probabilities from a target population, inferential statements can be made about that population based on the sample data. We will first examine cross-sectional data of this type in order to describe the relationship between marital status and subjective well-being, beginning with a sample of the adult population of the United States.

Differences among Adults of All Ages

The relationships between marital status and each of several measures of overall life quality, as reported by respondents in the 1978 Quality of Life study, are shown in Table 4–1. The two thirds of the respondents who were married (including the less than one percent who said that they were living with someone though not legally married) reported greater satisfaction than did the remaining one third. For most of the measures shown in the table, the average level reported by the married respondents was about one tenth of a standard deviation above the overall mean. Reporting the poorest quality of life were those who had separated from their spouses (about four tenths of a standard deviation below the mean, on the average). Intermediate between these extreme categories were, in order of declining average reported life quality: (2) widowed; (3) never married; and (4) divorced respondents.[1]

Differences among Young People

Turning to Monitoring the Future data in order to examine the subjective quality of life of young people, we find that the only marital statuses that can be distinguished are "married" and "not married." Preliminary inspection of the data, however, suggested that it would be useful to distinguish among the "not married" according to whether respondents said that they were engaged to be married. The proportion of respondents who were married increased from less than three percent at the base year (during their senior years in high school), to 12.5 percent at the first follow-up (one or two years after high school), and to 26 percent at the second follow-up (three or four years after high school); while the proportion who said that they were engaged stayed in the seven to nine percent range at all three points in time.

The average levels of satisfaction and happiness reported by persons who said that they were married, engaged, or neither at the time of the first and second follow-up data collections are shown in Table 4–2. This table shows that the major difference with respect to subjective quality of life is not between those young people who are and those who are not married, but between those who are either engaged to be married or already married and those who have not taken either step. At the first follow-up, those who were engaged were not quite as happy or as satisfied as those who were already married (the difference is not statistically significant). At the second

---

[1]It is of interest, but not central to this study, to note that while the five marital status groups are ordered in the above sequence with respect to the first two listed measures and on the average across all ten measures, there are divergent patterns for some of the other items. For example, never married respondents report experiencing both more positive *and* more negative events over the preceding two weeks than those in any other marital status. Widowed respondents report being highly satisfied with more domains of life than any other group, and also the lowest scores on the stress index; but on the other hand they report the fewest positive events.

follow-up, however, the reverse pattern is observed. Again, the difference is not statistically significant, but the pattern is suggestive of findings that will be observed as we go on to examine the effects of marital transitions more directly in later chapters.

Retrospective Data: Time since Marital Transitions

People who are in a particular marital status category share with one another a set of characteristics by virtue of being in that status, and they also share the fact that they all have been through a particular type of transition. All who are currently married have made the transition from being unmarried to being married; all who are divorced have made the transition from being married to being divorced; and so on. These two things are closely but not inextricably linked, because the time since the transition varies across people, and the effects of a transition on the quality of life of individuals may decline with time. The observation that those who are currently married are more satisfied than those who are separated or divorced, or who have never married, could be a consequence of the difference in status *per se* — being married and/or living with someone of the opposite sex may be a more satisfactory circumstance for most people than any of the alternative statuses. (It could also reflect differences in the kinds of people who are likely to enter a status — that is, a "selection" bias.) On the other hand, the covariation could reflect the more transitory consequences of transitions into and out of a marriage. If marriages are generally followed by a substantial "honeymoon" period, and if most separations and divorces are followed by a period of unhappiness for at least one of the former partners, it is conceivable that such transient consequences could account for the overall differences in satisfaction observed for all persons in these statuses. This hypothesis can be tested using cross-sectional data if the time since transition into the current status is ascertained. We will use such data from the 1978 Quality of Life survey in our first examination of the question.

Respondents in the 1978 Quality of Life survey were asked whether they had experienced each of a series of life events during the preceding five years. Included in the set of events were marital transitions: marriage, separation, divorce, and widowhood. For each type of event that was reported, the time of the most recent occurrence was also ascertained. If the difference in average level of life satisfaction is attributable to the short-term effects of these transitions, rather than to characteristics of the statuses *per se*, we would expect the differences to be strongest for persons in the period immediately after each type of transition.

The patterns actually observed are shown in Figure 4–1. There is little evidence from these data for transient effects of any marital transition except widowhood. In fact, none of the trends across the first five years fol-

Table 4-1
Differences in Life Satisfaction between Respondents in Different Marital Statuses
(1978 Quality of Life Data)

Measure	TOTAL		DEVIATIONS FROM OVERALL MEAN				
	Mean	St. Dev.	Married	Widowed	Single	Divorced	Separated
(a) Sat.-Dissat.	2.452	1.245	0.103	0.012	-0.214	-0.328	-0.491
(b) Thermometer	82.169	13.826	0.090	-0.008	-0.199	-0.256	-0.374
(c) Del.-Terr.	5.535	0.958	0.095	-0.175	-0.123	-0.356	-0.384
(d) General Affect	5.726	1.058	0.110	-0.122	-0.224	-0.224	-0.465
(e) Stress Index	1.668	1.309	0.034	0.154	-0.036	-0.324	-0.304
(f) Positive Affect	3.332	1.353	0.044	-0.403	0.051	-0.054	-0.273
(g) Negative Affect	3.483	1.469	0.120	-0.019	-0.350	-0.184	-0.271
(h) Affect Balance	7.072	2.102	0.113	-0.271	-0.212	-0.163	-0.365
(i) Domain Index	5.931	2.506	0.074	0.188	-0.220	-0.220	-0.433
AVERAGE			0.087	-0.072	-0.170	-0.234	-0.373

NOTES: The entries in the last five columns are in standard deviation units (using the standard deviation of the overall sample for each variable).

The measures were as follows (the variable numbers refer to the codebook for the archived data, Campbell and Converse, 1980):

(a) V425: "How satisfied are you with your life as a whole these days?" 1 = "Completely satisfied" . . . 7 = "Completely dissatisfied."

(b) V471: "Finally, where would you place your life as a whole?" 0 = "Terrible, as bad as you can imagine it" . . . 100 = "Perfect, as good as you can imagine it."

(c) V486: "How do you feel about your life as a whole?" 1 = "Terrible" . . . 7 = "Delighted."

(d) V671: Mean of eight semantic differential items; cf. Campbell et al. (1976, p. 45). Range is from 1 (very unfavorable) to 7 (favorable). (Reversed scoring.)

(e) V673: Recode of five items; cf. Campbell et al. (1976, pp. 403-405, but present index omits one of six items listed there). Range is from 0 (high stress) to 5 (low stress). (Reversed scoring.)

(f) V674: Count of "yes" responses to five items about positive experiences, from Bradburn (1969). Range is from 0 (none) to 5 (all).

(g) V675: Count of "no" responses to five items about negative experiences, from Bradburn (1969). Range is from 0 (none) to 5 (all). (Reversed scoring.)

(h) V676: Positive affect score - negative affect score.

(i) V683: Count of domains (out of ten) with which respondent reports being highly satisfied. Range is from 0 (none) to 10 (all).

Table 4-2

Differences in Life Satisfaction and Happiness
between Married, Engaged, and Unmarried Respondents
(Monitoring the Future Panel Data)

Marital Status	Follow-up 1 Data			Follow-up 2 Data		
	Proportion of Cases	Deviations from Overall Mean		Proportion of Cases	Deviations from Overall Mean	
		Life Sat.	Happiness		Life Sat.	Happiness
Overall mean (St. dev.)		4.825 (1.468)	2.143 (0.580)		4.868 (1.463)	2.169 (0.600)
Unmarried	.788	-.061 (.006)	-.081 (.006)	.656	-.100 (.009)	-.138 (.009)
Engaged	.087	.214 (.039)	.293 (.037)	.084	.226 (.040)	.305 (.039)
Married	.125	.235 (.032)	.306 (.031)	.261	.178 (.020)	.248 (.020)
Multiple R (adjusted)		.1158	.1605		.1371	.1898
Multiple R² (adjusted)		.0134	.0258		.0188	.0360

NOTE: The entries in rows 2 - 4 are deviations from the overall mean, divided by the overall standard deviation. The entries in parentheses are the standard errors of these deviations.

lowing these events is statistically significant.[1] The number of respondents who had experienced these events in the preceding five years is small
(about 400 married, about 150 each were divorced and widowed, and about
100 separated from their spouses and remained in that status at the time of
the interview), so the estimates for mean satisfaction level at each interval
following the event are not very precise. With this qualification, we conclude that these data, based on retrospective reports of marital transitions,
provide little support for the hypothesis that differences in life satisfaction of
persons in different marital statuses are attributable to transient effects of
the transitions from one status to another.

Panel Data

Panel data consist of information about a sample of individuals collected on two or more occasions. Such data can provide more compelling
evidence with respect to causal relationships than is possible with cross-
sectional data, including retrospective data of the type just examined. A
necessary condition for inferring a causal relationship is that the
hypothesized cause must precede the supposed effect. Retrospective data
are attractive because they permit temporal priority to be assessed from
cross-sectional data, but a nagging doubt that persists with retrospective
data is whether the hypothesized effect may not influence the self-report on
the prior level of the causal variable. Such doubts are compounded when
we start to consider competing causal hypotheses, such as the possibility
that an observed relationship is spurious rather than the consequence of one
variable influencing the other. For example, we noted earlier the possibility
that differences in satisfaction levels between those in different marital
statuses could reflect "selection" biases — differences in the kinds of people
likely to enter each status. To test such competing hypotheses, we would
like to know the prior levels of any variables that we think could produce a
spurious relationship, but again with retrospective data the best we can do
is rely on current self-reports on prior levels of those variables. Panel data
go a long way toward overcoming these problems of cross-sectional data,
since they allow the analyst to examine the relationship between
hypothesized causal variables as reported at one time and the hypothesized
dependent variables as reported at a later time. Specifically, panel data allow us to examine levels of satisfaction reported by the same respondents
before and after marital transitions. We will examine data from the small
number of persons in the 1971–78 Quality of Life panel who experienced
marital transitions during that time span, and from the much larger num-

---

[1]The difference in satisfaction levels of those widowed within the last five years and
those widowed for a longer time is statistically significant (t = 4.03, p < .01). The
analysis shown in Figure 4–1 was repeated using a different measure of life satisfaction
(with a 0–100 scale) and again using the index of general affect, with the same pattern of
results. The differences between those widowed for more and less than five years,
however, were not significant for either of these measures.

Figure 4-1
Average Level of Life Satisfaction of Respondents in Different Marital Transitions, by Time in that Status
1978 Quality of Life Data

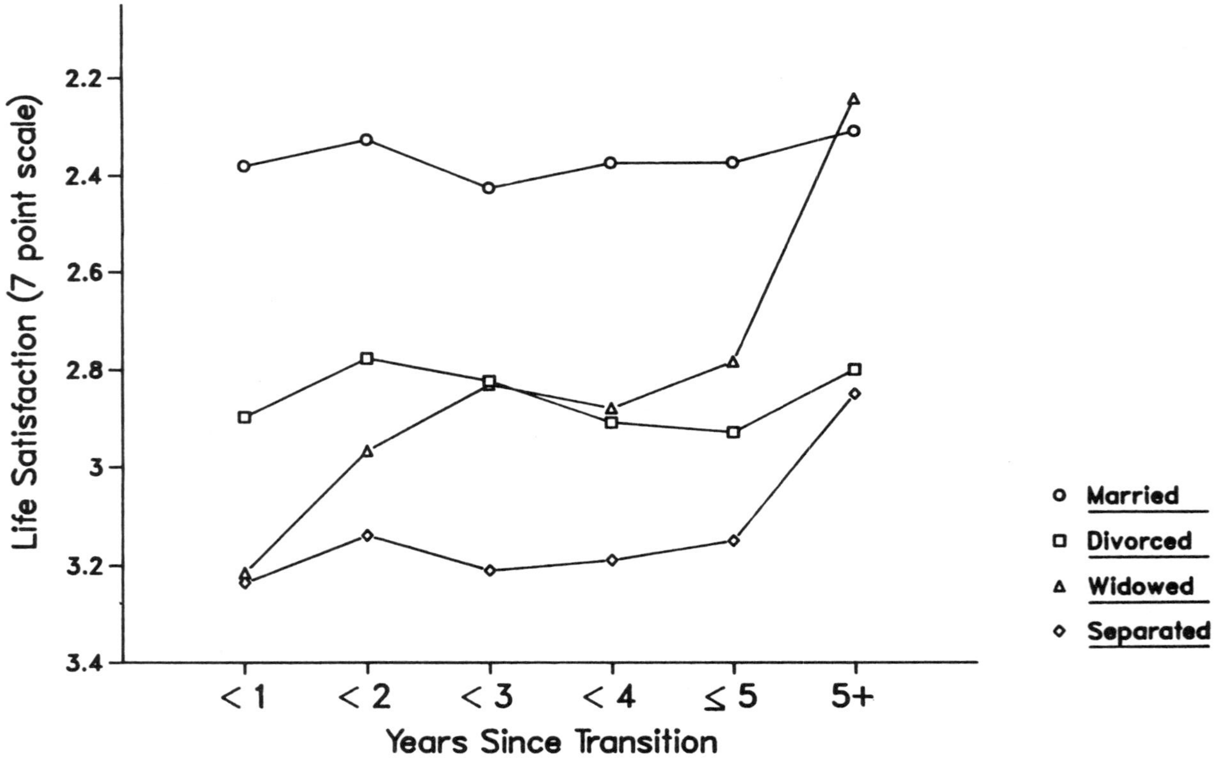

ber of respondents in the several Monitoring the Future panels who were married during the period of observation.

Transitions among Adults of All Ages

As explained in Chapter 1, almost 700 of the respondents in the 1971 Quality of Life survey were reinterviewed in 1978 and thus offer opportunities for panel data analysis. It was also noted, however, that these panel respondents are by no means a random sample of the adult population, since only persons who had not changed place of residence between 1971 and 1978 were reinterviewed. These respondents were cross-classified by their marital statuses in 1971 and 1978, and their levels of life satisfaction each of those years were examined. The findings are shown in Table 4–3. Unfortunately (for the purposes of this analysis, at least), the number of respondents who changed marital statuses is too small to permit analysis of change in life satisfaction which accompanies most types of marital transitions. Only eleven respondents changed from married to divorced or separated; 39 persons were widowed; and even fewer people made other types of transitions. This surely is a consequence of the nature of the panel, since many persons who change marital status also change place of residence. It may also underestimate the number of marital transitions even among those who did not change their place of residence, since it is based only on marital status as reported at the time of the two interviews, seven years apart. Anyone who experienced two or more transitions but ended up in the same status in 1978 as in 1971 — such as someone who divorced and remarried — is nonetheless classified as stable in this analysis.

Although our interpretation of the changes in life satisfaction shown in Table 4–3 must be severely tempered by the highly selected nature of the panel sample and the small number of cases making marital transitions, there are some suggestive findings that merit comment. In particular, the numbers of persons who *remain* in particular marital statuses are large enough to provide meaningful estimates of trends. Over half of the reinterviewed respondents were married in both 1971 and 1978 (464 persons, though all were not necessarily in the same marriage). These showed an average decline in life satisfaction which is statistically significant (p < .05). This can perhaps best be interpreted as a reflection of the increase in age between the two interviews, given our earlier observations on the apparent decline in satisfaction with age.

By contrast, those who were widowed at both interviews showed an average *increase* in life satisfaction that is larger in magnitude than the decline for those who remained married, but given the smaller number (77) in this group the increase is not statistically significant. This increase, assuming it is real and not just sampling variation, would be contrary to the general decline with age but is consistent with the pattern observed in the 1978 cross-sectional data reported in the previous section of this chapter: widowhood is followed by a period of some years during which life satisfaction is lower than that of married respondents, but subsequently returns to levels at least as high as those of married respondents. Indeed, further

Table 4–3
Changes in Life Satisfaction in Relation to
Marital Status from 1971 to 1978
(Quality of Life Panel Data)

| MARITAL STATUS IN 1971 | MARITAL STATUS IN 1978 | | | | Mean 1971 |
	Married	Widowed	Div/Sep	Single	
Married	−0.136 (464)	−0.462 (39)	−0.545 (11)	− (0)	2.22 (516)
Widowed	− (2)	0.234 (77)	− (1)	− (0)	2.29 (82)
Div/Sep	− (5)	− (5)	0.103 (29)	− (0)	3.05 (39)
Single	− (1)	− (0)	− (3)	0.000 (42)	2.83 (46)
MEAN, 1978	2.37 (477)	2.19 (126)	3.09 (45)	2.83 (42)	

NOTES: The differences are calculated so that a positive difference indicates *higher* average satisfaction in 1978 than in 1971.

Numbers in parentheses are case counts.

−: differences are not shown if case count is less than 10.

evidence for the reality of this pattern is obtained by examining the persons who were widowed between 1971 and 1978; the average life satisfaction of these persons declined by almost half a point on the seven-point scale. Again, there are too few people who experienced this transition (39) for the difference to be statistically significant, but the pattern is consistent with the analysis of retrospective data from the 1978 study.

Even fewer respondents remained divorced or separated and in the never married status, and the average changes in life satisfaction are small for both of these groups. The pattern for divorced and separated respondents is similar to that observed for widowed respondents, however: a slight increase in satisfaction for those who have remained in this status, and a large decline for those who went from being married to divorced or separated.

Panel data from the Monitoring the Future study do not have the limitations of panel data from the Quality of Life studies, in that the intention has been to obtain follow-up information from representative samples of each cohort of high school seniors. On the other hand, since these data were obtained from young adults within a few years after high school, they provide very few cases of transitions out of marriage, and the information about transitions into marriage is limited to those who married at fairly young ages. This limitation is particularly serious for subgroups whose members tend to marry at later ages: men, for example, and those who extend their educations beyond high school.

For this analysis, we included only persons who had participated in the base-year data collection (as high school seniors) and at least the first follow-up data collection. It will be recalled that the participants in these follow-ups were sampled from each class of high school seniors; that half were asked to return mailed questionnaires one-year after high school and the others after two years; and that those in each half-sample have been asked to participate in subsequent follow-ups at two-year intervals. For the following analysis we classified respondents according to their marital status at the time of each of two consecutive data collections, and for respondents in each pattern we calculated the average level of satisfaction and happiness at the second of those times. To increase the sample sizes in these marital status transition categories, we combined data from two pairs of data collections: (1) the base year and the first follow-up; and (2) the first and second follow-ups. Thus respondents who participated in all three data collections are represented twice in the following analysis. The age span of the respondents is approximately 18 through 22.

At each data collection, respondents were classified into one of the three groups distinguished earlier in this chapter: (1) those who were neither married nor engaged to be married (hereafter referred to simply as "unmarried"); (2) those who said that they were engaged to be married; and (3) those who were married. Taking into account the status of an individual at each of two points in time allows us to distinguish nine groups of respondents with different marital status patterns. Respondents in three of these groups remained in the same status at both times, while those in the other six groups made a transition of some type. More than 60 percent of the respondents were neither married nor engaged at either time; about 15 percent married during the interval, while less than 2 percent terminated marriages; and about 11 percent were married at both times.

The initial and final levels of happiness and life satisfaction of these groups are shown in Figure 4–2. As will be documented in Chapter 9 when we examine these data more analytically, the sizes of some of the groups are small and therefore their average levels of satisfaction have large sampling errors, so these figures should be taken only as a first descriptive look at the data. In particular, though, one of the groups — those who were married at time 1 and engaged at time 2 — included less than one tenth of one percent of the respondents, so the averages for this group are not meaningful enough to be shown in these figures.

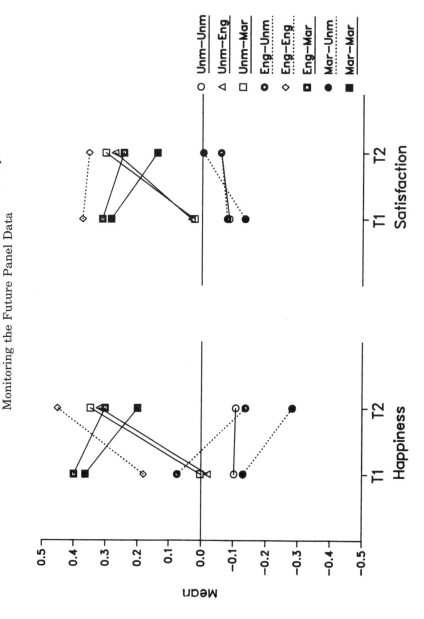

Figure 4-2
Patterns of Happiness and Life Satisfaction Reported by Respond-
ents in Each of Eight Marital Status Transition Groups
Monitoring the Future Panel Data

68

More than half of the respondents were unmarried (and unengaged) at both data collections, and there was practically no change in the average levels of happiness and satisfaction reported by these respondents. It was observed earlier in this chapter that respondents who were engaged to be married were as happy and as satisfied with their lives as those who were actually married, suggesting that it is the commitment to a marital partner that may enhance the subjective quality of life of these young people. This interpretation is reinforced by inspection of Figure 4-2. The most striking changes to be observed in this figure are the rises in satisfaction and happiness reported by those who were unmarried at the first of the two data collections but had become *either* married or engaged by the time of the second data collection. These respondents reported an increase of about a quarter to a third of a standard deviation unit in both their happiness and life satisfaction. The importance of the marital commitment is further emphasized when we note that those who made the transition from engaged to married reported *no* increase in their happiness or satisfaction; indeed, there was a small, non-statistically significant decline in each measure. Thus it seems that the enhancing effects of marriage are associated with the decision to marry rather than with the actual marriage.

Inspection of Figure 4-2 is also useful in distinguishing between two possible causal interpretations of the relationship between marital status and the subjective quality of life. One competing interpretation to the hypothesis that marital status has a causal influence on satisfaction is that level of satisfaction affects the probability of getting or staying married. Perhaps people in circumstances they find to be satisfactory are more likely to consider marriage, and/or to be successful in attracting a marital partner, than are those in less satisfactory circumstances. To test this hypothesis properly would require panel data from the full age spectrum, but Figure 4-2 does provide a modicum of support for this interpretation: among those who were unmarried at time 1, those who were married or engaged by time 2 were slightly happier and more satisfied (by about one tenth of a standard deviation unit) than those who remained unmarried. The differences are statistically significant ($p < .05$). On the other hand, these initial differences are considerably smaller than the *changes* observed among those who became engaged or married; so while it is possible that initial differences in the subjective quality of life influence the probability of marriage at a young age, the far greater effect on life quality appears to result from marital transitions.

Figure 4-2 shows a pattern that does not appear consistent with the cross-sectional differences examined earlier: those who were married at the time of the first as well as the second follow-up data collections showed a *decline* in happiness and life satisfaction that was about half as large as the *increase* observed among those who made the transition from unmarried to engaged or married. We did not observe such a pattern in the retrospective data from the 1978 Quality of Life data (Figure 4-1), and at first glance it seems to be inconsistent with the cross-sectional differences in average satisfaction levels of married and other respondents. It is, however, consistent with a pattern that was reported by Campbell et al. (1976, pp. 161 ff.). Using data from the 1971 Quality of Life survey, those investigators found that respondents whose marriages had taken place within six months or so of the interview reported high levels of satisfaction with those marriages, but that satisfaction dropped off considerably for those whose marriages had lasted somewhat longer. This decline was followed by a gradual increase, resulting in a check-shaped curve. A similar pattern was observed with respect to housing satisfaction following a residential move, and the authors speculated that this may be a fairly general pattern, perhaps induced by the dissonance which seems inevitable after committing oneself to a particular alternative, whether that be a spouse, a home, a job, or any other important choice. In the Monitoring the Future data, we do not have a long enough follow-up period to determine whether these respondents would show a gradual increase in satisfaction as their marriages continue for several years, but the initial pattern — an initial elevation followed by a sharp decline — is entirely consistent with the pattern observed in the 1971 retrospective data.

Summary

We began this chapter by examining the average levels of satisfaction reported by adults in five different marital status categories. We observed that those who seem most satisfied with their lives are those who are married and living with their spouses, while the least satisfied are those who are divorced, and to an even greater extent those who are separated from their spouses but not divorced. Intermediate in subjective well-being are those who are widowed and those who have never married. Among young adults (those in their late teens and early twenties), married respondents tend to be more satisfied than those who are neither married nor engaged to be married; but those who are engaged to be married feel about as well off as those already married.

Retrospective data about how long a respondent had been in his or her current marital status afforded us a first look at how satisfaction with life may vary, not just with marital status, but with time since the transition to that status; but there was little evidence of a dynamic process in these data. At least across those in the first five years in each marital status, there was no evidence of either decline or rise in life satisfaction.

Panel data are a more powerful tool for examining dynamic processes, however, and in the latter part of the chapter we examined data from a highly self-selected panel of adults from the 1971 and 1978 Quality of Life surveys and from representative samples of young adults from the Monitoring the Future study. Despite its small size and unrepresentativeness, the data from the panel of adults provides some suggestive patterns. Those who were married at both interviews, conducted seven years apart, showed a slight decline in life satisfaction, while those who remained widowed, divorced, or separated showed slight increases, and the few who went from married to unmarried showed large average declines.

Panel data from young adults in the Monitoring the Future also show interesting patterns. The majority of these respondents remained unmarried at both of two successive data collections, and they showed practically no average change in satisfaction or happiness. On the other hand, those who became either married or engaged during the interval between data collections reported substantial average increases in well-being. This provides confirmatory evidence for the hypothesis suggested by cross-sectional data, that it is the decision to marry someone which enhances the quality of life, not the actual marriage. The panel data suggest another pattern, however, that was not observed from the cross-sectional data: just as with the panel data from adults of all ages, those who were married at both data collections showed a decline in reported well-being. Another observation is that those who were married or engaged at the second but not at the first data collection were slightly more satisfied at the first data collection than those who remained unmarried and unengaged. This suggests that a relatively small part of the explanation for the higher satisfaction of married respondents may lie in the selection process whereby young people become married. Those in more favorable circumstances, or those with more positive outlooks on life, may be more likely to commit themselves to marriage, and to be more attractive as potential mates, than those in less favorable circumstances or with more negative outlooks.

In short, while the purpose of this chapter has been descriptive rather than explanatory, it has raised several suggestions for causal pathways that could account for some or all of the relationship between marital status and the subjective quality of life. We will return to these hypotheses in the second section of this report.

CHAPTER 5

THE RELATIONSHIP OF OTHER VARIABLES TO
THE SUBJECTIVE QUALITY OF LIFE

In the preceding chapter we considered in some detail the relationship between marital status and reported levels of satisfaction with life. There are any number of other characteristics of respondents that could be examined in similar fashion with respect to their impact on the subjective quality of life. In this chapter we shall focus on a few characteristics that, like marital status, frequently change during late adolescence and early adulthood. Young people often must adjust to a variety of major changes in their situations: for example, they may complete their education, start a job and a career, leave their parental home, and become a parent, all in the space of just a few years.

As in Chapter 4, we will examine both cross-sectionally observed differences in the subjective well-being of persons with different characteristics, and changes in levels of well-being reported by respondents in panel samples who have undergone transitions with respect to these characteristics. We will examine the patterns of subjective well-being associated with several characteristics, including employment or student status, living arrangements, and parenthood. In this chapter, as in Chapter 4, each of these relationships will be described in isolation, without taking into account the possibility of spuriousness and without trying to explain the relationships through the mediating effects of other variables.

Our treatment of these relationships will be more limited than our consideration of marital status, since the latter is the primary focus of this report. Our primary purpose in conducting these analyses is to give greater context to the effects of marital status, in two senses. First, the magnitude of the effects of marital status can better be judged when considered relative to the magnitude of the effects of other characteristics. Second, the decision to marry does not occur in a vacuum but rather as part of a general process whereby adolescents take on adult roles, and so it is possible that some of the differences in life quality that we have observed between marital statuses are more properly explained in terms of other characteristics that are associated with marriage. The latter possibility will not be taken up seriously until the second section of this report, but the descriptive data presented in this chapter lay the groundwork for the subsequent causal analysis.

The analyses reported in this chapter are based on data from respondents who participated in the base-year data collection as high school seniors in the years 1976 through 1980 *and* in both of the first two follow-up data collections during their first four years after high school. We will distinguish between male and female respondents in this chapter, conducting the analyses separately for each sex to permit distinctions to be observed in the effects of the various transitions.

Marital Status

We begin with marital status, the variable that was the focus of Chapter 4, in order to provide data for this characteristic that can be directly compared to data to be presented subsequently for other characteristics. The entries in the first row of Table 5-1 are the average levels of satisfaction and happiness reported by married respondents, expressed as deviations from the average for unmarried respondents, at the time of the second follow-up.[1] There are no surprises here; the pattern is familiar from Chapter 4. Among both men and women, those who were married reported levels of subjective well-being that were about 0.25 standardized units above the levels reported by the unmarried on these variables.[2] The difference in happiness was greater among women (.35 units) than among men (.18 units), but the general picture is the same for both sexes and both measures.

Living Arrangements

One of the transitions that often accompanies marriage is a change in living arrangements. For young adults in the age range considered here, marriage is often the occasion on which they first stop living with their parents. The departure from the parental home, however, may also occur independently of marriage; indeed, the first few years after high school are a period during which most young people do establish separate living arrangements. By the time of the first follow-up data collection (one or two years after their senior year), 46 percent of the men and 49 percent of the women were not living with their parents. Two years later these percentages had increased to 61 and 65, respectively. That there is a relationship between marital status and living arrangements is obvious; among women at the time of the second follow-up, only 3 percent of those living with their

---

[1]In this chapter we have had to drop one of the marital status distinctions drawn in Chapter 4: that between unmarried persons who are engaged and those who are not engaged. As we shall see, it is important to distinguish unmarried respondents according to whether or not they are living with their parents, and to have retained this distinction as well as that between engaged and unengaged single respondents would have resulted in subgroups with very small sample sizes.

[2]The coefficients shown in Table 5-1 and in all subsequent tables have been partially standardized by dividing them by the standard deviation of the dependent variable for the combined samples of five cohorts of high school seniors (those in the classes of 1976 through 1980, the cohorts from which the data analyzed in this chapter are taken). This partial standardization procedure eliminates arbitrary differences in the scale units for different dependent variables, while preserving comparable units for comparisons of the effects of different predictor variables and for men and women.

parents were married, whereas 41 percent of those *not* living with their parents were married; for men, the comparable percentages are 2 and 25.[1] It is appropriate to ask, therefore, the extent to which the observed differences between married and unmarried respondents reflect differences in living arrangements.

Cross-Sectional Differences

The deviations of those who were still living with their parents from those in other living arrangements are shown in the second row of Table 5–1. Comparing the entries in this row with those in the first row (for married respondents), we observe that the difference in well-being between those who had and those who had not left the parental home was almost as great as that between those who have and those who have not yet married. The general pattern suggests that at least part of the explanation for the higher levels of well-being reported by married respondents may lie with departure from the parental home rather than specifically with marriage, but that marriage may have its own unique effects as well. This is, however, only a first step toward isolating the unique effects of marriage.

Changes Observed in Panel Data

As our next step, we examined *changes* in the life quality measures that accompany transitions from one living arrangement or marital status to another. We will rely on data from the same respondents as in the cross-sectional analyses just reported, but now our reason for confining our attention to those who participated in the two follow-ups as well as the base-year data collection becomes apparent: we will examine changes in life satisfaction and happiness from base-year through the second follow-up for groups of respondents differentiated according to their marital status and living arrangements at all three data collections.

We distinguish three groups of respondents:

(1) not married, living with their parents;

(2) not married, *not* living with their parents; and

(3) married.

Making these distinctions at each of three data collections allows a total of 27 possible patterns, but only a few of these were represented by enough respondents to allow meaningful analysis. To begin with, almost all of the

---

[1]The questions about marital status and living arrangements refer to somewhat different times, as documented in the Appendix to this report, and so these percentages may underestimate the relationship between the two variables.

Table 5-1

Regression Analyses: Predicting Level of Life Satisfaction and Happiness from Current Characteristics (Monitoring the Future Panel Data)[1]

Predictor	Life Satisfaction		Happiness		Average[3]
	Females	Males	Females	Males	
Married	.223[2] (.049)	.227 (.063)	.354 (.046)	.184 (.061)	.247
Live with parents	-.204 (.046)	-.115 (.047)	-.280 (.043)	-.234 (.046)	-.208
Parent or not?	-.030 (.058)	.083 (.082)	-.101 (.055)	-.089 (.080)	-.034
Work/student status					
Student	.058 (.028)	.036 (.026)	.134 (.030)	.182 (.029)	.103
Working	-.002 (.023)	-.015 (.022)	-.031 (.024)	-.089 (.024)	-.034
Homemaker	.084 (.072)		.103 (.076)		.094
Unemployed	-.252 (.067)	-.167 (.073)	-.361 (.071)	-.426 (.080)	-.302
All others	-.025 (.046)	.043 (.052)	-.056 (.049)	.022 (.057)	-.004
Liberal political Orientation	-.077 (.030)	-.026 (.025)	-.120 (.028)	-.084 (.025)	-.077
Religion					
Church attendance	.056 (.028)	.021 (.030)	.123 (.027)	.087 (.029)	.072
Importance	.032 (.030)	.066 (.029)	-.018 (.028)	.027 (.029)	.027
Dating frequency	.099 (.015)	.094 (.017)	.140 (.014)	.112 (.016)	.111

NOTES: [1] The data are from participants in the base year of the Monitoring the Future study in 1976 through 1980 who also participated in the first two follow-ups. The variables shown in this table were all measured at the second follow-up. Definitions of the predictor variables are given in the Appendix.

[2] The entries are bivariate or multivariate regression coefficients for each variable or set of variables; that is, each variable or set of variables is considered in isolation, without controlling on the other variables. These regression coefficients and their standard errors have been partially standardized by dividing them by a constant: 1.458 for life satisfaction, and 0.552 for happiness. (These are the standard deviations of these variables for the entire sample in the base years of data collection for the samples represented here, 1976-80.) The standard errors of these coefficients are shown in parentheses.

[3] The entries in the right hand column are the simple average of those in the four preceding columns.

respondents were living with their parents at the time of the base year data collection, when they were high school seniors; the few who did not are omitted from this analysis. Furthermore, if we think of the three categories in the order listed above as an ordered sequence, only a small proportion took a step "backwards" by, for example, returning to live with their parents after marriage or another living arrangement; and those who did so are also omitted from this analysis.

These omissions leave us with just six groups to examine. Figure 5–1 displays the average levels of life satisfaction reported by respondents in each of these groups, plus the combined averages across all six groups, at each of the three data collections. As already noted in Chapter 2, the age trends for both of these global variables are weak at best, and are especially weak for men: for the sample of men as a whole, Figure 5–1 shows no change in satisfaction across the age range represented by these three data collections (about 18 through 22), while for women there is a slight positive trend. This lack of change is also observed for most of the subgroups distinguished in Figure 5–1, but there are some exceptions which are by now familiar. There are rather large increases (about 0.4 standard deviation units) for both men and women at the time of the data collection following marriage (all these transitions are shown by dashed lines). Some groups showed a *decline* in satisfaction between the base-year and the first follow-up, and these tended to be groups of respondents who continued to live with their parents at that time. Only one group of each sex showed a decline in satisfaction between the first and second follow-ups, however, and it should come as no surprise by now to observe that these were respondents who had already married by the time of the first follow-up (the "married-married" transition is shown by dotted lines, while other transitions are shown by solid lines). In other words, we are seeing again the pattern observed in Chapter 4 of an initial increase in satisfaction following marriage, and then a decline as the marriage continues.

For the most part, the patterns observed with respect to life satisfaction are replicated with respect to happiness, as shown in Figure 5–2. For three of four groups of respondents who married between the first and second follow-ups, there was a substantial rise in happiness across this interval, which for women was superimposed on a general upward trend. A decline in satisfaction is observed among women who were married at the time of both the first and the second follow-up, but *not* among men in this situation. We have no ready interpretation for the latter observation. The total number of young men in these samples who were married by FU1 was less than one hundred so that there may be considerable sampling variation in the estimates for this group.

Our final observation from Figures 5–1 and 5–2 is that, with just one exception, the groups of respondents who had married by the second follow-up reported above average levels of happiness and satisfaction at the base year. We observed this pattern in Chapter 4 as well, and noted there that this lends some support to the hypothesis that part of the explanation for the relationship between marital status and subjective life quality is earlier selection (by self and/or by prospective mates) of persons with more positive outlooks on life into the marital pool.

Figure 5–1
Patterns of Life Satisfaction Reported by Respondents in Each
of Six Marital Status/Living Arrangements Groups
Monitoring the Future Panel Data

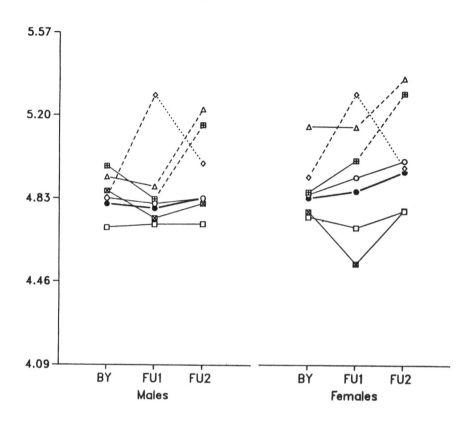

Living arrangements at...

	Follow-Up 1	Follow-Up 2	Male N	Female N
□	With Parents ...	With Parents	539	616
▣	With Parents ...	Other	245	239
⊞	With Parents ...	Married	117	232
○	Other ...	Other	588	515
△	Other ...	Married	110	158
◇	Married ...	Married	54	202
●	Total ...	Total	1652	1962

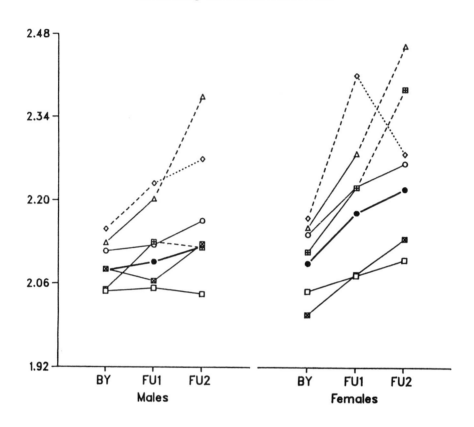

Figure 5-2
Patterns of Happiness Reported by Respondents in Each of
Six Marital Status/Living Arrangements Groups
Monitoring the Future Panel Data

Living arrangements at...

	Follow-Up 1	Follow-Up 2	Male N	Female N
□	With Parents ...	With Parents	695	780
▨	With Parents ...	Other	313	302
⊞	With Parents ...	Married	153	275
○	Other ...	Other	633	601
△	Other ...	Married	68	126
◇	Married ...	Married	73	267
●	Total ...	Total	1933	2351

Parenthood

Another transition that is related to marriage in the path toward adult responsibilities is that of becoming a parent. Only a small proportion of the respondents had made this transition by the time of the second follow-up: at that time, 17 percent of the women and 9 percent of the men said that they had one or more children. Moreover, those who had become parents at so young an age may not represent well the consequences of parenthood for the broader population, so the findings from the present analysis should not be generalized as estimates of the effects of parenthood at later ages.

Cross-Sectional Differences

The third row of Table 5–1 shows the differences between respondents who were parents at the time of the second follow-up and other respondents. The differences are all small, and not statistically significant at conventional levels, but three of the four are negative, suggesting that parenthood at a young age may tend to have a slight depressing effect on the subjective quality of life.

Changes Observed in Panel Data

The transition to being a parent is not accompanied by statistically significant changes in the well-being of young people, but there is an interesting, though small, sex difference. Among men there is an average *increase* in the measures of well-being, amounting to almost 0.2 standardized units for life satisfaction (data not shown), while among women there is an average *decrease* in both measures. Since the major responsibilities for the care of infants generally falls to their mothers, this would not be an inexplicable finding if it can be replicated.

Work and Student Status

In addition to changes in family life and living arrangements, young adults are also undergoing major transitions in their work lives. After high school, about half of the graduates continue at least part time as students; some of these quickly drop out, but others return to school after a few years of employment or military service. Of those who immediately enter the labor force, most are able to find jobs but some experience intervals of unemployment. Among the men in the Monitoring the Future study, at the time of the second follow-up 36 percent were primarily students, 44 percent were employed full-time, and 11 percent were unemployed (the remaining 9 percent could not be neatly classified into one of these categories). Among women, 31 percent were students, 41 percent were employed full-time, 7 percent were unemployed, and 6 percent were primarily homemakers.

From these numbers, it is clear that about two thirds of the respondents had made at least one major transition in their work careers: they had given up their roles as primarily students. Moreover, most of them had entered the labor force.

Cross-Sectional Differences

To examine the possible consequences of such transitions, we begin with consideration of the regression coefficients in Table 5–1. The coefficients shown for each status (student, employed, homemaker, and unemployed) are deviations from the overall mean at the time of the second follow-up data collection. The most striking and consistent pattern observed here is the relatively low happiness and satisfaction reported by those who were unemployed. In particular, unemployed men were 0.4 standardized units below the mean level on the happiness item. Those who had remained students were happier than others of their age, and men who had full-time jobs were somewhat below the average on both the happiness and satisfaction items. Women who were homemakers, on the other hand, tended to be somewhat above average on both items.

Changes Observed in Panel Data

We again can examine *changes* in the subjective quality of life reported by persons making transitions between the various work and student statuses. Only five (four for males) patterns across the three data collections were represented by enough respondents to be considered in this analysis:

> (1) those who were full-time students at both FU1 and FU2 (all respondents were students at the base year data collection);
>
> (2) those who were full-time students at FU1 but full-time employed at FU2;
>
> (3) those who were employed full-time at both FU1 and FU2;
>
> (4) those who were unemployed at FU2; and
>
> (5) women who were homemakers at FU2.

The average levels of life satisfaction reported by each of these groups, and by the total sample, are shown in Figure 5–3, and Figure 5–4 provides the same information about levels of happiness. These graphs are remarkable primarily for how similar the trends and levels are for each group, but there are some differences as well, in particular for those who were unemployed at the time of the second follow-up (FU2). Males in this category were considerably less satisfied and happy by FU2 than they had been in the base year; and while females in this category did not show much change, they started out at levels well below average and stayed there, suggesting that pre-existing conditions may account both for their subsequent unemployment and for their dissatisfaction and unhappiness. At the other extreme, males who were students at all three data collections started out and remained happier than other respondents. Intermediate are those who made the transition from full-time student to full-time worker between the first and second follow-ups; both males and females in this category showed slight declines in satisfaction.

Other Characteristics and Transitions

Young people differ on many characteristics besides those associated with the major transitions just listed. Indicators of a few such characteristics are included at the bottom of Table 5–1.

Political Orientation

High school graduates have generally reached the age of eligibility to vote, and their orientation to political parties and partisan issues may be in flux. One indicator of political orientation that was asked in the panel study is a question about their overall liberalism or conservatism. On a six-point scale, over half of the respondents either described themselves as "moderate" or did not classify themselves; one in every four or five males, and one in seven or eight females, described themselves as "conservative" or "very conservative"; one in five of each sex described themselves "liberal" or "very liberal"; and the last 1 to 4 percent described themselves as "radical." The regression coefficients for this variable indicate that those classifying themselves at the liberal end of this scale were somewhat less happy and satisfied with their lives than were their more conservative counterparts.

Changes Observed in Panel Data. Changes in happiness and satisfaction that accompany changes in political orientation (not shown) are even smaller than the cross-sectional differences observed in Table 5–1. The average coefficient across the two indicators and both sexes is less than 0.02 standard deviation units, and all four are statistically insignificant.

Religion

Two indicators of the religious commitment of the respondents included in the Monitoring the Future study are the frequency of attendance at religious services, and the importance of religion in their lives. These two variables are related to one another, but by no means perfectly (the correlation at FU2 was 0.6 for both males and females), so we consider their simultaneous influence on (i.e., relationship to) the measures of subjective well-being.

Figure 5–3
Patterns of Life Satisfaction Reported by Respondents in Each
of Five Employment/Education Transition Groups
Monitoring the Future Panel Data

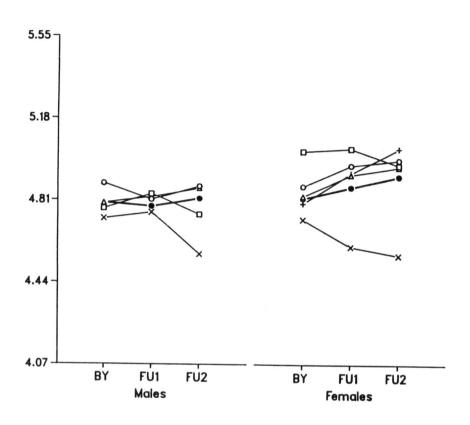

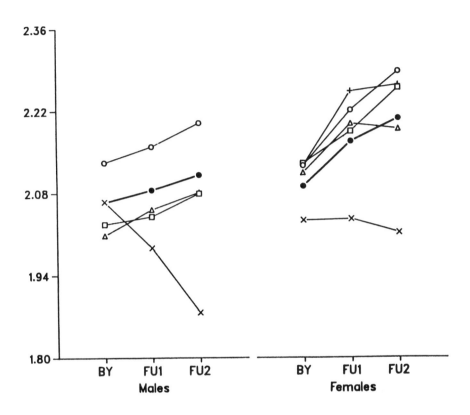

Figure 5–4
Patterns of Happiness Reported by Respondents in Each of
Five Employment/Education Transition Groups
Monitoring the Future Panel Data

Student/Employment Status at...

	Follow-Up 1		Follow-Up 2	Male N	Female N
O	Student	...	Student	696	754
□	Student	...	Employed	199	316
△	Employed	...	Employed	592	577
+	Any	...	Homemaker	(NA)	182
✗	Any	...	Unemployed	149	200
●	Total	...	Total	2267	2868

The proportion of respondents who said that they attended religious services on a weekly basis dropped from about 40 percent in the base year, when most of them were living at home with their parents, to about 25 percent at the second follow-up. Those who frequently attended religious services at the latter data collection were happier, and slightly more satisfied with their lives, than those who attended less often.[1] Despite the decline in attendance of formal religious services, there is no decline in the importance respondents attached to religion; on the contrary, there was actually a slight increase in the proportion who said that religion is "very important" in their lives (from about 29 percent in the base year to about 34 percent at the second follow-up). After controlling on variation in religious attendance, however, the relationship of this variable to the subjective quality of life is weak.

Changes Observed in Panel Data. Estimates of the relationships of changes with respect to these religious items and changes in the subjective well-being measures (not shown) are generally consistent with those between their static score counterparts, but there are differences worth noting. Increases in frequency of attendance at religious services are accompanied by very slight average reductions in satisfaction and increases in happiness, none approaching statistical significance. On the other hand, relationships involving the importance of religion estimated from change score analysis are more than twice as large as those based on static scores. If this can be replicated, it suggests that static score differences may underestimate the differences in well-being associated with the importance attached to religion by individuals.

Frequency of Dating

An indicator of at least the quantity of the social life of the respondents, if not its quality, is a self-report on the average frequency of going out with a date (or with their spouse if they were married). The proportion of respondents who never went out on dates declined markedly in the four years after high school, but the number who went out more than three times a week also declined, and thus there is no trend in the overall mean frequency of dating.

The differences in well-being that accompany a one-unit difference in dates per week average about 0.1 standardized units for satisfaction and slightly more for happiness. Thus, for example, if woman A dates more than three times a week (coded 6) and woman B dates two or three times a month (coded 3), then (other things being equal) A would be expected to be about 0.4 standardized units happier than B — which, as it happens, is similar to the difference between married and unmarried women.

---

[1]The regression coefficients shown in Table 5–1 indicate the difference on the dependent variable associated with a one-point increase on a four-point scale with categories ranging from "never" to "about once a week or more." The full scale is given in the Appendix to this report.

86

Changes Observed in Panel Data. Estimates of the effects of dating frequency on changes in well-being (not shown) are in the same direction as those based on static scores, but are weaker, averaging somewhat over half as large.

Summary

The intention of this chapter was to provide a context within which to interpret the differences in subjective well-being reported by married and unmarried respondents, and differences in the changes in well-being reported by respondents who experienced marital transitions.

Looking first at differences in levels of well-being, we observed that marital status is an important, but by no means overwhelming, factor relative to the other variables under consideration. The differences between married respondents and those who were unmarried averaged about a quarter of a standard deviation unit. The difference between young people living with their parents and those in other living arrangements (including those who were married) is almost as large as the difference between the married and unmarried respondents. The marital status difference is substantially larger than that observed between those who were full-time students and those who were working full-time, or between women who were full-time homemakers and those who were either students or employed outside the home. Across the work/student categories, only the differences associated with unemployment are larger than those associated with marriage.

Several other characteristics of respondents were examined, and most were associated with only rather small differences in satisfaction and happiness relative to those associated with marital status; these variables included parenthood, political orientation, and religiosity. The only exception, along with unemployment and living arrangements, is the number of dates per week.

Reviewing now the patterns of change revealed by panel data, we observed increases in satisfaction and happiness among those who made the transition from unmarried to married. Transitions across other categories of the marital status/living arrangements variable for the most part showed no particular pattern, except for those who remained married; consistent with the observation in Chapter 4, these respondents tended to show a decline in well-being.

For those who made changes in their work and student roles, there was considerable stability at least at the average level; but men who were unemployed at the later data collection showed substantial declines in well-being and women who were unemployed appear to have been relatively unhappy and dissatisfied even as high school students. Changes in well-being associated with changes in the importance attached to religion suggest that cross-sectional differences may underestimate the strength of the relationship between this variable and the quality of life, while changes associated with frequency of dating suggest that cross-sectional differences may overestimate the effects of the latter variable.

Across the entire set of regression coefficients displayed in Table 5-1, the differences in subjective life quality associated with marital status are larger than those associated with any of the other characteristics considered except for unemployment or a substantial change in the frequency of dating. We also noted that respondents who had left their parental home reported considerably higher levels of satisfaction and happiness than those who were living with their parents. The pattern suggested that part of the explanation for the elevated well-being reported by married respondents may be the transition from a child in the parental home to the greater independence found by establishing a separate household.

The pattern just noted involving marital status and living arrangements returns us to the question of how marital status is related to the other variables. Even though Table 5-1 presents the relationships of each of these variables in isolation from the others, they are not really independent. In addition to the obvious relationship between marital status and living arrangements, marital status is also related to parenthood and to adoption of the homemaker role by some women. To what extent can the higher life quality reported by married persons be explained by such relationships between marital status and other transitions? We also might question the extent to which preexisting differences between those who marry at relatively young ages and other respondents may explain these marital status differences in subjective life quality. It is to such questions that we turn our attention in the next section of this report.

SECTION II CAUSAL ANALYSIS

CHAPTER 6

APPROACHES TO CAUSAL ANALYSIS

Introduction

We now take up the question of how to interpret the relationships observed in the chapters in the first section of this report, and in particular that between marital status and the subjective quality of life. Causal analysis is a topic that has concerned scientists and philosophers of science for centuries; we do not treat this topic at length here, but we do consider some of the issues involved in causal analysis that are particularly relevant to our own analyses.

Any statement about relationships among variables is inevitably tinged by, if not explicitly formulated in terms of, a causal model: an assumption, that is, about why the variables are associated in the way they are. Humans think in causal terms; the observation of a relationship between two types of phenomena generally prompts inferences about why that relationship exists. It thus behooves the author of a scientific discourse to deal explicitly with questions of causality, since if a statement about a relationship is made without discussion of the causal model adopted by the author, then most readers will search for and supply their own. In the latter case, it often turns out that the model supplied by the reader is not identical to the implicit model of the author, and misunderstandings may proliferate. In the social sciences, at least, there is ample room for such alternative explanations of just about any observed relationship.

The situation can be illustrated with the relationship that is central to the research described in this report: that between marital status and the subjective quality of life. An interpretation of this relationship that immediately comes to mind is that marital status has a causal influence on life satisfaction: the married state is more satisfying than the nonmarried state, at least for most people. A slight modification on this interpretation is one that elaborates the relationship in terms of one or more intervening variables: for example, that being married is directly responsible for greater fulfillment of the need for affiliation, or for sexual intimacy, or any number of other biological and/or psychological needs; and that the extent to which such needs are met in turn has a causal influence on life satisfaction.

This is not, however, the only plausible interpretation of the relationship between marital status and life satisfaction. One alternative is that the causal flow is in the reverse direction: those who are more satisfied with their lives are more likely to enter into, and remain in, the married status. Indeed, it is entirely possible that both causal mechanisms are at work.

Nor have we by any means exhausted the list of possible interpretations of the simple relationship between two variables. Another possibility is that the relationship is entirely or partially spurious, reflecting not a causal influence of either variable on the other, but the influence of one or more other variables on both of these observed variables. For example, one could posit a personality characteristic which influences both the probability of marriage and the level of life satisfaction. If that personality characteristic has been measured, then the plausibility of that interpretation can be tested (although again, its truth cannot be confirmed, only disconfirmed) by examining the relationship between marital status and life satisfaction after controlling on that characteristic, either statistically or by cross-tabulations.

A specific form of the interpretation just mentioned is that measurement errors are responsible for the observed relationship. It is highly probable that survey measures of both marital status and life satisfaction are less than perfect reflections of the concepts those measures were intended to capture. Life satisfaction measures, in particular, may be expected to contain a substantial proportion of measurement error. The topic of errors in survey measures is a large one, and we will not try to review it here; excellent books and articles on the topic are available (for example, Andersen et al., 1979; Schuman and Presser, 1981). For our purposes, it is sufficient to note that although some of the measurement error is certainly random, and so would not account for the observed relationship with marital status, some of the error may be systematic and so could account for part if not all of the relationship with marital status. For example, unmarried respondents may differ from married respondents in being more willing to admit to problems and dissatisfactions.

Some of these possible explanations for an observed relationship can be tested if measures of relevant concepts are available in the data set that is being analyzed. Possible sources of spurious correlations can be controlled, for example, if measures of such variables are available. In practice, however, it is never possible to measure all such variables. In the experimental sciences, the solution to this dilemma is to randomly assign cases to different treatments, so that variation on unmeasured variables can be assumed to be uncorrelated with type of treatment (within limits of sampling variation) and so ignored as a source of bias in the estimates of the effects of treatment on the dependent variables. Ethical and practical considerations make experimental studies inappropriate for most questions of interest to social scientists, however, and so we must rely on statistical techniques to alert us to possible sources of bias and to reduce and eliminate such biases.

Panel data — i.e., repeated measurements on the same respondents — have often been regarded as the social scientist's answer to the experimental techniques available to natural and physical scientists. Unfortunately, panel data are not a panacea, and it has come to be recognized that the causal interpretation of relationships observed with panel data depends just as surely as in the case of cross-sectional data on the imposition of a causal model. For example, in the 1950s and 1960s it was commonly thought by social scientists that panel data would permit empirical methods to distinguish between two hypotheses concerning the causal relationship of two variables: does X cause Y, or does Y cause X? Beginning with the analysis of turnover tables by Lazarsfeld (1948) and then extended to the analysis of continuous variables through the cross-lagged panel correlation technique developed by Campbell (1963) and by Pelz and Andrews (1964), the notion was that the relative strengths of two relationships[1] — that between X at time 1 and Y at time 2, vs. that between Y at time 1 and X at time 2 — are sufficient to establish the causal path. The fallacy of this notion was pointed out by Duncan (1969; see also Heise, 1970). In order for such an inference to be drawn, strong assumptions must be made, in particular about the relative stabilities over time of X and Y and about the lags in the effects of these variables on one another.

The cross-lagged panel correlation approach has more recently been popular as a means of testing for, or even controlling for, spuriousness (Duncan, 1972; Kenny, 1973). Kessler and Greenberg (1981) review this approach, and conclude (p. 72) that it is only "a very limited test of a narrowly specified null hypothesis without any serious implications for parameter estimation in structural models. . ." and that it is inappropriate as a method to control for spuriousness.

These past misuses of panel data for causal analysis should not be taken to mean that panel data are of no value for causal analysis. To the contrary, although panel data do not obviate the need for specification of a causal model and for the imposition of untestable assumptions implied by such a model, under certain circumstances, at least, they do offer important advantages over cross-sectional data in the estimation of the parameters of such a causal model.

In particular, while we agree with Kessler and Greenberg (1981) that the cross-lagged panel correlation technique is inappropriate as a method of removing the effects of spuriousness, we nonetheless shall argue that another approach to the analysis of panel data does offer the opportunity to remove the effects of spurious sources of covariance if it can be assumed that those characteristics do not change over time. For example, if personality factors are suspected of contributing to the covariance of marital status and life satisfaction, and if it is assumed that those personality factors do not change with age among adult respondents, then the relationship between *changes* in marital status and *changes* in life satisfaction across time would not be influenced by those personality factors (cf. Liker, Augustiniak, and Duncan, 1985). This example illustrates one type of additional opportunity for exploring causal relationships that are offered by panel data as compared to cross-sectional data, or by a series of cross-sectional data sets without a panel component. At the same time, it also illustrates the fact that panel data do not completely remove the ambiguities inherent in attempts to establish causal relationships. It may be possible to make weaker, more plausible assumptions if panel data are available, but it is not possible to avoid the necessity of such assumptions.

Another strength of panel data as compared to cross-sectional data is the increased opportunity they offer for estimation of dynamic causal

---

[1]Or the relative strength of the partial correlations between these variables, an approach suggested by Pelz and Andrews (1964) to control for differences in the stabilities of these variables.

models. Most of the interpretations of causal relationships that we have enumerated up to this point have been basically static in nature: for example, that one marital status is more satisfying than another, or that some kinds of people are more likely than others to give socially desirable answers to interview questions. Other types of explanations are more dynamic, including one that we have already mentioned: some people may be more likely to marry at relatively young ages than others, and this could result in a spurious relationship between marital status and life satisfaction. Causal hypotheses of this type are commonly estimated through use of retrospective data (event histories), but panel data offer definite advantages by establishing clearer evidence concerning the timing of events.[1]

For examining other types of dynamic models, panel data may be essential. If the model involves subjective phenomena, such as attitudes or evaluations, or events the occurrence or timing of which are soon forgotten, then retrospective reports may easily be distorted by subsequent events. For example, it would be foolhardy to use retrospective data to test the hypothesis that dissatisfaction with marriage increases the probability of divorce. Even if a strong relationship were found between level of marital satisfaction, as reported retrospectively for some time in the past, and subsequent probability of divorce, an obvious alternative explanation would be that respondents' memories of their feelings about a marriage (or their reports of those feelings) may have been influenced by the subsequent disposition of that marriage. Panel data, on the other hand, would not suffer from this limitation. The relationship between self-reported marital satisfaction on one occasion and subsequent probability of divorce, as measured on later occasions, would offer solid evidence for a causal relationship. This is not to say that there would not be other competing explanations to explore, but only that the obvious competing explanation of faulty recall would not be at issue.

The distinction between static and dynamic models is probably largely artificial, an accident imposed by the fact that much of social science data is cross-sectional with only crude approximations of temporal variation. As panel data become more widely available, and as techniques for estimation of explicitly dynamic models become more widely known, the distinction may become less important. Nevertheless, we still find it useful to distinguish between causal explanations that focus on the states that individuals are in at a particular time and those that focus on the process by which individuals come to be in those states, including factors that influence the probability of changing from one discrete state to another and those that influence the rate at which a continuous variable is changing. Returning to the example of the relationship between marital status and satisfaction with life, we have already considered the first type of explanation: the married state may be intrinsically more satisfying for most people than any other

---

[1]Techniques for estimation of dynamic models are reviewed in several recent articles and books, most notably Tuma and Hannan (1984). Other references include Allison, 1982, 1984; Coleman, 1964, 1968, 1981; Kessler and Greenberg, 1981; and Tuma, 1982.

marital status. A possible dynamic explanation for the observed relation-ship is that the transition from the single to the married status produces a positive gradient in satisfaction for most people. In other words, perhaps it is not that marriage as a state is more satisfying than any other status, but rather that the marriage *event* produces a large, though possibly transient, surge in satisfaction.

In this chapter we will consider alternative approaches that have been taken to the causal analysis of survey data. We will illustrate these approaches in subsequent chapters as we undertake the causal analysis of several relationships observed in Chapters 4 and 5. The purpose of this chapter is not substantive, however, but expository.

Static Models

In order to quantify the impact of one state on another, it is neces-sary to specify a causal model and to estimate the parameters of that model. The simplest models involve just one dependent variable (the "effect") and one independent variable (the "cause"). Such a model can be written in general form in terms of the following expression:

$$Y_i = f_1(X_i) + \epsilon_i \tag{6.1}$$

where Y_i is the level of individual i on Y, the dependent variable; X_i is that individual's level on the independent variable; f_1 is an unspecified functional form, say a simple linear relationship or some more complex pattern; and ϵ_i is a term to signify all sources of variation in Y that is *not* explained by X.

Consider, for example, the relationship between marital status and reported life satisfaction as summarized in Table 4–1 in Chapter 4. To represent the hypothesis that this relationship reflects the causal influence of marital status on satisfaction, we can write the following specific version of expression (6.1):

$$Y_i = \sum_{j=1}^{J} \beta_j D_{ij} + \epsilon_i \ . \tag{6.2}$$

Here the independent variable, marital status, is simply a set of categories and so is represented by a set of dummy variables, D_{ij}, each of which is equal to 1 if individual i is in marital status j, 0 if that individual is in any other marital status. For individuals in marital status j, the model specifies that their expected satisfaction is a particular value represented by the parameter β_j. This parameter can be estimated very simply by finding the average satisfaction level of the individuals in the sample who are in status

j. ϵ_i, then, is the deviation of the satisfaction reported by individual i from the average for all persons in his or her marital status.

Single predictor models of the general type given by expression (6.1) can readily be expanded to models with multiple predictors of the following general form:

$$Y_i = f_1(\underline{X}_i) + \epsilon_i \tag{6.3}$$

where $\underline{X}_i$ now is a vector of observations on an arbitrary number, K, of state variables, $\{X_{1i}, X_{2i}, \ldots X_{Ki}\}$ and f_1 is an arbitrary function of those variables. Commonly the function is taken to be a simple weighted sum, and the model can be written in the following matrix notation:

$$Y_i = \underline{X}_i\gamma + \epsilon_i \tag{6.4}$$

where γ is a vector of parameters which are generally estimated using multiple regression analysis. Specifically, the model for differences in satisfaction between respondents in different marital statuses can be expanded to take account of other characteristics of the respondents thought to influence levels of satisfaction:

$$Y_i = \sum_{j=1}^{J} \beta_j D_{ij} + \underline{X}_i\gamma + \epsilon_i \ . \tag{6.5}$$

More elaborate versions of causal models could be specified by, for example, assuming that certain characteristics act as "intervening variables" in explaining the relationship between other variables; for example, that marital status has a causal influence on things such as economic resources and frequency of social activities, which in turn have causal influences on subjective well-being, thereby explaining some or all of the relationship between marital status and well-being. In this report we will in general not explicitly specify any such elaborations of the basic two-step model, although some of our interpretations of the estimates of multivariate models will be in terms of such possible causal paths.

Possible Consequences of Model Misspecification

How much confidence can we place in estimates of the effects of one variable on another, such as the multiple regression coefficients that could be obtained as estimates of the β and γ parameters in expression (6.5)? There are several sources of possible error in such estimates. A familiar example, sampling variance, results from the use of a sample of cases to represent a population, and is relatively straightforward to estimate, allowing confidence intervals to be placed about point estimates. Other sources of error are more troublesome and less easily quantified. A major concern in the estimation of any model is the possibility that the model has been *misspecified*. If one or more of the causes of variability in the dependent variable have not been included in the causal model that is being estimated, and if those variables are related to the causal variables that *are* included in the model, then the magnitude of the model parameters may be biased either upward or downward depending on the pattern of covariances among the variables. In a real sense, this is an insoluble problem with observational (as opposed to experimental) data; it is impossible to prove that an important cause of the dependent variable has *not* been omitted from a model. As pointed out in the introduction to this chapter, however, the use of panel data allows us to make some headway if it is reasonable to make certain assumptions.

Consider the model specified by the following expression:

$$Y_i = \sum_{j=1}^{J} \beta_j D_{ij} + \underline{X}_i \gamma + \underline{Z}_i \lambda + \epsilon_i \ . \tag{6.6}$$

This model is identical to that specified in expression (6.5) except for the inclusion of a set of M additional predictors, $\underline{Z}_i = \{Z_{1i}, Z_{2i}, \ldots, Z_{Mi}\}$. If the λ coefficients are not all zero and the covariances of these Z variables with the marital status and transition variables are also not zero, then parameter estimates based on expression (6.5) would be biased. We can use expression (6.6) to estimate models that include such additional variables, either on the basis of a theory which hypothesizes causal effects of certain variables or on the basis of covariances observed in the sample data, but such a strategy can only deal with Z variables that have been measured for the sample of cases being analyzed. If panel data are available, two strategies have been proposed to cope with the problem of unmeasured Z variables. We will consider both of these strategies.

Including Prior Level of the Dependent Variable as a Predictor of Current Level

The strategy that is probably most commonly used in the analysis of panel data is to include the dependent variable as measured at one or more previous times as a predictor of the current level. Too often, this procedure is adopted without considering the justification for it, so it is appropriate for us to consider the rationale before exemplifying the use of this procedure in subsequent chapters.

One inducement for including past level of the dependent variable as a predictor of current level may be simply to increase the proportion of explained variance. More often than not, the strongest correlate of the current level of a variable is the past level of that same variable, and so the predictive power of a regression model is greatly enhanced by including past level as a predictor; so it might seem obvious that it *should* be so included. This is not a compelling rationale, however; within the present context of estimating causal models, the objective of regression analysis is to enhance our understanding of causal processes, not to maximize predictive power. The best predictor of a person's eye color today is certainly that person's eye color yesterday, but no one would argue that yesterday's eye color in any sense "causes" today's eye color. For some variables, a convincing argument can be made that prior level is a proximate determinant of current level. An example is the level of use of addictive drugs, such as nicotine. A person reports heavy cigarette use at one time at least in part *because* of heavy use at a prior time. While this may be true, it is nevertheless not very helpful to use prior smoking behavior as a predictor of current smoking behavior if our objective is not simply to predict who smokes and who does not, but to understand *why* certain people are more likely to smoke than others. Whatever the dependent variable, it is difficult to make a convincing case that our understanding of its basic causes is enhanced by estimation of a model that includes as a predictor past level of that variable. This statement runs so counter to conventional practice, however, that it merits further discussion.

The assertion rests on the assumption that the past level of a variable is not a cause of current level. We cannot prove this as a general principle, but another example may be helpful. Consider an economic variable, income. The best predictor of labor income in year t is probably labor income in year t-1, but it is a long step from such correlational evidence to the inference that past income *causes* current income; and to draw that inference would be to cut short the search for the factors that are in a more basic sense causes of income level: that is, the characteristics of individuals, of occupations, of industries, of societies, and so on that produce the wide variance in income levels. The same argument applies to psychological and sociological variables, such as intelligence, alienation, or (to take the present focus) subjective well-being. People who were satisfied with their lives last year are often satisfied this year as well, as we saw from our estimates of stability coefficients in Chapter 3, and we can postulate causal paths that could account for some of that stability. For example, those who are satisfied with their lives may be better able to establish and maintain good marriages, jobs, and so on, which in turn contribute to higher levels of satisfaction at a later time. Nevertheless, the basic causes of satisfaction are those other factors, such as good marriages and stable jobs and the personal characteristics which aid in getting into and staying in those situations. To estimate a causal model that includes past level of the dependent variable as a cause of present level may only serve to obscure the search for those more basic causes.

One explanation for the stability of a variable such as life satisfaction is the stability of the factors that cause that variable. The exploration of the reasons for the stability of those determinants may be other acts in the same play. That is, these characteristics may be stable not because the past determines the present but because of the stability of *their* determinants. Clearly, to avoid an infinite regress we must assume that certain characteristics are inherently more-or-less stable. Such characteristics may differ by scientific discipline: what social psychology takes as given may be the focus of exploration of physiological psychology, which in turn takes as given biological characteristics, and so on. For example, differences in intelligence may be taken as a given in one context, but explanations for such differences are sought in genetic makeup or child-rearing practices in another context, while explanations for variations in genetic makeup are sought in a third context. Whatever the context, however, the principle is the same: whatever it is that one is trying to explain, it rarely (if ever) is plausible to include levels of that variable in the past as a cause of its present level.

Another rationale that has been offered for including past levels on the dependent variable in the regression model is a practical one: not that the past is itself a cause of the present, but that the past level is correlated with unmeasured causes of the present level. In terms of the model given by expression (6.6), the dependent variable at the earlier time is correlated with the omitted Z variables. The previous level is included, then, as a kind of instrumental variable for the Z variables. It is not a proper instrument, however, unless it can be safely assumed to be *un*correlated with the predictors that *are* included in the regression (controlling on the omitted Z variables). This rarely is a sensible assumption, since the reason for including those variables in the regression model is precisely because they are thought to be related to the current level of the dependent variable; this being the case, it is difficult to argue that, after controlling on the unmeasured Z variables, they would be unrelated to the level of the dependent variable at an earlier time.

It still might be argued that, as a practical matter, it may be better to include the past level of the dependent variable in the prediction equation because it is better to include even an improper instrument for unmeasured variables than to ignore entirely the possibility of such unmeasured causes. One approach to this question is to use simulation techniques, whereby the true causal model is known because it is specified by the simulator, and to determine how well the parameters of that true causal model are estimated if the regression model includes the past level of the dependent variable. Another approach is to ask whether there are alternative procedures for dealing with the possibility of misspecified models because of unmeasured Z variables. At least one such procedure has been proposed, and it is to a description of that procedure that we now turn.

Analysis of Change Scores

An alternative strategy that has been used with panel data to cope with the problem of possible unmeasured Z variables is to predict *change* rather than current level on the dependent variable. The rationale for this strategy is straightforward. The critical assumption is that the relevant Z variables do not change between data collections. This is most reasonable for characteristics which remain more or less fixed across the lifetime, or at least the adult lifetime, of an individual, as is often assumed about many personality characteristics. If expression (6.6) is written for two waves of data collection, say $t=1$ and $t=2$, and if the expression for time 1 is subtracted from the expression for time 2, the following difference equation is obtained:

$$\Delta Y_i = Y_{2i} - Y_{1i}$$

$$= \sum_{j=1}^{J} \beta_j (D_{2ij} - D_{1ij}) \tag{6.7}$$

$$+ (\underline{X}_{2i} - \underline{X}_{1i})\gamma + \epsilon_{2i} - \epsilon_{1i} \; .$$

The important feature to note about expression (6.7) is the disappearance of the Z variables. That is, conditional on the validity of the assumption that any omitted causal variables do not vary across data collections, parameter estimates for the marital transition variables derived from the change score expression (6.7) are unbiased.

The use of change scores offers a clear advantage over the use of static scores by reducing the potential for misspecified models. There is a price, however: in general, the standard errors of estimates based on change scores are greater than those based on static scores. The conventional wisdom tells us that this increase is likely to be large and that for this reason the use of change scores to estimate static models is to be eschewed. The conventional wisdom is wrong, however. For reasonably large sample sizes, and for a wide range of stabilities of the true values and measurement errors in the predictor variables, the ratio of the sampling errors for estimates based on change scores to those based on static scores is *not* excessively large. For now, we are basing this assertion on mathematical considerations which are developed in an appendix to this chapter, but in subsequent chapters we will put the assertion to empirical tests.

Dynamic Models

A general form of a dynamic model is as follows:

$$\frac{dY_{ti}}{dt} = f_2(\underline{X}_{ti}) + \epsilon_{ti} \; . \tag{6.8}$$

This is identical to expression (6.1) for the general form of a static model except that the left hand side, $\dfrac{dY_{it}}{dt}$, is the instantaneous rate of change in the dependent variable (for individual i at time t) rather than its level at a particular time. In general, of course, we are not able to measure the instantaneous rate of change of any variable, and in particular with survey data we usually must rely on measurements obtained at intervals of weeks, months, or years. More tractable versions of dynamic models can be derived from expression (6.8) through integration across a time interval. The following version assumes that the effects of the predictor variables are additive and linear, as we also assumed in expression (6.4) for static models:

$$
\begin{aligned}
\Delta Y_i &= \int_{t=0}^{\Delta t} \frac{dY_{ti}}{dt} dt \\
&= \int_{t=0}^{\Delta t} (\underline{X}_{ti}\underline{\gamma} + \epsilon_{ti}) dt \\
&= [\int_{t=0}^{\Delta t} \underline{X}_{ti} dt]\underline{\gamma} + \int_{t=0}^{\Delta t} \epsilon_{ti} dt .
\end{aligned}
\tag{6.9}
$$

Now if we assume that for each individual i the set of X variables change linearly from their values $\underline{X}_{1i}$ observed at time t_1 to their values $\underline{X}_{2i}$ observed at time t_2 $(= t_1 + \Delta t)$ so that at any intervening point in time their values $\underline{X}_{ti}$ are equal to $\underline{X}_{1i} + \underline{\alpha}_i t$ for a set of individual slopes $\underline{\alpha}_i,$[1] then the expression can be rewritten as:

$$
\begin{aligned}
\Delta Y_{ti} &= [\int_{t=0}^{\Delta t} (\underline{X}_{1i} + \underline{\alpha}_i t) dt]\underline{\gamma} + \int_{t=0}^{\Delta t} \epsilon_{ti} dt \\
&= \underline{X}_{1i}\underline{\gamma}\Delta t + (\Delta t)^2 \underline{\alpha}_i \underline{\gamma}/2 + v_i \\
&= \underline{X}_{1i}\underline{\gamma}\Delta t + \Delta t \underline{\Delta X}_i \underline{\gamma}/2 + v_i \\
&= \underline{X}_{1i}\underline{\gamma}\Delta t + \underline{\Delta X}_i \underline{\mu} + v_i
\end{aligned}
\tag{6.10}
$$

with a new set of parameters $\underline{\mu} = \Delta t \underline{\gamma}/2$ and a new stochastic term, $v_i = \int_{t=0}^{\Delta t} \epsilon_{ti} dt$. That is, if the rate of change in Y is a linear additive function of a set of X variables, then change in Y from one time to the next, t_1 to t_2, can be expressed as a linear additive function of the initial level and of the change in each of those X variables. The parameters in an expression such as (6.10) can be estimated using ordinary regression techniques. In reaching this simplification of the general model, we have assumed that measures of the predictor variables, $\{X_{1ti}, X_{2ti}, \ldots, X_{Kti}\}$, are available only at the beginning and end of the interval (t_1 and t_2 respectively), that the range of

---

[1] $\underline{\alpha}_i = (\underline{X}_{2i} - \underline{X}_{1i})/(t_2 - t_1) = \underline{\Delta X}_i/\Delta t.$

possible values for each X variable is a continuum, and that any change in an X variable between observations is linear over that interval.

A somewhat different version of the model is necessary if some of the X variables are discrete rather than continuous. With such a variable, the assumption that any change observed between two observations is linear over the interval between them is nonsensical, and we must deal with such variables in another fashion. To be specific, consider the classification of young adults developed in Chapter 5 according to their marital status and, if unmarried, their living arrangements. Since this is a categorical variable, it could be represented in expression (6.10) by a set of dummy variables. Moreover, we observed in Chapter 5 that the average change in life satisfaction and happiness varies according to the pattern of marital status and living arrangements at the beginning and end of a two-year period between successive data collections. For this reason, we want to incorporate the possibility of interaction effects involving initial and final status, rather than just the additive effects of these two states. One way to allow such interaction effects to be estimated is to incorporate into the model dummy variables which represent each transition of interest. This is illustrated by the following expression, where a person, i, who makes the transition from marital status j at time t_1 to marital status j' at time t_2 is given a value of 1 on the dummy variable $D_{jj'i}$ and 0 on the dummy variables representing other transition patterns:

$$\frac{dY_{ti}}{dt} = \sum_{j=1}^{J} \sum_{j'=1}^{J} \beta_{jj'} D_{jj'i} + \underline{X}_{ti}\gamma + \epsilon_{ti} \ . \tag{6.11}$$

Since the dummy variables representing each transition type have values of either 1 or 0, we assume that if the value of such a variable is observed to be different at observation times t_1 and t_2, there was an instantaneous jump from one value to the other at some point in the interval. Specifically, if (in the present example) $D_{jj'i}$ has a value of 1, then individual i was in marital status j at t_1 and remained in that status until, at some unknown time t_c, s/he entered status j', in which s/he remained through the second observation at t_2.[1] Suppressing the notation for other variables and the disturbance term, the model for change in the dependent variable for such an individual can be obtained through integration in parts:

---

[1] Or for all that can be known from observations only at t_1 and t_2, s/he may have switched statuses any (odd) number of times during the interval. We ignore this possibility; for the marital events considered in this report, such multiple events would be rare.

$$\Delta Y_i = \int_{t=t_1}^{t_2} \frac{dY_{ti}}{dt} dt$$

$$= \int_{t=t_1}^{t_2} \sum_{j=1}^{J} \sum_{j'=1}^{J} \beta_{jj'i} D_{jj'i} dt \qquad (6.12)$$

$$= \int_{t=t_1}^{t_c} \beta_{jj} dt + \int_{t=t_c}^{t_c+dt} \beta_{jj'} dt + \int_{t=t_c+dt}^{t_2} \beta_{j'j'} dt$$

$$= \beta_{jj}(t_c - t_1) + \beta_{jj'} dt + \beta_{j'j'}(t_2 - t_c)$$

$$= \beta_{jj'}^{*}$$

for a new parameter, $\beta_{jj'}^{*}$, defined for each pair of states j and j'. Expanding this to incorporate respondents in all transition patterns, and putting the X variables and error term back in, we have:

$$\Delta Y_i = \sum_{j=1}^{J} \sum_{j'=1}^{J} \beta_{jj'}^{*} D_{jj'i} + \underline{X}_{1i}\gamma\Delta t + \Delta\underline{X}_i\mu + v_i \; . \qquad (6.13)$$

Thus, although the underlying change process may be complex, the estimable function from a two-wave panel data set turns out to be simple and intuitive: the average change in the dependent variable is estimated for each distinct transition pattern, taking account of marital status at t_1 and t_2 (including the patterns of remaining in the same status at both times).

Alternative Models

The reader who is familiar with the literature on the estimation of dynamic models may have been puzzled by the divergence of our specification of such models, and the procedures for estimating them, from the treatment of these models by others, and it is time that we make these differences explicit along with our rationale.

The usual expression of a dynamic model for a continuous dependent variable (see Tuma and Hannon, 1984, p. 36 and p. 333 ff.; Kessler and Greenberg, 1981, p. 165 ff.) includes the level of the dependent variable as a predictor of its rate of change, and thus would add a term to our expression (6.8):

$$\frac{dY_{ti}}{dt} = f_3(\underline{X}_{ti}, Y_{ti}) + \epsilon_{ti} \ .$$

(6.14)

The rationale for including current level of the dependent variable as a *cause* of the rate at which it is changing is no more obvious to us than the rationale for including prior level of the dependent variable as a cause of its current level. We have no doubt that there is often a correlation between level and rate of change, but we would tend to regard this as an annoyance to be avoided wherever possible by suitable transformation of the dependent variable. For example, the rate of change of income is undoubtedly correlated with level of income, if income is measured in dollars, but this relationship might well be weakened if not eliminated by a logarithmic transformation. In any case, correlation does not imply a causal influence, and we suspect that including level of the dependent variable in the causal model only introduces bias into the estimated effects of true causal variables. We would not argue that it is *never* appropriate to include current level of a variable as a cause of its rate of change, but we would argue strongly against what seems to be the common practice of doing so automatically and thoughtlessly.

The inclusion of current level of the dependent variable in the causal model for the rate of change makes integration of the model over time somewhat more complex, as is apparent from comparison of the sources cited earlier (e.g., expression [7a] on page 338 in Tuma and Hannan, 1984) with our expressions (6.10) and (6.13). Moreover, whereas the dependent variable used in the estimation procedures we have proposed is *change* from one observation to another, the dependent variable used in other estimation procedures is the level at the time of the most recent observation. The estimation procedure developed for a causal model of the type given by expression (6.14) turns out to be remarkably similar to the procedure for estimating the parameters of a model which includes prior level of the dependent variable as a predictor of current level (see expression [4] on page 36 of Tuma and Hannan, 1984). In subsequent chapters, we will compare the estimates of causal effects derived from those models to estimates derived from models of the type given by expressions (6.1) and (6.8) as developed in this chapter.

Summary

In this chapter we described various approaches to the causal analysis of survey data, and in particular panel data. One basic distinction that we draw is between *static* and *dynamic* models. Static models have been much more common in the social sciences at least in part because most data available for analysis lacks adequate measurement of temporal variation. We began by briefly considering the estimation of static models using cross-sectional data, and then went on to consider the advantages of panel data for estimation of static models.

We observed that more powerful techniques for causal analysis can be employed if panel data are available. We described two competing approaches that have been advocated for such analyses. In the more conventional approach, current level of the dependent variable is predicted from past (and possibly present as well) levels of the independent variables; and, in addition, prior level of the dependent variable is included in the estimation model. We examined several possible justifications for including prior level of the dependent variable as a predictor of current level, and found none of them convincing. We then described an alternative approach to the causal analysis of panel data, in which the dependent variable is *change* rather than current level. Although this approach has often been dismissed because of the higher proportion of error variance in change scores relative to static scores, it offers the important advantage of reducing the possibility of biased estimates due to misspecified models. Moreover, the increase in sampling errors of estimates derived from change scores is generally rather minor.

We then considered dynamic models, which are concerned with the rate of *change* rather than *level* of the dependent variable. Dynamic models can be estimated from retrospective data obtained in a cross-sectional study, but there are definite advantages offered by panel data. We introduced some fairly simple dynamic models, and discussed methods for estimating the parameters of such models through the use of panel data which do not allow observation of instantaneous rates of change in the dependent variable, but only measures of overall change that accumulates over the period between successive observations.

In subsequent chapters we shall estimate several causal models, with particular attention to the effects of marital status, and of changes in marital status, on the subjective quality of life. We shall consider both static and dynamic models, estimating both types of models using each of two approaches described in this chapter: one in which the dependent variable is level at the final observation, and the other in which the dependent variable is change from one observation to the next.

Appendix to Chapter 6:

Comparison of Estimates from Cross-sectional and Panel Data

The accuracy of estimates of the causal influence of one variable on another depends on, among other factors: (1) whether the causal model has been properly specified; (2) the amount of measurement error and random variance in the dependent variable relative to the variance predicted by variables included in the causal model; and (3) the size of the sample. The relative accuracy of estimates based on panel as compared to cross-sectional data depends on how the design impacts on these and other factors. In this appendix, we specify several models and for each compare the accuracy of estimates from panel data to those from cross-sectional data. By definition, any model is a simplification of reality; and all of the models considered here are especially simple. The purpose is to explore the characteristics of models that would tend to favor panel data over cross-sectional data, or vice versa.

Model 1: One X Variable

We begin with an elementary model, with just one causal variable:

$$y_{ti} = \alpha + \beta x_{ti} + \epsilon_{ti} \ . \tag{6A.1}$$

It is assumed that the parameters (α and β) of this model are time-invariant, that the variances of the exogenous variables (σ_x^2 and σ_ϵ^2) are also time-invariant, and that the random term at time t, ϵ_{ti}, is independent of the X terms at the same and every other time and of the random terms at every other time. Given these assumptions, the following equalities hold:

$$\sigma_{y_t}^2 = \beta^2 \sigma_{x_t}^2 + \sigma_{\epsilon_t}^2 \tag{6A.2}$$

(by assumption, this is invariant across time);

$$\sigma_{y_t x_t} = \beta \sigma_{x_t}^2 \tag{6A.3}$$

(the correlation of X and Y at time t, which is also assumed to be invariant across time);

$$\sigma_{y_2 x_1} = \beta \sigma_{x_1 x_2} \tag{6A.4}$$

where $\sigma_{x_1 x_2}$ is the covariance of X_1 and X_2 at two times, $t=1$ and $t=2$;

$$\sigma_{y_1 x_2} = \beta \sigma_{x_1 x_2} \qquad (6A.5)$$

and

$$\sigma_{y_1 y_2} = \beta^2 \sigma_{x_1 x_2} . \qquad (6A.6)$$

Our objective, it is supposed, is to estimate the coefficient β, which represents the causal effect of X on Y according to the model specified by expression (6A.1). The data from which we propose to obtain such an estimate consist of two or more waves of panel data, but initially we will ignore the panel dimension of the data and estimate the parameter from cross-sectional data. The ordinary least squares estimate of β is given by the following expression:

$$\qquad (6A.7)$$

$$\hat{b} = s_{yx} / s_x^2 ,$$

where s_{yx} is the covariance of the Y and X variables observed in the data and s_x^2 is the variance of the observations on the X variable. If the model is properly specified by expression (6A.1), $\hat{b}$ is an unbiased estimator of β, and its variance can be written as:

$$\qquad (6A.8)$$

$$\sigma_{\hat{b}}^2 = (\sigma_y^2 - \beta^2 \sigma_x^2)/n\sigma_x^2$$

where n is the sample size.

Now we ask whether we could improve the estimate of β by taking into account that we have panel data: we have observed the values of the X and Y variables on the same set of cases at two or more times. Specifically, we consider change scores, obtained from panel data by subtracting observations at one time (say $t=1$) from those at another time ($t=2$). The model can then be written as follows, directly from expression (6A.1):

$$\Delta y_i = y_{2i} - y_{1i}$$

$$= \beta \Delta x_i + \Delta \epsilon_i . \qquad (6A.9)$$

If we assume that there is no autocorrelation in ϵ (i.e., $\sigma_{\epsilon_1 \epsilon_2} = 0$), the variances and covariances of the change scores are given by:

$$\sigma^2_{\Delta y} = \sigma^2_{y_1} + \sigma^2_{y_2} - 2\sigma_{y_1 y_2}$$ (6A.10)

$$= 2\beta^2(1 - \rho_{x_1 x_2})\sigma^2_x + 2\sigma^2_\epsilon ,$$

$$\sigma^2_{\Delta x} = 2(1 - \rho_{x_1 x_2})\sigma^2_x ,$$ (6A.11)

and

$$\sigma^2_{\Delta x \Delta y} = 2\beta(1 - \rho_{x_1 x_2}) \sigma^2_x ,$$ (6A.12)

where $\rho_{x_1 x_2}$ is the population value of the correlation between x_{1i} and x_{2i}. The least squares estimator from change data is:

(6A.13)

$$\tilde{b} = s_{\Delta y \Delta x} / s^2_{\Delta x} .$$

where $s_{\Delta y \Delta x}$ is the covariance of changes on the Y and X variables observed in the data and $s^2_{\Delta x}$ is the variance of the observed changes on the X variable. Like the least squares estimator from cross-sectional data, the least squares estimator from these change data is unbiased if the model is properly specified by expression (6A.1), and its variance can be written as:

$$\sigma^2_{\tilde{b}} = (\sigma^2_{\Delta y} - \beta^2 \sigma^2_{\Delta x})/n\sigma^2_{\Delta x} = \sigma^2_{\hat{b}}/(1 - \rho_{x_1 x_2}) ,$$ (6A.14)

where $\rho_{x_1 x_2}$ is the population value of the correlation between x_{i1} and x_{i2}.

Since $\rho_{x_1 x_2}$ is generally positive, expression (6A.14) tells us that the causal influence of X on Y is more accurately (i.e., with less variance) estimated from cross-sectional data than from change scores if the model is correctly specified by expression (6A.1). Indeed, the advantage of estimates from cross-sectional data is even greater than might first appear from inspection of expression (6A.14). If two waves of panel data are available, the regression coefficient β can be estimated from either change scores or by treating the panel data as two cross-sections. In the latter case, the total

sample size is on the order of twice as large as that for change scores.[1]
The relative advantage of cross-sectional data in this situation diminishes as
the number of waves of data collection increases; for example, with three
waves of data, the effective sample size for static score analysis would be on
the order of 3n (i.e., three times the size of the sample at each data collection), while the effective sample for change score analysis across one time
unit would be approximately 2n, or 2/3 that for static score analysis.

Another analysis strategy that has been so frequently advocated and
used with panel data in the social sciences as to have become the standard
(e.g., Harris, 1963; Cronbach and Furby, 1969; Kessler and Greenberg,
1981) is to introduce values of both the X and the Y variables from previous
times as predictors to current levels of Y:

$$y_{i2} = \alpha + \beta_1 x_{i1} + \beta_2 x_{i2} + \beta_3 y_{i1} + \epsilon_{i2} \ . \tag{6A.15}$$

It should be emphasized that this is not merely a different method for
estimating the coefficients in the model described by expression (6A.1), but
a different model: one that assumes the causal effect of X on Y is lagged
rather than simultaneous. As Liker et al. (1984) point out, the use of
change scores in their paper, and in the preceding discussion, is not intended
to estimate the parameters in a truly dynamic model but only to improve on
the estimation of a static model through the use of longitudinal data.

In this important sense, the choice between the use of change scores
and time 2 scores as the dependent variable depends on the assumption the
analyst chooses to make about the time lag of the effect of one variable on
another. For the type of data analyzed in this monograph, it makes more
sense to assume that the causal lag is "simultaneous" rather than "lagged."
The quotations in the preceding sentence are intended to imply that these
terms are relative, not absolute: that is, given that the waves of data collection are at intervals of at least a year, we are saying that the time lag of
causal effects for the variables we have considered is closer to zero than to a
year. With other types of data (for example, time series with a substantial
number of observations for each individual, or something approaching continuous observations), it would be possible to test empirically the time lag of
causation; but with the small number of observations and the length of time
between observations available to us this is not a feasible goal.

Apart from the difference in the assumption about the presence or absence of a time lag in effect of X on Y, there is also an important conceptual
distinction between the models specified by expressions (6A.1) and (6A.15).
The latter model introduces a prior measurement of the Y variable as a
predictor of its current level. Various justifications for this re-specification

---

[1]The effective sample size for the cross-sectional analysis is not, in general, fully
twice as large as that for change score analysis; since the observations in the two waves
are not independent, the effective sample size is reduced. Change scores, on the other
hand, can only be calculated for cases with non-missing observations at both times, so if
there is substantial sample attrition at the second data collection, or if there is a substantial proportion of item missing data, the sample size for change scores will be considerably
smaller than the sample size for just one wave of static scores.

of the causal model have been offered, including both concerns about measurement error and arguments based on the alleged necessity to take account of the correlation between the initial value of a variable and change on that variable. These justifications have been critically reviewed by Liker et al. (1985), who found them less than compelling for most types of data. Specifically with respect to the quality of life and life event data we have considered in this report, we find it difficult to justify the model specified in expression (6A.15). Our concern is with levels of satisfaction, with evaluations of one's life and of various domains of life; it is difficult to imagine in what sense satisfaction at one point in time can be considered a cause of satisfaction at a later time. This is not to imply that there is no stability in satisfaction levels; we have presented considerable evidence to the contrary. We interpret such stability, however, as evidence for the stability of situational factors and personal characteristics that influence satisfaction. We described our justification for this interpretation in the text of Chapter 6. We do not claim to have proven our case, however. Short of the perhaps unattainable goal of specifying the causes of satisfaction in sufficient detail to permit us to explain most if not all of its stability in terms of those causes, our interpretation, as well as the alternative, rests on assumption, not observation.

Model 2: One X Variable and One Z Variable

Our second model differs from the first only by inclusion of a second predictor:

$$y_{ti} = \alpha + \beta x_{ti} + \gamma z_i + \epsilon_{ti} \ . \tag{6A.16}$$

The same assumptions concerning time invariance of the coefficients and variances are made here as for Model 1; and it is also assumed that the Z variable does not change over time — that is, it refers to a stable characteristic of the units of analysis. To complete the specification of the model, let the correlation of the X and Z variables be noted by ρ_{xz}, which is assumed to be independent of t.

Now suppose that again our objective is to estimate the causal effect of X with respect to Y, and that we have panel data which include observations on X and Y for a set of n units; Z is unmeasured. The variance of the estimate of β from cross sectional data remains the same (see expression [6A.8]), but unlike the case for Model 1, such an estimator is generally *not* unbiased. The expected value of this estimator is given by:

$$E(\hat{b}) = \beta + \gamma \rho_{xz} \sigma_z / \sigma_x \ ; \tag{6A.17}$$

that is, the bias is zero only if Z has no causal influence on Y (i.e., $\gamma = 0$) *or* if X and Z are uncorrelated (i.e., if $\rho_{xz} = 0$). The variance of this estimator is:

$$\sigma_{\hat{b}}^2 = (\sigma_y^2 - \beta^2\sigma_x^2 - 2\beta\gamma\sigma_{xz})/n\sigma_x^2 \ . \tag{6A.18}$$

If we use change scores instead of static scores, we note that the Z variable drops out of the equation for Y; the estimator given by expression (6A.13) is unbiased whether the true model is 1 or 2. We are confronted with a choice between an estimator ($\hat{b}$) that may be biased and another ($\tilde{b}$) that is unbiased but which generally has greater variance. To permit an overall comparison of the two estimators, we evaluate the mean square error of each, where mean square error is defined as the sum of the variance of the estimator and the square of its bias. The mean square errors of the two estimators are given by the following expressions:

$$MSE(\hat{b}) = \frac{\sigma_y^2 - \beta^2\sigma_x^2 - 2\beta\gamma\sigma_{xz}}{2n\sigma_x^2} + (\gamma\rho_{xz}\sigma_z/\sigma_x)^2 \tag{6A.19}$$

and

$$MSE(\tilde{b}) = \frac{\sigma_y^2 - \beta^2\sigma_x^2 - \gamma^2\sigma_z^2 - 2\beta\gamma\sigma_{xz}}{n\sigma_x^2(1 - \rho_{x_1x_2})} , \tag{6A.20}$$

if the effective size of the sample available for making the estimate of $\hat{b}$ is 2n, twice as large as the sample available for estimating $\tilde{b}$. Given these conditions, $\hat{b}$ is a better estimator of β than is $\tilde{b}$ if the following condition holds:

$$n < \sigma_x^2 \frac{(\sigma_y^2 - \beta^2\sigma_x^2 - 2\beta\gamma\sigma_{xz})(1 + \rho_{x_1x_2}) - 2\gamma^2\sigma_z^2}{2\gamma^2\sigma_{xz}^2(1 - \rho_{x_1x_2})} . \tag{6A.21}$$

If, for greater intuitive clarity, the X, Y, and Z variables are all standardized, this inequality can be rewritten as:

$$n < \frac{(1 - \beta^2 - 2\beta\gamma\rho_{xz})(1 + \rho_{x_1 x_2}) - 2\gamma^2}{2\gamma^2 \rho_{xz}^2 (1 - \rho_{x_1 x_2})} .$$

(6A.22)

From (6A.22) it is seen that level score estimates are more accurate than change score estimates if $\gamma = 0$, $\rho_{xz} = 0$, or $\rho_{x_1 x_2} = 1$ — that is, if the omitted Z variable has no effect on Y, or if Z is uncorrelated with X, or if the X variable is completely stable across data collections. If none of these conditions is true, then as the sample size increases the change score estimates eventually become more accurate.[1] The minimum sample size at which the change score estimate is more accurate than the level score estimate depends on each of the parameters. It is generally smaller (and therefore change score estimates are more likely to be *better* than level score estimates) for *larger* absolute values of β and γ (the standardized regression coefficients for X and Z, respectively, on Y) and of ρ_{xz} (the correlation of X and Z); and for *smaller* algebraic values of $\rho_{x_1 x_2}$ (the stability of X over time).

To go beyond this generalization, it is useful to plug some reasonable values into expressions (6A.22). For example if we assign values of 0.5 to the parameters β, γ, $\rho_{x_1 x_2}$, and ρ_{xz}, then any reasonable sample (specifically, n > 4) would lead one to prefer the estimate based on change scores.

The accuracy of the estimate of β derived from change scores *decreases* as the stability of the X variable increases. This is somewhat counter intuitive, perhaps, but it follows from the fact that if X is highly stable, then the variance in the *change* in X is small, and therefore the random error term becomes relatively more important as a determinant of Y. To give an example, if we retain the values of β, γ, and ρ_{xz} at 0.5 but increase the value of $\rho_{x_1 x_2}$ from 0.5 to 0.9, a sample size for change scores of more than 36 is required to give an estimate with lower mean square error than that from static scores (with twice the sample size). If X has a stability of 0.99 (that is, if it is very nearly perfectly stable), a sample size of more than 396 cases is required.

Higher values of β — that is, given that Y and X are standardized, higher correlations between X and Y — increase the relative attractiveness of change score estimates, but *lower* values of β (i.e., lower than 0.5) have only a slight effect. Lower values of γ or of ρ_{xz} — that is, lower correlations

---

[1] This is true because, while the variances of both estimators of β are inversely proportional to sample size, the bias in the estimator from static scores is independent of sample size.

of the Z variable with the Y and/or the X variables — reduce the advantage for change score estimates; in the limit, if either of these correlations is zero, model 2 reduces to model 1, since the Z variable can safely be ignored, and in such a case the estimate based on static scores is preferable. The problem, of course, is that we are supposing that Z is an unmeasured variable, and in general there is no way to assure that all unmeasured variables are unrelated to the dependent and/or independent variables. The use of change scores does not free us from untestable assumptions, but it does make these assumptions somewhat weaker: that each such variable either (1) is unrelated to the dependent variable; *or* (2) is unrelated to the independent variable(s); *or* (3) does not change over the time between measurements.

Measurement Error

In Models 1 and 2, we assumed that the X and Y variables were measured without error. This is not a reasonable assumption for most social science data, so we now consider the consequences of measurement error on parameter estimates from cross-sectional and change data.

Measurement errors may arise from any number of sources, including misunderstanding of the question by the respondent, misunderstanding of the answer by the interviewer, and memory lapses or deliberate misrepresentations on the part of the respondent. The possible implications of measurement errors on estimates of all types of parameters from panel data are immense, matched only by our general ignorance about the nature and pervasiveness of such errors. We are, indeed, aware of only one study in which measurement errors have been assessed with respect to panel survey data.[1] We shall consider the assumptions that are typically made about measurement errors by analysts using panel data, the implications of violations of those assumptions, and the extent to which our proposed study will enable us to test those assumptions.

To facilitate our discussion of these implications, it is useful to distinguish between measurement errors that are random (by which we mean errors that are distributed independently of any other variable of interest in the context of a particular analysis); and those that are systematic, that is, those that are related to other pertinent variables including the autocorrelation over time in a single variable. To anticipate what will be discussed more thoroughly in a subsequent section, random errors do not introduce systematic biases into many statistics, including measures of central tendency and the covariances among different items. Random errors in measures of the independent variables in causal models do, however, introduce bias into estimates of causal effects, and they also lead to overestimates of the variances of items, and increase the standard errors of most statistics including means, covariances, and regression coefficients. Random errors may

---

[1]Presser and Traugott (1983) report a study of response errors with respect to voting in each of three elections by respondents in a 1972–74–76 election panel study.

be even more troublesome with respect to the analysis of panel data than is true for cross-sectional data. This follows from the fact that the focus of analysis with panel data is often on changes and trends at the level of individuals, and with many types of survey questions it may be found that true change during the interval between successive data collections is small compared to random error variance in the measure of change.

The potential consequences of systematic errors with respect to estimates from panel data are even more disturbing than those of random errors. It is also true, however, that in certain cases systematic errors, if they are stable over time, may actually improve the consistency of some estimators. There are numerous sources of systematic errors, and we shall make no attempt to review all such sources, but mention just two examples and their potential consequences with respect to estimates from panel data. One source of systematic errors is any general tendency to distort memories of the occurrence or timing of past events. On the other hand, there is evidence that if respondents are asked to report whether or not an event has occurred during a fixed interval preceding the interview, events that occurred somewhat outside that interval are often reported, a type of error referred to as "telescoping." Such a memory distortion could, if not detected and taken into account, lead to overestimation of the tendency for events to recur across time. On the other hand, some events may be forgotten and so underreported and it is difficult to predict the combined effects of these two types of distortion. It must also be recognized, however, that panel data offer some leverage with respect to these types of error. It may be possible to detect, and therefore delete, inappropriately reported events in second and subsequent waves if the same event seems to have been reported on two successive occasions. Moreover, the use of a panel design may make it possible to ask about events over a shorter interval (i.e., the interval since the previous interview), thereby reducing underreports due to forgetting.

As a second example of a source of systematic errors, consider the characteristics of particular interviewers which influence the distribution of responses they elicit from respondents. Interviewer effects, if they are consistent across two or more questions, introduce biases into measures of the relationships among those variables. With respect to panel data, if some or all of the respondents are interviewed by the same interviewer on two or more occasions (as happens frequently if the interviews are conducted face-to-face by a national interviewing staff), substantial autocorrelations may be incorporated into the error terms for the measured variables.

The Effects of Measurement Error on Estimates of Net Change

Before taking up the effects of measurement error on estimates of the parameters of causal models, it is useful to consider two more basic statistics: the net (aggregate) change in a variable from one time to another within a population, and the stability of a concept at the individual level across time.

Net change on a variable can be estimated either from two independent cross-sections of the target population, or from a panel study that collects data from a single sample at both times.[1] In both cases, assume that the response of each individual, i, at time t with respect to a variable, x_t, includes measurement error, v_{ti}, so that the observed score is given by:

$$x^*_{it} = x_{ti} + v_{ti} \ . \tag{6A.23}$$

Change from one time (say t = 1) to another (say t = 2) is estimated by the difference in the mean observed scores at times 1 and 2: $\Delta \bar{x}^* = \bar{x}^*_2 - \bar{x}^*_1$, the expected value of which is:

$$E(\Delta \bar{x}^*) = E(\bar{x}_2 - \bar{x}_1) + E(\bar{v}_2 - \bar{v}_1) \ . \tag{6A.24}$$

If we assume variances and covariances among these variables are equal at times 1 and 2, the variance of the estimated change is given by:

$$\sigma^2_{\Delta \bar{x}^*} = [2\sigma^2_{x_t} - 2\sigma_{x_1 x_2} + 2\sigma^2_{v_t} - 2\sigma_{v_1 v_2}$$

$$+ 2\sigma_{x_t v_t} - \sigma_{x_2 v_1} - \sigma_{x_1 v_2}]/n \tag{6A.25}$$

where n is the sample size.[2]

With data from independent cross-sectional samples, the cross-time covariances in expression (6A.25) have expected values of zero, but in general the covariance of the true scores, $\sigma_{x_1 x_2}$, will be positive if the data are from a panel design, so that differences estimated with greater precision (lower variances) if a panel design is used rather than successive cross-sections. Moreover, correlated measurement error ($\sigma_{v_1 v_2} > 0$) also reduces the variance of the estimate of change. Presser and Traugott (1983), in the panel study of measurement error mentioned earlier, found that errors in reporting voting behavior in three elections were quite stable across a four-year period, so what little evidence is available suggests that measurement error may indeed enhance the advantage of panel designs over cross-sectional designs in the estimation of change.

---

[1]Or from a mixed design which includes both a panel and independently drawn cross-sections at each data collection. In this exposition, which focuses on measurement error in the data from respondents, complications due to nonresponse, including panel attrition, are ignored.

[2]A similar derivation is given in Ashenfelter, Deaton, and Solon (1986), except that those authors assume that the covariance terms involving X and V are all zero — that is, that measurement error is unrelated to the true values of the variable.

The Effects of Measurement Error on Estimates of Stability

Data from successive cross-sections can be used to estimate net change in a variable from one time to another, although, as shown in the previous section, generally not as accurately as is possible with panel data. Cross-sectional data, however, can tell us nothing about gross change — change at the individual level. To examine mobility at the individual level (or the converse, stability), data with temporal dimension (i.e., retrospective or panel data) are required. Measurement error, however, may bias estimates of mobility.

To show this, suppose again that the observed score for individual i is given by expression (6A.23). Then it is straightforward to show that the stability of the observed scores from t=1 to t=2 is given by:

$$\rho_{x_1^* x_2^*} = (\rho_{x_1 x_2} \sigma_x^2 + \rho_{v_1 v_2} \sigma_v^2$$

$$+ \ \rho_{x_1 v_2} \sigma_x \sigma_v + \rho_{x_2 v_1} \sigma_x \sigma_v)/\sigma_{x^*}^2 \tag{6A.26}$$

(assuming again that variances and covariances are the same at both times). If the lagged and unlagged correlations of measurement errors with the true scores are all zero, the last two terms in expression (6A.26) drop out and the entire expression simplifies to one that is equivalent, except for notation, to one given by Ashenfelter et al. (1986, p. 51, expression [20]). As those authors note, this indicates that the stability in observed scores from time 1 to time 2 is a weighted average of the stability of the true scores and the stability of the measurement errors, with the weights being given by the proportion of valid to total variance in the measure. Under these assumptions, then, the estimate of mobility with respect to X may be biased either upward or downward depending on the stability of the true scores relative to the stability of measurement error. The possibility of correlations between measurement errors and true scores, which we do not think should be overlooked, makes it even harder to predict the direction or size of the bias in estimated stability.

Model 3: One X Variable, Measurement Error in the Dependent Variable

Effects on estimates from cross-sectional scores. For a simple linear model, measurement error in the Y variable does not introduce any new issues. Suppose that the true causal relationship between an X and Y variable is given by expression (6A.1) but that there are errors in the measure of Y, so that the observed values of Y, call them y* values, are related to the true values as follows:

$$y_{it}^* = y_{ti} + u_{ti} = \alpha + \beta x_{ti} + \epsilon_{ti} + u_{ti} \ . \tag{6A.27}$$

114

If the error term, u_{ti}, is independently distributed relative to the predictor variable, x_{ti}, it does not introduce any bias into the estimate of the β coefficient.[1] If, on the other hand, there is a correlation between the error term and the predictor variable, the standard OLS estimator, $\hat{b}$, of the regression coefficient of Y on X, β, is biased:[2]

$$E(\hat{b}) = \beta + \sigma_{u_t x_t} / \sigma^2_{x_t} .$$

(6A.28)

That is, measurement error in the dependent variable that is correlated with the independent variable has the same effect as an unmeasured stable causal (Z) variable (compare expressions [6A.19] and [6A.28]).

Effects on estimates from change scores. The model given by expression (6A.1) can be estimated from panel data by the use of change scores in order to eliminate biases due to unmeasured causal factors (Z variables) which might be correlated with the X variable:

$$\Delta y_i = \Delta \alpha + \beta \Delta x_i + \Delta \epsilon_i .$$

(6A.29)

If the measure of Y includes errors, as in expression (6A.27), the change in the measure also includes errors:

$$\Delta y^*_i = \Delta y_i + \Delta u_i$$

(6A.30)

$$= \Delta \alpha + \beta \Delta x_i + \Delta \epsilon_i + \Delta u_i .$$

The OLS estimate of β based on change scores is given by:

(6A.31)

$$\tilde{b} = \sigma_{\Delta y^* \Delta x} / \sigma^2_{\Delta x} .$$

This is an unbiased statistic unless the errors of measurement with respect to Y at either time are correlated with the values of X at either time:

---

[1] If u_{ti} is uncorrelated with x_{ti}, its effect on the estimate of the regression coefficient cannot be distinguished from that of the stochastic term, ϵ_{ti}; neither term introduces a bias into the estimate, and both increase the standard error of that estimate. Note that this is true even if the error term is correlated with the stochastic term and therefore with the true values of the Y variable.

[2] Although the assumption of independence between measurement error in Y and the true level of X is nearly universal, Duncan and Hill (1985) provide evidence that it is *not* warranted in the case of a simple model of earnings determination. Specifically, a fairly sizable negative correlation between the measurement error of ln(earnings) and the true level of job tenure imparted a 30 percent bias to the regression coefficient for job tenure.

$$E(\tilde{b}) = \beta + \frac{\sigma_{\Delta u \Delta x}}{\sigma_{\Delta x}^2}$$

$$= \beta + \frac{2\sigma_{u_t x_t} - \sigma_{u_1 x_2} - \sigma_{u_2 x_1}}{\sigma_{\Delta x}^2} . \qquad (6A.32)$$

Note that this implies that β tends to be overestimated by $\tilde{b}$ if the covariance between measurement error in Y at a particular data collection is more strongly (positively) correlated with the level of X at the same time than with the levels of X at the preceding and succeeding times. As with the estimates from static scores, covariance of the measurement errors with the stochastic term, ϵ, does not introduce any bias into the estimate of β, although it does increase or decrease (depending on whether the covariance is positive or negative) the standard error of that estimate. Similarly, autocorrelation of the measurement error from one data collection to the next does not introduce a bias, but a positive autocorrelation does reduce the standard error of the estimate.

Model 4: Multiple X Variables, Measurement Error in the Dependent Variable

If there is more than one predictor variable, and if the error in measurement of Y covaries with any of those predictors, the estimates of the causal effects of all of the predictors on Y may be biased. This can be illustrated by examining the biases in the regression coefficients for two predictors, X and W. If the population parameters for these predictors are β_1 and β_2, respectively, the biases in their OLS estimates are as follows:

$$E(\hat{b}_1) = \beta_1 + \frac{\sigma_w^2 \sigma_{xu} - \sigma_{xw} \sigma_{wu}}{\sigma_x^2 \sigma_w^2 - \sigma_{xw}^2}$$

$$= \beta_1 + \frac{\rho_{xu} - \rho_{xw} \rho_{wu}}{1 - \rho_{xw}^2} \cdot \frac{\sigma_u}{\sigma_x} \qquad (6A.33)$$

116

$$E(\hat{b}_2) = \beta_2 + \frac{\sigma_x^2 \sigma_{wu} - \sigma_{xw}\sigma_{xu}}{\sigma_x^2\sigma_w^2 - \sigma_{xw}^2}$$

$$= \beta_2 + \frac{\rho_{wu} - \rho_{xw}\rho_{xu}}{1 - \rho_{xw}^2} \cdot \frac{\sigma_u}{\sigma_w}$$

(6A.34)

Whether the estimates tend to over- or understate the true parameters depends on the particular configuration of covariances and variances in the above expressions, and so cannot in general be taken into account without explicit information about the existence, direction, and magnitude of the covariances between the errors in the dependent variable and the values of all of the predictor variables. Rarely is such information available, however, and so it is generally simply assumed that these covariances are zero and that therefore the estimators are unbiased.

The mean square error in the estimator of β_1 from cross-sectional scores is:

$$MSE(\hat{b}_1) = \frac{\sigma_\epsilon^2 + \sigma_u^2}{2n\sigma_w^2(1 - \rho_{xw}^2)}$$

(6A.35)

$$+ \frac{\sigma_u^2}{\sigma_x^2}\left(\frac{\rho_{xu} - \rho_{xw}\rho_{wu}}{1 - \rho_{xw}^2}\right)^2 .$$

Effects on estimates from change scores. The estimates of β_1 and β_2 for X and W, the two predictors of Y in the above example, as obtained from change scores are given by the following expressions:

$$E(\tilde{b}_1) = \beta_1 + \frac{(1 - \rho_{w_1w_2})\Omega_{xu} - \Omega_{xw}\Omega_{wu}}{(1 - \rho_{x_1x_2})(1 - \rho_{w_1w_2}) - \Omega_{xw}^2}$$

(6A.36)

$$E(\tilde{b}_2) = \beta_2 + \frac{(1 - \rho_{x_1 x_2})\Omega_{wu} - \Omega_{xw}\Omega_{xu}}{(1 - \rho_{x_1 x_2})(1 - \rho_{w_1 w_2}) - \Omega_{xw}^2} \tag{6A.37}$$

where $\Omega_{xu} = (\rho_{x_1 u_1} + \rho_{x_2 u_2} - \rho_{x_1 u_2} - \rho_{x_2 u_1})$, and Ω_{xw} and Ω_{wu} are defined in similar fashion. From these expressions it can be seen that there is no bias in the estimate of either coefficient if: (1) there is no measurement error (i.e., $\sigma_u^2 = 0$); or (2) the measurement errors are independent of *both* X and W (i.e., $\rho_{x_t u_{t'}} = \rho_{w_t u_{t'}} = 0$ for all t, t'); or (3) the measurement errors are perfectly autocorrelated across time (i.e., $\rho_{u_1 u_2} = 1$, and therefore Ω_{xu} and Ω_{wu} both $= 0$). If none of these conditions holds, and if measurement error in Y is more strongly correlated with the true values of the X variable at the same time than at different times (i.e., $\Omega_{xu} > 0$), this introduces a positive bias into $\tilde{b}_1$ and a negative bias into $\tilde{b}_2$ (other things being equal).

The mean square error in the estimator of β_1 from change scores is:

$$MSE(\tilde{b}_1) = \left(\frac{\sigma_\epsilon^2 + \sigma_u^2(1 - \rho_{u_1 u_2})}{n\sigma_w^2(1 - \rho_{w_1 w_2}) - \dfrac{\Omega_{xw}^2}{4(1 - \rho_{x_1 x_2})}} \right) + \frac{\sigma_u^2}{\sigma_x^2}\left(\frac{(1 - \rho_{w_1 w_2})\Omega_{xu} - \Omega_{xw}\Omega_{wu}}{(1 - \rho_{x_1 x_2})(1 - \rho_{w_1 w_2}) - \Omega_{xw}^2} \right)^2 . \tag{6A.38}$$

Model 5: One Independent Variable, with Measurement Error

Suppose that the true causal relationship between an X and a Y variable is given by expression (6A.1), but that there are errors in the measurement, not of the Y variable, but of the X variable, so that the observed values of X are related to the true values as follows:

118

$$x^*_{it} = x_{ti} + v_{ti} \ .$$
(6A.39)

Expression (6A.1) can be rewritten in terms of the observed values, x^*_{it}, as follows:

$$y_{ti} = \alpha + \beta x^*_{it} - \beta v_{ti} + \epsilon_{ti} \ .$$
(6A.40)

If the errors in the observed values of the X variable are independent of the true values of the X variable and of the stochastic term, ϵ (and therefore of the Y variable as well), the limiting value of the OLS estimate of the regression coefficient, β, as the sample size increases is given by:

$$E(\hat{b}) = \beta \left(\frac{\sigma^2_{x_t}}{\sigma^2_{x_t} + \sigma^2_{v_t}} \right) \ .$$
(6A.41)

That is, the magnitude of the regression coefficient is underestimated in the ratio of the variance of the true scores to the variance of the observed scores on the X variable. If the measurement errors covary with the true X values (and, by implication, with the Y values as well), the limiting value of the OLS estimate is:

$$E(\hat{b}) = \beta \left(\frac{\sigma^2_{x_t} + \sigma_{x_t v_t}}{\sigma^2_{x_t} + \sigma^2_{v_t} + 2\sigma_{x_t v_t}} \right) \ .$$
(6A.42)

If the measurement errors covary with the stochastic term (and again, therefore, with the Y values), the limiting value of the OLS estimate is:

$$E(\hat{b}) = \beta \left(\frac{\sigma^2_{x_t}}{\sigma^2_{x_t} + \sigma^2_{v_t}} \right) + \frac{\sigma_{v_t \epsilon_t}}{\sigma^2_{x_t} + \sigma^2_{v_t}} \ .$$
(6A.43)

Expressions (6A.41) to (6A.43) indicate the potentially devastating consequences of incorrect assumptions about measurement error in an independent variable, even in the elementary model considered. Unfortunately, the absence of information about the magnitude of measurement errors, and the extent to which they covary with the true values, leaves most analysts with no alternative to making arbitrary assumptions. Moreover, the possibilities for incorrect assumptions, and the potential consequences of those misspecifications, increase rapidly when we move from the simple bivariate model just considered to the more typical model with multiple predictor variables.

Awareness of these consequences is reflected in the increasing emphasis placed on the specification of measurement models along with causal models, and the popularity of techniques, such as the LISREL computer program (Jöreskog and Sörbom, 1984), which allow simultaneous estimation of measurement and substantive models. To illustrate, consider the advantages of having two parallel ("tau equivalent," to use the terminology of psychometrics; see Novick and Lewis, 1967) indicators of the independent variable in a bivariate causal model. We rewrite (19) with an additional subscript, $j = 1,2$, to differentiate between these indicators:

$$x^*_{ijt} = x_{it} + v_{ijt} .$$ (6A.44)

We further assume, for the time being, that the measurement errors in these two indicators are independent of one another. Then an unbiased estimator of β is as follows:

$$\hat{B}_{jt} = s_{y_t x^*_{jt}} / s_{x^*_{1t} x^*_{2t}} .$$ (6A.45)

Effects on estimates from change scores. We now consider the effects of errors in the measurement of the X variable on estimates based on change scores from panel data. Again, we assume that the observed value of X, call it x^*, is equal to the true value plus a measurement error term, call it v, which is independent of the other variables. If we estimate the causal effect of X on Y by regressing change scores in Y on change scores in x^*, this estimate is biased:

$$E(\tilde{b}) = \beta\sigma^2_{\Delta x} / (\sigma^2_{\Delta x} + \sigma^2_{\Delta v}) .$$ (6A.46)

This can be rewritten, after some algebraic manipulations, as

$$E(\tilde{b}) = \beta\sigma^2_x / (\sigma^2_x + \sigma^2_v \psi) ,$$ (6A.47)

with $\psi = (1 - \rho_{v_1 v_2}) / (1 - \rho_{x_1 x_2})$ and with $\rho_{x_1 x_2}$ being the correlation of the true scores on X at times 1 and 2, and $\rho_{v_1 v_2}$ the correlation of the measurement errors at these two times. ψ is never negative, so the expected value of $\tilde{b}$ is never greater in absolute value than β, given the stated assumptions. Inspection of expression (6A.41) tells us that $\tilde{b}$ greatly underestimates the absolute value of β if the variance of measurement error is large relative to the true score variance; and/or if the stability of the true values of X is large relative to the stability of measurement error in the observed values of X. Comparison with expression (6A.41) shows that the bias of the estimator from static scores is also influenced by the first of these ratios (the variance of error relative to the true variance), but the relative (in)stability of the error terms and the true scores is relevant only to the bias of the estimator from change scores. The implication is that estimates from change scores are less attractive relative to estimates from static scores to the extent that true scores on the predictor variable are more stable than errors in the measurement of that variable.[1]

As with cross-sectional scores, an unbiased estimate of β can be obtained if parallel measures of X are available at both waves of data collection:

$$\tilde{B}_j = s_{\Delta y \Delta x_j^*}/s_{\Delta x_1^* \Delta x_2^*} \cdot \tag{6A.48}$$

Model 6: Multiple Independent Variables, with Measurement Error

If there are errors in measurement in any of the independent variables in an explanatory model, the estimates of the regression coefficients for *all* of the independent variables will generally be biased. This is true to a greater extent if the errors of measurement are correlated with the true values of any of the explanatory variables, but also holds true even if the measurement errors are randomly distributed. The algebra gets lengthy even if there are just two predictor variables, and little would be gained from inspection of the expressions for the limiting values of the estimates in the presence of measurement error aside from renewing the conclusion that measurement errors can have important consequences on the accuracy of the estimates of explanatory models and that for this reason it is important to increase our understanding of measurement error.

---

[1]This is obvious in the extreme: if the true scores are perfectly stable, then change scores reflect nothing except measurement error. For a less extreme example, suppose that $\sigma_x^2 = 1$ and $\sigma_v^2 = 0.5$. From expression (6A.41) it follows that $E(\tilde{b}) = 0.667\beta$. If $\rho_{v_1 v_2} = \rho_{x_1 x_2}$, $E(\tilde{b}) = 0.667\beta$ as well. If $\rho_{x_1 x_2} = 0.75$ and $\rho_{v_1 v_2} = 0.5$, then $E(\tilde{b}) = 0.500\beta$, and if $\rho_{v_1 v_2} = 0.25$, $E(\tilde{b}) = 0.400\beta$. On the other hand, if the stability of the true scores were *lower* than the stability of the measurement errors, then the estimates based on change scores would be *less* biased than those based on static scores. If the variances of the true scores and measurement error are as before, but $\rho_{x_1 x_2} = 0.5$ and $\rho_{v_1 v_2} = 0.75$, $E(\tilde{b}) = 0.8\beta$.

Errors in the measurement of any of the predictors in a causal model may also cause biases in the estimated coefficients of all of the predictors based on change scores. Again, the algebra gets lengthy even with just two variables, so we do not give explicit expressions for the biases. As in the bivariate case, the effects of measurement errors are reduced, however, if these errors are stable from one data collection to the next.

CHAPTER 7

ESTIMATING THE EFFECTS OF MARITAL
STATUS ON SUBJECTIVE WELL-BEING

As we pointed out in Chapter 6, there are several possible explanations for any relationship observed in cross-sectional data. In particular, we
pointed out that differences between persons in different marital statuses
could be explained in several ways other than that the marital state is
somehow more satisfying than the alternatives. We will consider some of
these competing explanations in this chapter.

As we consider these possible explanations for the relationship between marital status and the subjective quality of life, it is important to
remember that they are not mutually exclusive. It is entirely possible that
the relationship is partly spurious, partly a reflection of the influence of
marital status on life satisfaction, and partly a reflection of the influence of
life satisfaction on marital status. Another limitation of our analysis is perhaps obvious but still worth emphasizing: our ability to test various possible
hypotheses is restricted by the availability of measures of relevant concepts
and the quality of those measures.

Is the Relationship Spurious?

One class of possible explanations is that the relationship is spurious;
that is, married people may be more satisfied with their lives not because of
any causal influence of one of these variables on the other, but because both
are influenced by some other variable or variables. Many specific variables
could be mentioned as potential sources of such a spurious relationship. For
example, consider age. If married (and widowed) persons are on the
average somewhat older than those who have never married or who have
divorced or separated, and if satisfaction with life increases with age, then
the apparent relationship between marital status and satisfaction could be
explained (partially, at least) by age. Another type of spurious relationship
would arise if self-reports on level of satisfaction are influenced by a tendency of respondents in an interview situation to give socially desirable answers
to questions, and if the answers of married respondents are more affected by
this tendency than those of unmarried respondents.

Compositional Differences

Our first exploration of the hypothesis that the relationship between
marital status and life satisfaction is spurious is rather crude in terms of the

characteristics included as potential predictors. We consider a set of demographic variables: age, sex, race, and educational attainment. We are, then, asking whether what can be thought of as differences in the composition of those in different marital statuses account for the observed differences in the satisfaction levels of those groups.

The findings are shown in Table 7-1. Since we are interested in differences between groups rather than absolute levels of satisfaction, the average levels of satisfaction are expressed in terms of deviations from the average for all married respondents. Without controls on any variables, divorced and separated respondents report average life satisfaction about 0.5 unit below the average for married respondents (on the 7-point satisfaction scale). After controlling on the four demographic characteristics, this difference actually *increases* to 0.7 unit, so the lower satisfaction cannot be interpreted in terms of differences between married and divorced persons with respect to any of these demographic characteristics. If anything, such differences as do exist only suppress the relationship, making it appear weaker than it would otherwise.

Table 7-1
Marital Status Differences in Life Satisfaction, with Controls on
Compositional Differences and Level of Personal Efficacy
(1978 Quality of Life Data)

MARITAL STATUS	No Controls	Control on Demographics	Control on Pers. Comp.
Married	0	0	0
Widowed	0.116	0.226	0.018
Single	−0.396	−0.287	−0.323
Div/Sep	−0.507	−0.692	−0.377

Never married respondents have average satisfaction scores about 0.4 unit lower than those of married respondents. Controlling on the set of four demographic characteristics decreases that difference to about 0.3 unit, indicating that perhaps a quarter of the difference between these two groups can be explained in terms of differences in their demographic composition — primarily, it turns out from inspection of the coefficients for individual variables, from differences in the age distributions. Younger people are less likely to be married, and they also report somewhat lower levels of satisfaction.

124

The difference between married and widowed respondents is not statistically significant ($p > .10$), but the sample data indicate a somewhat higher average satisfaction level for widowed than for married respondents. Controlling on the four demographic characteristics does not decrease this difference. In fact, the difference *increases* to a statistically significant ($p < .05$) 0.2 unit, suggesting that, as with the comparison between never married and married respondents, compositional differences may actually suppress the difference between married and widowed respondents. Differences in the age distribution, and to a lesser extent educational attainment, are the relevant factors in this suppression.

To summarize the findings with respect to this limited set of compositional differences between marital status groups, it appears that the younger ages of most never married respondents may account for about a quarter of the difference in their average levels of satisfaction relative to married respondents, but that compositional differences may in fact suppress the differences in satisfaction levels for the divorced and separated, and for the widowed, relative to married respondents.

Personality Factors

Another possible source of a spurious relationship between marital status and life satisfaction is that there are personality characteristics that influence both marital status and level of satisfaction. The suggestion here is that certain types of people enjoy life more than others, quite apart from the objective circumstances in which they find themselves, and that such people are more likely than other types to marry and to stay married. The suggestion is plausible, but for the most part is not amenable to testing with data from the quality of life surveys, since measures of relevant personality characteristics are not available. The only measure that comes close in this respect is an indicator of personal efficacy: the extent to which respondents feel that they have control over what happens in their lives as opposed to being at the mercy of external forces and events.

The findings from a regression analysis in which we controlled on a six-item index of personal efficacy (cf. Campbell et al., 1976, p. 59) are shown in the last column of Table 7-1. The differences in average satisfaction levels of unmarried respondents compared to married respondents are somewhat reduced by this procedure. In particular, the difference between separated and divorced respondents and married respondents shrinks from .51 to .38 unit. The discrepancy for never married respondents is reduced slightly, from .40 to .32 unit; and the discrepancy for widowed respondents, which is not statistically significant even without the control, drops from .12 to .02 unit. It appears, therefore, that some of the relationship between marital status and life satisfaction could be explained by differences in the feelings of personal efficacy expressed by persons in those statuses. Married persons express higher levels of personal efficacy (average = 21.9 on a scale that ranges from 0 to 60, with low scores reflecting high personal efficacy) than do widowed (mean = 25.5) or never married (mean = 24.6) respondents, while divorced and separated respondents express the lowest levels (mean = 30.5). We do not feel confident in asserting that the association with personal efficacy implies that the relationship between marital status and life satisfaction is at least partly spurious, however, since it is not obvious how to interpret the relationships between personal efficacy and the other two variables. To interpret the effect as spurious, it is necessary to assume that feelings of personal efficacy have causal influences on both marital status and life satisfaction. This is plausible, but other plausible interpretations of the relationships can also be posited. In particular, becoming widowed, divorced, or separated may lead an individual to feel more at the mercy of external forces and events.

In sum, our investigation provides only limited support for the possibility that the relationship between marital status and life satisfaction may be spurious because of personality factors that influence both variables. The only characteristic that might be regarded as a personality characteristic for which we have a measure is that of personal efficacy, and while it does appear that the relationship between marital status and life satisfaction is weaker after controlling on this factor, it is not obvious that personal efficacy is such an enduring characteristic that other interpretations of the relationships can be ignored.

Method Factors

Another possible source of bias in estimates of the relationship between two measures is that respondents in different marital statuses may differ in how they interpret questions and answer scales, and that this affects their answers to particular questions regardless of content. For example, questions about satisfaction in the Quality of Life and Monitoring the Future studies almost all use a scale with extreme categories which are labelled "completely satisfied" and "completely dissatisfied." If any of these words — "satisfied," "dissatisfied," or "completely" — mean different things to different respondents, there could be systematic differences in their answers that have nothing to do with the underlying levels of satisfaction. If such differences in interpretation of the scales are related to marital status, the observed covariance of marital status and satisfaction would be distorted because of the methods factor.

If all of the items are measured by the same method, the possible contribution of that method to the covariances of the items cannot be distinguished from the covariances attributable to the relationships among the concepts the items are intended to measure. Therefore, to be able to assess the existence and strength of a methods factor, and to obtain estimates of the underlying relationships among the theoretical concepts that are corrected for such methods factors, it is necessary to have measured at least some of the concepts using two or more methods. This is the logic that underlies the notion of the multitrait-multimethod matrix (Campbell and Fiske, 1959). Although the inferential rules originally proposed by Campbell and Fiske depend on assumptions that are often unwarranted (in particular, the lack of correlation of the methods factors: cf. Althauser and Heberlein, 1970), data of this form can be analyzed through the specification of structural equations, without making such assumptions, and this is the procedure we have followed.

The data for this analysis are from the 1978 Quality of Life survey. In addition to the standard seven-point satisfaction scale already described, two other methods for assessing satisfaction were used in this study. One method involved a thermometer-like scale on which the respondents were asked to evaluate several life domains. On this scale, the respondent was told that a score of 100 would mean that he or she found the situation with a particular domain was "perfect — as good as you can imagine it being," while a score of 0 was to be given if the situation was "terrible, as bad as you can imagine it being." The third method was taken from earlier quality of life surveys by Andrews and Withey (1976), who developed a seven-point satisfaction scale with extreme categories which were labelled "delighted" and "terrible."

In order to estimate the effects associated with these three types of scales, it is necessary to include several concepts in the causal model, with each concept measured by two or more of the three methods. For this reason, we include levels of satisfaction with several domains of life, such as work, friendships, and health, as well as overall life satisfaction. The effect of marital status on the true level of satisfaction with each concept is assumed to take the following form:

$$\eta_{ji} = \gamma_j \xi_i + \zeta_{ji} \; , \tag{7.1}$$

where η_{ji} is the satisfaction of person i with domain j; ξ_i is that person's marital status (here taken to be a dichotomous variable; specifically, we will distinguish married and widowed persons from all others); and ζ_{ji} represents all other sources of variance in satisfaction with that domain. (Intercept terms are ignored here, so the expression applies to scores expressed in terms of deviations from the mean.)

Overall life satisfaction is assumed to depend on satisfaction with specific domains of life as well as on marital status. Thus, the structural equation for the true level of life satisfaction (η_{Li}) includes more predictors:

$$\eta_{Li} = \gamma_L \xi_i + \sum_j \beta_j \eta_{ji} + \zeta_{Li} \; . \tag{7.2}$$

It is assumed that the residual variance in life satisfaction (ζ_{Li}) is uncorrelated with anything else in the model.

We allow for the possibility that marital status may also influence individual tendencies in the use of measurement scales:

$$\eta_{ki} = \gamma_k \xi_i + \zeta_{ki} \; , \tag{7.3}$$

127

The residual variance of method k (ζ_{ki}) may, it is assumed, be correlated with the residual variance for other methods but with nothing else in the model.

Finally, the expression relating the latent (unobserved, or true) levels of satisfaction to the self-reports of satisfaction is assumed to be:

$$y_{jki} = \lambda_{jk}\eta_{ji} + \lambda_k\eta_{ki} + \epsilon_{jki} \; , \tag{7.4}$$

where ϵ_{jki} (the residual variance in each such self-report — i.e., the variance not explained either by true satisfaction level or by the method factor) is assumed to be unrelated to anything else in the model. The link from true to self-reported satisfaction, represented by the parameter λ_{jk}, is allowed to differ across both domains and methods, but the link from a method factor to a self-report, λ_k is assumed to be equal for all self-reports based on that method.

The model described by expressions (7.1) − (7.4) is shown in diagrammatic form in Figure 7–1. To estimate these parameters, we used the maximum likelihood procedure described by Jöreskog (1973) and implemented in the computer program LISREL IV (Jöreskog and Sörbom, 1978). The estimates of the parameters are shown in Table 7–2.[1]

The fit of the model to the data is not perfect. The chi square statistic from the LISREL analysis is 374.4, with 75 degrees of freedom, which is highly significant (p < .001). The statistical significance of the lack of fit is almost inevitable, given the large sample size (3692). However, the deviations of the observed covariances among the items from the covariances predicted by the model are almost all small. This is reflected in a summary measure, the "critical N" statistic, proposed by Hoelter (1983), as an indicator of fit that is independent of sample size. For this model, the value of the critical N statistic is 947 (for p = .05), which by Hoelter's criterion indicates an adequate fit.[2]

The estimates from this analysis suggest that measurement error and method effects, far from explaining the relationship between marital status

---

[1]The model was estimated from unstandardized data — the observed variances and covariances among the variables — since the constraint that the method effects be equal across all items using a particular method makes sense only if those items are measured in a common unit. The underlying satisfactions and method factors (the η_j and η_k variables) are standardized to unit variances.

[2]Hoelter (1983) states that, based on his inspection of a variety of models, a critical N that is at least 200 (for analysis of a single group) indicates an adequate fit of the model to the data. That is, in his experience, if it would take a sample of more than 200 cases to reject the model, given the deviations of the observed covariances from those predicted by the model, the lack of fit generally lacks substantive importance. Any such criterion has an arbitrariness to it, and thus should not be followed blindly, but our own experience concurs with that of Hoelter in suggesting that 200 is a reasonable threshold value.

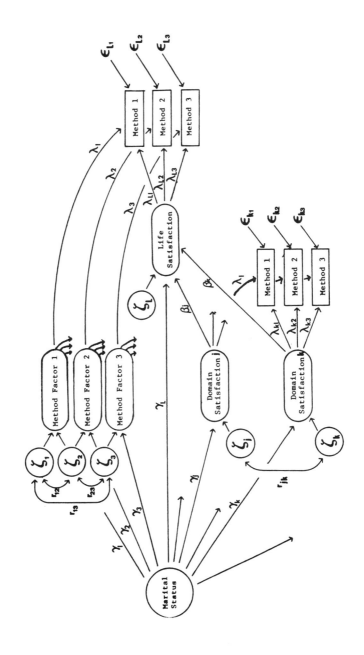

Figure 7-1
Model for Effect of Marital Status on True and Measured Levels of
Satisfaction with Domains and with Life as a Whole

129

Table 7-2

LISREL Estimates of Parameters for Model Relating Marital Status to Domain and Life Satisfaction Measures
(1978 Quality of Life Data)

DOMAIN	Marital Status Effect on Domain Sat.	Domain Effect on Life Sat.	METHOD	Concept Loading	Method Loading
Work	0.63	0.15	Satisfied-Dissatisfied	1.03	0.47
			Thermometer	15.45	7.79
Dwelling unit	0.57	-.02	Satisfied-Dissatisfied	1.20	0.47
			Thermometer	17.07	7.79
			Delighted-Terrible	1.02	0.47
Health	0.12	0.19	Satisfied-Dissatisfied	1.14	0.47
			Thermometer	17.58	7.79
Friendships	0.42	0.28	Satisfied-Dissatisfied	0.89	0.47
			Thermometer	12.24	7.79
Standard of living	0.68	0.38	Satisfied-Dissatisfied	1.24	0.47
			Thermometer	13.36	7.79
			Delighted-Terrible	0.80	0.47
Life as a whole			Satisfied-Dissatisfied	0.96	0.47
(a) Direct	0.35		Thermometer	9.20	7.79
(b) Indirect	0.48		Delighted-Terrible	0.67	0.47
(c) Total	0.83				

NOTE: The total effect of marital status on overall life satisfaction is split into "direct" and "indirect" components, where the indirect component is defined as the effect that is mediated by the domain satisfactions listed above.

and life satisfaction, instead suppress that relationship. Since the units of measurement differ for the three measures of life satisfaction, and the scale of measurement of the underlying latent concept is arbitrary, we will assess the effect of marital status in terms of differences in standard deviation units. On this common metric, the average level of life satisfaction reported by married and widowed respondents is about 0.3 standard deviation units higher than that reported by other respondents.[1] The true difference in the life satisfaction of these two marital status groups, as estimated based on the model sketched in Figure 7-1, is 0.83 standard deviation units: more than twice as large as the observed differences on the individual items.

Part of the explanation for the larger difference between marital statuses as estimated by the structural equation model as compared to what is observed on individual items is, of course, random measurement error. The modelling approach estimates a common factor that underlies the three observed measures, and such a factor is purified of the unique variance associated with each item. Another part of the explanation lies with the methods factor incorporated into the model. The latent satisfaction factor is also stripped of at least some of the "methods" effects associated with differences in how individual respondents use the three types of satisfaction scales. What the estimates obtained based on this model imply is that such method effects do exist, and that they do have substantial effects on the measures; but the estimates also imply that, rather than accounting for some or all of the observed differences between marital status groups, the method effects apparently suppress those differences.

The estimation of the model provides some additional information which, while secondary to the primary objective of estimating the effects of marital status on life satisfaction, is nevertheless of interest: the effects of marital status on levels of satisfaction with the several domains of life included in the model in order to obtain estimates of the method effects. As shown by the entries in the second column of Table 7-2, married and widowed respondents are considerably more satisfied with their work, with their standard of living, and with their dwelling units. They are also more satisfied with their friendships, though the difference is smaller than for the three domains just enumerated; and very slightly more satisfied with their health. These effects of marital status on satisfaction with specific domains of life mediate more than half of the total effect of marital status on overall life satisfaction. More than half of this mediated effect is through the effect of marital status on satisfaction with standard of living, suggesting that economic factors are a major (but by no means the only) reason for the relative dissatisfaction of divorced, separated, and never married respondents.

---

[1]More specifically, the difference between these two groups is 0.38 s.d. units when life satisfaction is assessed by the seven-point "completely satisfied – completely dissatisfied" item; 0.31 s.d. units when measured on the thermometer item; and 0.28 s.d. units when measured on the "delighted – terrible" item.

Multivariate Effects of Marital Status on Subjective Well-being, as Estimated from Static Scores

In this section we turn to Monitoring the Future panel data, and we include a range of additional variables in estimation models intended to assess the effects of marital status on subjective well-being. In particular, we include the characteristics considered in Chapter 5 (and listed in Table 5–1), plus the set of background variables described in that chapter. The relevance of some of these variables to subjective well-being and to marital status is obvious and has already been demonstrated: for example, marriage is often the occasion of a change in living arrangements, and it is important to try to separate the effects of these two types of transitions. Similarly, changes in work status are often associated with marital transitions, sometimes directly as with those who wait until their education is completed before considering marriage, other times more indirectly because of the greater importance of a job when a person has a family to support. Other variables, such as political orientation, may have less relevance to marital status but are included here as part of a more comprehensive set. With the size of samples available for these analyses, little is lost by including irrelevant variables and it is better to err in the direction of over- than of under-inclusiveness.

None of the models that will be estimated in this and the remaining chapters is at all complex or precisely defined with respect to the causal relationships among the variables included as predictors of subjective well-being. We suspect that some of these relationships are reciprocal rather than unidirectional. It is also likely that some of the predictors are better interpreted as intervening variables which partially explain the relationship between marital status and subjective well-being, while others may contribute to a spurious relationship. We will occasionally comment on such competing interpretations, but our analyses treat the predictors as a parallel set of exogenous variables and thus take the relationships among them as given.

In all of the following regression analyses, we focus on the coefficients that estimate the difference in well-being between married and unmarried respondents. The findings from the regression analyses are summarized in Table 7–3. The first row of this table is taken from the first row of Table 5–1: the difference in life satisfaction and happiness between married and unmarried men and women, with no controls on the other variables. The remaining rows list the multivariate regression coefficients for marital status when considered simultaneously with various combinations of other variables.

Background Variables

We first introduce a set of background variables into the estimation model. The consequence, as shown by comparison of the first two rows in Table 7–3, is *not* a reduction in the regression coefficients for current marital status in predicting either satisfaction or happiness. To the contrary, there is a slight *increase* in the estimated difference in happiness between married and unmarried respondents, and similarly with respect to the difference in satisfaction among men, though not among women. Whatever background differences are associated with early marriage, at least among the set considered here, they do not help to explain the higher level of satisfaction or happiness reported by married respondents. If anything, such differences somewhat suppress the relationship between marriage and well-being.

Prior Marital Status

Consistent with the notion introduced in Chapter 5 that some causal effects may be lagged rather than simultaneous, or more specifically that duration in a particular marital status may influence the subjective quality of life, we next introduce marital status at the first follow-up ("lagged" marital status) along with marital status at the second follow-up ("current" marital status) as a predictor of satisfaction at the second follow-up. When we compare the entries in the third row of Table 7–3 with those in the first row, we detect no support for the hypothesis that the effects of marital status are lagged *rather than* simultaneous. In fact, all four of the estimated differences between married and unmarried respondents *increase* when prior marital status is introduced into the model. Moreover, if we compare the entries in the fourth row with those in the second, we observed that all four coefficients increase at least slightly even after controlling on the background variables. The increase in the explanatory power of "current" marital status when "lagged" marital status is controlled is slight for males, but substantial for females.

The coefficients for prior marital status are shown in the columns labelled "lagged." The fact that they are all negative suggests that life satisfaction and happiness decline with the duration of marriage (but see the discussion of this issue in Chapter 4 based on data from the Quality of Life surveys). The relative sizes of these lagged coefficients indicate that the decline may be greater among women than among men.

Prior Level of Subjective Well-being

In the fifth row of Table 7–3 are shown the regression coefficients for current marital status if prior level on the dependent variable (Y1) is also included as a predictor of its current level. As expected (but not shown in the table), this substantially increases the proportion of variance explained. As *is* shown by a comparison of the entries in the fifth row with those in the first row, the estimated effects of current marital status *decrease* in all four instances when the prior level of the dependent variable is added to the model. The decrease is appreciable. Nevertheless, most of the estimated effects of marital status remain (i.e., row 5 estimates are about 70 percent as large as row 1 estimates). Moreover, inspection of the entries in row 6, which differ from those in row 5 by the addition of background variables

133

Table 7-3

Multiple Regression Analyses: Contemporary and Lagged Effects of Marital Status on Levels of Life Satisfaction and Happiness, with Controls on Other Variables (Monitoring the Future Panel Data)

	Life Satisfaction				Happiness				Average	
	Females		Males		Females		Males			
Variables Controlled	Current	Lagged	Current	Lagged	Current	Lagged	Current	Lagged	Current	Lagged
Nothing	.223 (.049)		.227 (.063)		.354 (.046)		.184 (.061)		.247 (.055)	
Bkgrnd	.222 (.051)		.255 (.065)		.382 (.046)		.252 (.062)		.278 (.056)	
Lagged	.313 (.057)	-.222 (.074)	.255 (.069)	-.109 (.112)	.438 (.054)	-.208 (.069)	.202 (.068)	-.067 (.109)	.302 (.062)	-.152 (.091)
Bkgrnd, Lagged	.300 (.058)	-.206 (.074)	.276 (.071)	-.084 (.112)	.436 (.053)	-.143 (.068)	.255 (.068)	-.010 (.107)	.317 (.063)	-.111 (.090)
Y1	.155 (.048)		.187 (.061)		.228 (.044)		.133 (.059)		.176 (.053)	
Bkgrnd, Lagged, Y1	.246 (.056)	-.236 (.072)	.241 (.069)	-.116 (.109)	.355 (.051)	-.239 (.065)	.209 (.065)	-.042 (.103)	.263 (.060)	-.158 (.087)
Living arrangements plus:										
Nothing	.162 (.053)		.198 (.066)		.278 (.050)		.097 (.064)		.184 (.058)	
Bkgrnd	.187 (.055)		.243 (.069)		.349 (.051)		.195 (.066)		.244 (.060)	
Lagged	.268 (.061)	-.266 (.078)	.225 (.073)	-.107 (.114)	.407 (.057)	-.318 (.073)	.137 (.071)	-.118 (.111)	.259 (.066)	-.094 (.094)
Bkgrnd, Lagged	.269 (.062)	-.226 (.078)	.258 (.075)	-.068 (.115)	.427 (.057)	-.218 (.072)	.207 (.072)	-.039 (.110)	.290 (.067)	-.138 (.094)
Y1	.107 (.052)		.160 (.064)		.180 (.048)		.060 (.061)		.127 (.056)	
Bkgrnd, Lagged, Y1	.220 (.061)	-.251 (.076)	.220 (.073)	-.101 (.112)	.351 (.055)	-.301 (.069)	.164 (.069)	-.068 (.105)	.239 (.065)	-.180 (.091)
Whether parent plus:										
Nothing	.290 (.054)		.254 (.072)		.484 (.051)		.281 (.070)		.327 (.062)	
Bkgrnd	.254 (.056)		.263 (.074)		.442 (.051)		.303 (.070)		.316 (.063)	
Lagged	.338 (.060)	-.161 (.078)	.265 (.075)	-.060 (.124)	.503 (.056)	-.076 (.073)	.252 (.073)	.154 (.121)	.340 (.066)	-.036 (.099)

Table 7-3 (continued)
Effects of Marital Status on Well-Being

Variables Controlled	Life Satisfaction				Happiness				Average	
	Females		Males		Females		Males			
	Current	Lagged	Current	Lagged	Current	Lagged	Current	Lagged	Current	Lagged
Bkgrnd, Lagged	.307 (.060)	-.188 (.078)	.275 (.077)	-.066 (.124)	.469 (.055)	-.095 (.072)	.278 (.073)	.139 (.119)	.332 (.066)	-.053 (.098)
Y1	.215 (.053)		.205 (.070)		.341 (.049)		.218 (.067)		.245 (.059)	
Bkgrnd, Lagged, Y1	.249 (.059)	-.218 (.076)	.236 (.075)	-.126 (.121)	.382 (.053)	-.197 (.069)	.230 (.070)	.099 (.114)	.274 (.064)	-.111 (.095)
Work/student status plus:										
Nothing	.305 (.055)		.273 (.066)		.509 (.051)		.314 (.064)		.350 (.059)	
Bkgrnd	.268 (.055)		.269 (.067)		.468 (.051)		.300 (.064)		.326 (.059)	
Lagged	.363 (.061)	-.120 (.079)	.295 (.072)	-.096 (.112)	.556 (.056)	-.032 (.073)	.317 (.069)	-.037 (.108)	.383 (.065)	-.071 (.093)
Bkgrnd, Lagged	.324 (.061)	-.135 (.079)	.281 (.073)	-.084 (.112)	.502 (.056)	-.030 (.072)	.287 (.069)	-.011 (.106)	.349 (.065)	-.065 (.092)
Y1	.219 (.054)		.230 (.064)		.355 (.049)		.234 (.061)		.259 (.057)	
Bkgrnd, Lagged, Y1	.261 (.060)	-.190 (.077)	.249 (.071)	-.116 (.109)	.409 (.054)	-.138 (.069)	.229 (.067)	-.044 (.102)	.287 (.063)	-.122 (.089)
Complete set plus:										
Nothing	.242 (.062)		.222 (.078)		.470 (.057)		.256 (.075)		.298 (.068)	
Bkgrnd	.216 (.063)		.216 (.079)		.430 (.057)		.233 (.075)		.274 (.069)	
Lagged	.278 (.068)	-.151 (.085)	.236 (.082)	-.034 (.126)	.493 (.062)	-.080 (.078)	.218 (.079)	.155 (.121)	.306 (.073)	-.028 (.103)
Bkgrnd, Lagged	.257 (.068)	-.169 (.085)	.228 (.083)	-.042 (.127)	.459 (.062)	-.102 (.078)	.194 (.079)	.130 (.120)	.285 (.073)	-.046 (.102)
Y1	.179 (.061)		.189 (.076)		.351 (.055)		.193 (.072)		.228 (.066)	
Bkgrnd, Lagged, Y1	.218 (.067)	-.217 (.083)	.212 (.081)	-.103 (.124)	.400 (.059)	-.201 (.075)	.161 (.076)	.087 (.115)	.248 (.071)	-.109 (.099)

NOTES: The entries are partially standardized (as described in the Notes to Table 5-1) regression coefficients from analyses in which reported levels of life satisfaction and happiness at FU2 were predicted by marital status at FU2 and the other variables listed in the first column. The entries in the columns labeled "Current" estimate the deviation of respondents who were married at FU2 from unmarried respondents, after controlling on the indicated variable(s). Similarly, the entries labelled "Lagged" estimate the deviation of respondents who were married at FU1 from those who were unmarried at that time. The standard errors of these coefficients are given in parentheses.

"Bkgrnd": background variables. These include race (black, white, or other); average years of education of parents; region of the country; degree of urbanization of place of residence; average grades in school; and days of truancy from school.

"Lagged": marital status and the other predictors included as unlagged predictors (i.e., living arrangements, parenthood, and work status) are also included as measured at the previous data collection.

"Y1": the level of satisfaction or happiness at the previous data collection.

"Living arrangements": whether respondent was living with his or her parents.

"Whether parent": whether respondent reports being the parent of one or more children, regardless of living arrangements.

"Work status": a set of dummy variables for whether respondent is (1) a student; (2) working part- or full-time; (3) unemployed; or (for women only) (4) a homemaker.

"Complete set": The "living arrangements," "whether parent," and "work status" variables described above, plus the following: (1) frequency of dating; (2) political orientation (liberal-conservative); and (3) religious involvement (attendance at religious services, and importance of religion).

and lagged marital status as predictors, shows that the coefficients for current marital status bounce back toward their bivariate levels, suggesting that controlling just on prior level of the dependent variable may somewhat overadjust the estimates for marital status effects.

Living Arrangements

The frequent concurrence of a marriage among young people and their initial departure from their parental household was noted in Chapter 5, where we wondered to what extent the difference in well-being associated with marriage might actually represent effects of such changes in living arrangements. We noted that the difference in well-being between those who had left their parental home and those still living with their parents was almost as large as that between married and unmarried respondents, and observed that most married respondents had indeed left their parental home.

The next set of regression analyses includes both marital status and living arrangements as predictors, so that the effects of each can be assessed after controlling on the other variable. The entries in the seventh row of Table 7–3 are the multiple regression coefficients for marital status, controlling (only) on whether or not the respondents were living with their parents. These coefficients are considerably smaller (by an average of about 25 percent) than the bivariate coefficients shown in the first row, confirming the overlap between these two variables. It is also true, however, that the estimated effects of marital status remain substantial; at best, living arrangements can account for only a limited proportion of the elevated well-being of married respondents. This to some extent excuses our failure to specify a causal relationship between marital status and living arrangements, since it appears that whatever assumption we were to make, a substantial direct effect (i.e., one not mediated by living arrangements) would be estimated between marital status and well-being. It is likely that there is a reciprocal relationship between marital status and living arrangements, and given such an assumption more data would be required for estimation of those causal paths than were available for the present analysis.

The eighth through twelfth rows add in other variables and sets of variables in the same order as in the second through sixth rows. Controlling on the background variables considerably reduces the effect of living arrangements on the marital status coefficients. The entries in the eighth row average about seven eighths as large as those in the second row, whereas those in the seventh row are only about three fourths as large as those in the first row. Otherwise, the patterns observed with respect to controlling on the lagged effects of marital status (and now of living arrangements as well) and on prior level of the dependent variable are largely replicated.

Parenthood

We have observed that respondents who had become parents at a relatively young age tended to be somewhat less satisfied with their lives than other respondents. As with living arrangements, it is likely that a reciprocal relationship exists between marital status and parenthood: the occurrence of a transition on either status often produces a transition in the other status. Again, the data are not adequate for estimating those causal paths, but regardless of the explanation, the fact that there is a relationship between parenthood and marital status raises the possibility that the apparently positive effect of marriage might to some extent be offset by a negative effect of becoming a parent.

To test this hypothesis, we estimated regression models that included parental as well as marital status as predictors of the quality of life indicators. The estimates of the effects of marriage, controlling on parenthood, are shown in the thirteenth row of Table 7–3, and seem to confirm that parenthood does indeed suppress the effects of marriage. The estimated effect of marriage, particularly on reported happiness, is considerably larger if parental status is included as a predictor (i.e., the coefficients for predicting happiness in row 13 are one third to one half larger than those in row 1). Taken at face value, this would seem to confirm the hypothesis that parenthood takes at least some of the shine off marital bliss. The subsequent rows of Table 7–3 lead to more caution in our interpretation, however. For example, the differences between the coefficients in rows 2 and 14, in which the background variables have been controlled, are much smaller than the differences between rows 1 and 13. This suggests that much of the apparent suppression effect of parenthood may really be accounted for by preexisting differences between those who had children at young ages and other respondents. Moreover, comparison of rows 3 and 15, in which prior marital status is controlled, suggests that the apparent suppressive effect of parenthood also reflects the fact that those who became parents had, on the average, been married longer than those not yet parents. If *both* the background variables *and* prior marital status are controlled (rows 4 and 16), the apparent suppression effect of parenthood all but disappears.

Work and Student Status

We now consider the extent to which the effect of marital status is explained or mediated by work and student status. As indicated earlier, our analysis of this issue is not as specific as we would like, since we are not able to describe the sequence of marital and work status transitions with much precision. Our initial analysis is limited to including work and student status dummy variables along with marital status in the regression model. The estimated effects of marital status on happiness increase markedly when work and student status are taken into account (comparing rows 1 and 19 of Table 7–3). The differences in the estimates for life satisfaction are smaller, but in the same direction. Our conclusion is that work and student status do not to any degree explain the higher levels of satisfaction expressed by married respondents, but that to the contrary differences in the distribution of married and unmarried respondents across the work and student status categories may actually somewhat suppress the extent of the improved quality of life expressed by married respondents. However, comparison of rows 20 through 22 with rows 2 through 4 of Table 7–3 indicates that if background variables and earlier marital status are also controlled, then the apparent suppression effect of work status largely disappears.

All Predictors

The final six rows of Table 7–3 display the regression coefficients for marital status when all of the variables listed in Table 5–1 in Chapter 5 are included along with marital status as predictors of satisfaction and happiness. These predictors include the variables discussed in the preceding paragraphs, plus position on a political dimension (liberalism-conservatism), religiosity, and frequency of dating. Comparison of the estimates in the first row of the table, for a model that includes *no* predictors besides current marital status, with those in the last row, which includes *all* of the predictors we have considered, shows very similar estimates of the differences between married and unmarried respondents.

Multivariate Effects of Marital Status on Subjective Well-being, as Estimated from Change Scores

The rationale for estimation of a model in which the dependent variable is *change* rather than static *level* was provided in Chapter 6: Change scores are unaffected by failure to include relevant causal factors if there has been no change in those factors. This strength of the analysis of change scores must be weighed against a cost that is incurred in the form of the higher proportion of measurement error that generally characterizes change scores, and the consequently higher standard errors of the estimates of model parameters. Our discussion in Chapter 6 led us to conclude that this disadvantage of change scores has been overemphasized. With reasonable sample sizes the loss in the precision of estimates from change scores relative to static scores is small and a price well worth paying in order to reduce the possibility of biased estimates due to a misspecified model. It is from this perspective that we now undertake to estimate the causal influence of marital status on levels of the subjective quality of life.

We repeated the relevant regression analyses reported in the previous section, but now using changes in the indicators of well-being as the dependent variables. The predictor variables are now change scores, as well: for example, the change in marital status from the first to the second follow-up data collection (FU1 to FU2). The regression coefficients for change in marital status are shown in Table 7–4.

The first row gives the simple bivariate coefficients. The interpretation of this coefficient is the average increase in satisfaction (or happiness) from FU1 to FU2 among respondents who married between these data collections, relative to the average change for those who did not change their marital status. These coefficients can be compared to those in the first row

139

of Table 7–3. Such a comparison shows that the effects of marital status as estimated from change scores are considerably smaller than the estimates based on static scores. Across both satisfaction and happiness, and men and women, the estimates from change score analysis are only about sixty percent as large as those from static score analysis.[1] Moreover, the standard errors of the estimates based on change scores are about thirty percent larger than those based on static scores. This reflects the higher proportion of error variance in change scores, which is a major reason for the reluctance of most analysts to use change scores but one that we consider to have been overemphasized, as discussed in Chapter 6. The increase in standard errors in the present analysis is substantial, but not overwhelming; for the bivariate estimates of marital status effects, the thirty percent increase in standard errors corresponds to about a forty percent reduction in effective sample size. Obviously, no one wants this reduction in precision, and if we are confident that our causal model has been properly specified there is no need to resort to the use of change scores in estimating the parameters of that model. We rarely are justified in such confidence, however.

Living Arrangements

In the remaining rows of Table 7–4 we show the estimates for marital status when other variables are included as predictors. In the second row, the transition from living with parents to other arrangements is included as a predictor. This has only a very slight effect on the estimates for marriage. This is in contrast to the situation observed based on the analysis of levels at FU2, where the estimated effects of marital status were visibly reduced when we controlled on living arrangements. We suspect that the reason for this difference may well be the feature which recommends the use of change scores: estimates based on change scores are not biased by the omission of relevant causal variables, as long as those omitted variables do not change between data collections. Living arrangements have changed, it is true, but it may well be that *unchanging* characteristics of respondents are related to the probability of leaving the parental home among these young people, and that it is these characteristics, rather than the actual living arrangements, which have effects on subjective well-being. To give a specific example, suppose that persons whose parents are highly educated are more likely to leave their parents' home at a young age, and that parental education also is positively related to subjective well-being. These relationships with

---

[1]Some of the regression analyses summarized in Table 7–3 for static scores were not repeated for change scores. Background variables were not included in these models because they were assumed to be constant over the two data collections, and indeed were only measured once, at the base-year data collection. The lagged predictor variables could in principle have been included in these models (using lagged change scores), but were not because of a limitation of these particular data: there was very little variation on most of these variables at the base-year data collection, when the respondents were high school seniors. (All were students, almost all were living with their parents, and very few were married.)

140

Table 7–4

Multiple Regression Analyses: Contemporary Effects of Marital Status on Levels of Life Satisfaction and Happiness, as Estimated using Change Scores, with Controls on Other Variables (Monitoring the Future Panel Data)

Variables Controlled	Life Satisfaction		Happiness		Average
	Females	Males	Females	Males	
Nothing	.141 (.068)	.128 (.084)	.245 (.058)	.068 (.075)	.146 (.071)
Living arrangements	.133 (.072)	.108 (.088)	.261 (.062)	.061 (.079)	.141 (.075)
Whether parent	.145 (.069)	.139 (.089)	.266 (.060)	.068 (.080)	.155 (.075)
Work/student status	.140 (.069)	.137 (.084)	.233 (.060)	.068 (.075)	.145 (.072)
Complete set	.188 (.075)	.153 (.093)	.329 (.064)	.085 (.084)	.189 (.079)

NOTES: The entries are partially standardized regression coefficients from analyses in which changes in reported levels of life satisfaction and happiness from FU1 to FU2 were predicted by change, over the same interval, in marital status and the other variables listed in the first column. The dependent variable is the signed value of the difference in satisfaction or happiness: the report at FU2 minus the report at FU1. (Cases with missing data at either time were deleted.) The difference in marital status is the difference in dummy variables at FU1 and FU2, both coded 1 if married at the time, 0 otherwise. The other variables are also change scores, for variables that are defined in the Notes to Table 7–3.

The predictor variables are described in the Notes to Table 7–3.

The entries in the right hand column are the simple averages of those in the four preceding columns.

141

parental education would introduce a spurious relationship between the living arrangements variable and the measures of subjective well-being, as measured cross-sectionally, but since parental education is generally constant over this age range it would have no effect on the covariance of the change scores for living arrangements and well-being.

There is some support for this interpretation in Table 7–3. From comparison of rows 1 and 2 with rows 7 and 8 we saw that much of the shrinkage of the apparent effects of marital status which came upon controlling for living arrangements disappeared when we also controlled on a set of background variables. Such background variables are precisely the type of variables that we have in mind when we advocate the analysis of change scores over static scores: variables which do not change over time, and therefore variables the omission of which do not cause a bias in estimates based on change scores — contrary to their potential for producing biases in estimates based on static scores.

Parenthood

In row 3 of Table 7–4 we show the estimates for marriage effects when change in parental status is included as a predictor. Again these estimates, based on change scores, are much more similar to the bivariate coefficients (in row 1) than was the case for the estimates based on static scores (comparing rows 1 and 13 in Table 7–3). The earlier analysis suggested that parenthood might be suppressing to some extent the marital status effects, since the coefficients for the latter became larger when we controlled on parenthood; but there is no hint of this suppression effect from the analysis of change scores. We interpret this as further evidence for the superiority of the change score estimates. Support for this interpretation is again found in Table 7–3, where we observed that controlling on background variables substantially reduced the impact of including parenthood as a predictor.

Work and Student Status

When changes in work and student status were included as predictors, we obtained the estimates of marriage effects that are shown in the fourth row of Table 7–4. The pattern is by now familiar: the estimated effects of marriage are only slightly changed by adding these predictors to the causal model. And once again, this stability is in contrast to the case for estimates based on static scores. Marital status effects were estimated to be much larger when we controlled on work and student status (comparing rows 1 and 19 in Table 7–3). Here, controlling on background variables only slightly reduced the effect of controlling on work/student status. Our interpretation of the different patterns observed with change scores relative the static scores is the same as for the patterns observed for living arrangements and parenthood: change score estimates are less likely to be biased because of misspecified models.

142

All Predictors

In the last row of Table 7–4 we show the estimated effects of marriage when the variables just discussed (living arrangements, parenthood, and work and student status), plus change in political orientation, change in religiosity, and change in dating frequency are all included as predictors. We finally see some movement: the estimates for marriage are somewhat larger, especially for women, when we control on all of these variables. This suggests that the simple (bivariate) model may indeed be misspecified, and that some of the variables omitted are *not* constant over time. We have already noted that some of these predictors — living arrangements, parenthood, and work/student status — can be omitted from the change score model with relative impunity, since their inclusion has little impact on the estimated effects of marital status. We will return to this topic in Chapter 8, in which we will consider the effects of all of these predictors on subjective well-being. For now, suffice it to say that inspection of the coefficients for the other variables reveals that it is the omission of the frequency of dating variable which is most critical with respect to possible bias in estimating the effects of marital status. Moreover, one interpretation of these data is that frequency of dating is an intervening variable: it is influenced by marital status, and in turn influences well-being. If this is the correct causal model, the change in coefficient for marital status when frequency of dating is included as another predictor does *not* reflect misspecification of the original model, but the difference between the total effect of marital status and that part of its effect that is not mediated by dating frequency.

Another observation concerning the model with all the other predictor variables is that the ratio of the standard errors of the estimates based on change scores relative to those based on static scores is not as large (ratio of average values is 1.16) as the ratio of the standard errors for the bivariate statistics (ratio of average values is 1.29). This apparently reflects higher covariances between static levels of the predictor variables than between changes on those predictors. The result suggests that as the causal model becomes more complex, the loss in precision of estimates because of the use of change scores becomes less important.

Including Prior Level on the Dependent Variable as a Predictor of Current Level

The more traditional approach to estimating causal effects from panel data is to control on the prior level of the dependent variable by including it as a predictor in the multiple regression analysis. The various rationales that have been offered for this approach were discussed in Chapter 6, and we did not find them convincing. We are now in a position to compare estimates of effects based on this approach to those based on the analysis of change scores. These comparisons are summarized in Table 7–5.

The estimates for marital status effects as estimated from levels at FU2, with no controls on other variables, were shown in the first row of Table 7–3; their average value is the first entry in the first column of Table

143

Table 7–5

Comparison of Estimated Effects of Marital Status on Levels of Life Satisfaction and Happiness Based on Analyses of Change and Static Scores (Monitoring the Future Panel Data)

Variables Controlled	Dependent Variable		
	Static Scores (Y2)	Y2, Control on Y1	Change Scores
Nothing	.247 (.055)	.176 (.053)	.146 (.071)
Living arrangements	.184 (.058)	.127 (.056)	.141 (.075)
Whether parent	.327 (.062)	.245 (.059)	.155 (.075)
Work/student status	.350 (.059)	.259 (.057)	.145 (.072)
Complete set	.298 (.068)	.228 (.066)	.189 (.079)

NOTES: Each of the entries is the average of four partially standardized regression coefficients, predicting life satisfaction and happiness separately for men and women. The entries in the second column are based on analyses in which the dependent and predictor variables are all their levels at FU2. Those in the third column are the same as the second, except that level of the dependent variable at FU1 is included as a predictor of level at FU2. Those in the fourth column are based on analyses in which the dependent variable is change from FU1 to FU2.

The predictor variables are described in the Notes to Table 7–3.

7-5. The estimates obtained when prior level of the dependent variable was included as a predictor were shown in row 5 of Table 7-3; their average value is the first entry in the second column of Table 7-5. Finally, the estimates based on the change scores from FU1 to FU2 were shown in the first row of Table 7-4; their average value is the first entry in the last column of Table 7-5. The remaining rows of Table 7-5 are the average of estimates based on each of these three types of model when other predictors are added to the regression analyses.

We have already noted that the estimated bivariate effects of marital status derived from change scores are considerably smaller than the estimates derived from static scores. The overestimation (as we would view it) of the static score coefficients is markedly reduced by introducing prior level of the dependent variable as a predictor of current level. These estimates remain larger than those based on change scores, but not by much. In this respect, the introduction of the prior level of the dependent variable as a predictor of current level is an improvement in the model.

In other respects, this procedure is less successful in reducing bias in estimates of marital status effects. We noted earlier that estimates based on change scores were not affected much at all by adding living arrangements, parenthood, or work and student status to the regression model. This was in contrast to the substantial impact of including these variables on the estimates based on static scores. Adding the prior level of the dependent variable as well does not improve this situation much; the differences between entries in the second column of Table 7-5 are almost as great as the differences between entries in the first column. We interpreted this variation to the omission of relevant variables from the static score models. If some of these omitted variables did not change between FU1 and FU2, as appears to be the case, then their omission from the change score models is irrelevant.

Summary

The intention of this chapter was to test several hypotheses that would explain the differences in subjective well-being reported by persons in different marital statuses that we observed in Chapter 4. We began by considering the possibility that the relationship between marital status and subjective life quality is spurious rather than indicative of a causal influence. We found that, across the full age spectrum of adults, the younger age distribution of never married respondents may account for a portion of their relatively low satisfaction level, and that differences in levels of personal competence may account for part of the lower satisfaction of all unmarried respondents relative to those who are married. The interpretation of the latter finding is ambiguous, however; and in any case, a large proportion of the marital status differences remain unexplained by the compositional and personality differences that we were able to test.

The possibility that differences in the use of the response scales might account for the higher satisfaction reported by married respondents was explored by estimating a structural equation model that combined a measure-

145

ment model with a causal model. We found evidence that there are indeed rather strong method effects: respondents in the Quality of Life study apparently did differ in how they used the satisfaction scales, and such differences tended to vary according to the marital status of the respondent. Such response tendencies, however, far from explaining the differences in the subjective well-being of married and unmarried respondents, apparently *suppressed* those differences; if it were not for differences in the use of the satisfaction scales, we estimate that the marital status differences in well-being might have been two or three times larger than the observed differences.

The possible sources of a spurious relationship between marital status and the quality of life have by no means been exhausted by the few that we could explore using the Quality of Life surveys for the full age range of adults. Moreover, even if the relationship is not spurious, we would like to know much more about why it exists. In the rest of the chapter we used data from the Monitoring the Future study to explore the relationship of marital status to other characteristics of young adults, including employment status, living arrangements, and social activities.

From our examination of bivariate relationships in Chapter 5, we observed that marital status is an important though by no means overwhelming predictor relative to the other variables under consideration. Substantial differences were also found between respondents in different situations with respect to schooling and employment; living arrangements; and social activities. Smaller, but often statistically significant, differences were found to be associated with several other characteristics. In particular, we observed that differences in average levels of happiness and satisfaction between respondents who had moved out of their parents' home and those still living with their parents were almost as great as the differences between married and unmarried respondents, and we wondered to what extent the marital status differences could be explained by differences in the living arrangements and other characteristics of married respondents relative to those still unmarried.

We explored this question in this chapter through a series of multivariate analyses, and found that if anything, the marital status differences are suppressed, rather than explained, by the associations between marital status and other variables including the work/student status, parenthood, and other variables listed in the previous paragraph and a limited set of background characteristics.

We then repeated these regression analyses, using change scores rather than static scores but still in order to estimate the same static model: the effect of marital status on level of subjective well-being. The estimates of marital status effects derived from change scores were generally smaller than the estimates derived from static scores, though consistently in the same direction. Moreover, the marital status effects as estimated from change scores were considerably more robust than the estimates derived from static scores; introducing various other predictor variables had little influence on the change score estimates, but often substantial influence on the static score estimates. We interpret this increased robustness as a consequence of the advantages offered by change scores, as we described them in Chapter 6.

Finally, we compared estimates in which prior level of the dependent variable was included as a predictor of current level to those based on change scores. These estimates were closer in magnitude to the change scores than the simple static score estimates, but they were almost as labile as the static score estimates in the face of introducing additional predictor variables.

CHAPTER 8

EFFECTS OF OTHER VARIABLES ON SUBJECTIVE WELL-BEING

In the preceding chapter we focused our attention on estimating the effect of marital status on the subjective quality of life. In the latter half of that chapter we examined estimates of this effect when various other factors were included in multivariate regression models. In this chapter we return to those same multivariate analyses, but shall now focus on the effects of the other factors. We shall not present the full set of regression estimates as we did for marital status, but will show estimates based on both static and change scores. We shall also compare the estimated effects of each variable based on a multivariate model, one that includes the effects of background variables and other variables, to the bivariate regression coefficients of those variables shown in Table 5–1.

Living Arrangements

Respondents who were still living with their parents at FU2 (i.e., three or four years after high school) were somewhat less happy and satisfied than those who had left their parental homes. As shown in the first row of Table 8–1, which is repeated from Table 5–1, these respondents reported levels of well-being that were about 0.2 standardized units below that reported by others. Controlling on the former level of the dependent variable reduces this discrepancy somewhat; as shown in the second row of Table 8–1, the average coefficient is now about −.16. This suggests (and inspection of the covariances confirms) that these respondents were somewhat below average in well-being at FU1 as well as at FU2.

In the third row of Table 8–1 are shown the coefficients for the living arrangements variable from a model which includes the whole set of predictors, (including the dependent variable at FU1). The estimated effect of living arrangements is reduced to less than half of the bivariate relationship: the average across the four columns is −.08. This suggests that much of the difference between respondents living with their parents and others can be attributed to other differences between these groups.

We repeated the estimation of the effects of living arrangements on well-being, but using change from FU1 to FU2 instead of level at FU2 as the dependent variable. The coefficients shown in the last two rows of Table 8–1 are for a variable which represents change on the dummy variable for living arrangements from FU1 to FU2, and thus can have values of 0 (for those who remained with their parents or remained in other living arrangements), −1 (for those who moved out of their parents' home), or +1 (for the few respondents who moved back into their parents' home). The interpretation of these coefficients is the same as for those in the first three rows of

Table 8–1
Estimates of the Effects of Living Arrangements
on Life Satisfaction and Happiness
(Monitoring the Future Panel Data)

Model	Life Satisfaction		Happiness		Average
	Females	Males	Females	Males	
Static Scores:					
Bivariate	−.204	−.115	−.280	−.234	−.208
	(.046)	(.047)	(.043)	(.046)	(.046)
Include Y1	−.154	−.102	−.181	−.192	−.157
	(.044)	(.046)	(.041)	(.044)	(.044)
All predictors	−.099	−.040	−.078	−.115	−.083
	(.050)	(.050)	(.045)	(.047)	(.048)
Change Scores:					
Bivariate	−.051	−.063	−.031	−.028	−.043
	(.051)	(.054)	(.045)	(.048)	(.050)
All predictors	−.002	−.044	.037	−.010	−.005
	(.055)	(.057)	(.047)	(.051)	(.053)

NOTES: The entries in the first three rows are partially standardized
regression coefficients from analyses in which the dependent variable was level of satisfaction or happiness reported at FU2 and
the predictors were also levels at FU2. The entries in the last
two rows are also regression coefficients, but from analyses in
which the dependent variable was change in the level of satisfaction or happiness from FU1 to FU2, and the predictors were also
changes.

The entries in the first row are bivariate regression coefficients
for a dummy variable that was given a value of 1 if the respondent was living with his or her parents, 0 otherwise.

Entries in the second row are regression coefficients for the living
arrangements variable when level of the dependent variable at
FU1 is included as a predictor of level at FU2.

Entries in the third row are regression coefficients for the living
arrangements variable when prior level of the dependent variable
and the following additional variables are included as predictors:
(1) marital status; (2) parenthood; (3) work/student status (was
the respondent a full-time student, employed full-time, a
homemaker, unemployed, or in some other situation or combina-

150

tion); (4) political orientation; (5) religiosity (frequency of attendance at religious services, and importance of religion); and (6) frequency of dating.

Entries in the fourth row are bivariate regression coefficients for change in the dummy variable representing living arrangements from FU1 to FU2, predicting change on the dependent variable.

Entries in the fifth row are multivariate regression coefficients for change in the dummy variable for living arrangements when changes on the other variables listed above are included as predictors of change in the dependent variable.

Entries in the last column are simply averages of the entries in the four preceding columns.

the table: the estimated effect of living with one's parents vs. living in some other situation.

The fourth row of Table 8-1 shows that, based on the analysis of change scores, the bivariate coefficients are all very small; none approach statistical significance, and their average value is only −.04. Controlling on changes in the other variables reduces the estimated effect of living arrangements even further: the fifth row shows the coefficients from these multiple regression analyses. Their average value is −.005. We also note from comparisons of the rows in Table 8-1 that the standard errors of the estimates derived from the analysis of change scores are only slightly larger than those derived from the analysis of static scores.

Our conclusion, based primarily on the analysis of change scores, is that the effects of living arrangements on the subjective quality of life are minimal. If these effects are estimated through the analysis of static scores, a bias is introduced such that we might have concluded that continuing to live with one's parents several years after high school has a deleterious effect on the well-being of young people. This bias is reduced by controlling on prior level of the dependent variable, and by controlling on other relevant variables, but persists even with these controls.

Parenthood

In Chapter 5 we observed only small differences between those who were parents and other respondents, with those who were parents showing just a slight tendency toward lower quality of life. The multivariate estimates of the effects of parenthood are shown in the second and third rows of Table 8-2. If we control on all of the other variables in the set, the estimated effects of parenthood on happiness are somewhat stronger than the bivariate coefficients in the first row.

If we base our estimates on the analysis of change scores, however, there is virtually no evidence of any effect of parenthood on the subjective well-being of young people. The inclusion of other variables has virtually no impact on these estimates (comparing the fourth and fifth rows of Table 8–

151

Table 8–2
Estimates of the Effects of Parenthood on Life Satisfaction and Happiness
(Monitoring the Future Panel Data)

Model	Life Satisfaction		Happiness		Average
	Females	Males	Females	Males	
Static Scores:					
Bivariate	−.030	.083	−.101	−.089	−.034
	(.058)	(.082)	(.055)	(.080)	(.069)
Include Y1	−.050	.077	−.124	−.094	−.048
	(.056)	(.079)	(.052)	(.076)	(.066)
All predictors	−.058	−.012	−.148	−.159	−.094
	(.068)	(.090)	(.061)	(.085)	(.076)
Change Scores:					
Bivariate	.007	.017	−.070	.032	−.004
	(.086)	(.108)	(.074)	(.097)	(.091)
All predictors	.008	−.007	−.093	.046	−.012
	(.092)	(.115)	(.079)	(.103)	(.097)

NOTES: The entries are partially standardized regression coefficients for a
dummy variable that is set to 1 if the respondent was a parent, 0
if not. The regression analyses are parallel to those in Table 8–1,
and the Notes to that table apply to this one as well.

2). We thus conclude that parenthood, even at a relatively young age, has
little influence on the subjective quality of life.

Work and Student Status

We next consider the importance of the status of young people with
respect to their educational and occupational careers. We classified the
respondents according to whether they were a full-time student, working
full-time, a homemaker (for women), unemployed, or in none of these
categories (e.g., a part-time student). In the following analyses of the effects of work and student status on the quality of life that are based on
static scores, dummy variables representing all of these categories are included as predictors, and the coefficients shown in the tables represent
deviations of those in a particular category from the overall average on the

dependent variable. In the analyses using change scores as the dependent variable, the coefficients are for change on the particular variable, but changes with respect to the other categories are included as predictors in the regressions.

Students

Those respondents who were still students at FU2 reported above average levels of happiness, and very slightly above average levels of satisfaction, as shown by coefficients given in Table 5-1 and repeated in the first row of Table 8-3. Controlling on prior level of the dependent variable (row 2) slightly reduces the coefficients. More important are controls for the other variables: among women, controlling on these variables *enhances* the estimated effects of being a student, whereas among men what slight change there is shows a tendency for the controls to reduce the differences.

When we estimate the effects of student status from change scores, we find a generally similar pattern suggesting a possible positive impact of this status on well-being. The change score estimates tend to be smaller than those based on static scores, are less volatile in the face of introducing other variables into the regression model, and mostly fall short of statistical significance. Overall, we conclude that the student status has rather little impact, once other variables are adequately controlled.

Full-time Workers

Those who were working full-time at FU2 were very close to the average levels on the measures of subjective well-being, except that working men were somewhat less happy than average (first row of Table 8-4). Controlling on prior level of happiness or satisfaction has little effect on these estimated differences (row 2), but controlling on the other predictor variables increases the estimated negative effects of employment on young men.

When we estimate these effects from change scores (rows 4 and 5 of Table 8-4), we observe essentially no influence of employment status on the subjective quality of life. There is a negative coefficient of $-.11$ with respect to the satisfaction of men, but it is not statistically significant and is not observed with respect to happiness.

Homemakers

Among those who were neither full-time students nor employed, women who said that they were full-time homemakers were somewhat above average in subjective well-being (first row in Table 8-5). The differences are not statistically significant, and become even smaller after controlling on prior level of the dependent variable and on other predictors (rows 2 and 3 of the table).

Table 8–3
Estimates of the Effects of Student Status on
Life Satisfaction and Happiness
(Monitoring the Future Panel Data)

Model	Life Satisfaction		Happiness		Average
	Females	Males	Females	Males	
Static Scores:					
Bivariate	.058	.036	.134	.182	.103
	(.033)	(.031)	(.031)	(.030)	(.031)
Include Y1	.052	.035	.112	.145	.086
	(.032)	(.030)	(.029)	(.028)	(.030)
All predictors	.125	.008	.235	.134	.126
	(.069)	(.074)	(.063)	(.070)	(.069)
Change Scores:					
Bivariate	.146	−.014	.056	.090	.070
	(.069)	(.074)	(.060)	(.064)	(.067)
All predictors	.151	−.014	.072	.104	.078
	(.069)	(.075)	(.060)	(.067)	(.068)

NOTES: The entries are partially standardized regression coefficients for
a dummy variable that is set to 1 if the respondent was a full-
time student at FU2, 0 if not. The coefficients are relative to
the overall average across all of the following categories: full-
time student, employed full-time, homemaker, unemployed, or
other. Dummy variables for all of these categories were
entered simultaneously in the regression models, including those
for the rows somewhat misleadingly labelled "bivariate." The
regression analyses are parallel to those in Table 8–1, and the
Notes to that table apply to this one as well.

Estimates of the effects of the homemaker role based on change scores
are about twice as large as those based on static scores (row 4 of Table 8–5).
Moreover, these estimates are not reduced substantially when we control on
other variables (row 5). We conclude that the homemaker role tends to
have a positive influence on the quality of life of women, and one that is not
explained by the other variables which we are considering nor by any
unchanging characteristics of the respondents.

Table 8–4
Estimates of the Effects of Employment Status
on Life Satisfaction and Happiness
(Monitoring the Future Panel Data)

Model	Life Satisfaction		Happiness		Average
	Females	Males	Females	Males	
Static Scores:					
Bivariate	−.002	−.015	−.031	−.089	−.034
	(.026)	(.026)	(.025)	(.025)	(.026)
Include Y1	−.002	−.017	−.026	−.060	−.026
	(.026)	(.025)	(.023)	(.024)	(.025)
All predictors	.017	−.104	−.004	−.103	−.049
	(.064)	(.071)	(.058)	(.067)	(.065)
Change Scores:					
Bivariate	.059	−.112	.044	.007	−.001
	(.067)	(.072)	(.058)	(.060)	(.064)
All predictors	.034	−.109	.006	.027	−.011
	(.067)	(.072)	(.058)	(.065)	(.066)

NOTES: The entries are partially standardized regression coefficients for a
dummy variable that is set to 1 if the respondent was employed
full-time at FU2, 0 if not. The coefficients are relative to the
overall average across all of the following categories: full-time
student, employed full-time, homemaker, unemployed, or other.
Dummy variables for all of these categories were entered simultaneously in the regression models, including those for the rows
somewhat misleadingly labelled "bivariate." The regression
analyses are parallel to those in Table 8–1, and the Notes to that
table apply to this one as well.

Unemployment

Men and women who were unemployed were considerably below
average on the subjective quality of life measures, as shown by the bivariate
coefficients in the first row of Table 8–6. Controlling on prior levels of the
dependent variables reduces these coefficients somewhat (second row), and
controlling on the other predictor variables reduces them still further for

Table 8-5
Estimates of the Effects of Status as Homemaker
on Life Satisfaction and Happiness
(Monitoring the Future Panel Data)

Model	Life Satisfaction		Happiness		Average
	Females	Males	Females	Males	
Static Scores:					
Bivariate	.084		.103		.094
	(.083)		(.078)		(.081)
Include Y1	.074		.051		.063
	(.081)		(.074)		(.078)
All predictors	.049		.027		.038
	(.107)		(.096)		(.102)
Change Scores:					
Bivariate	.181		.231		.206
	(.111)		(.096)		(.104)
All predictors	.135		.189		.162
	(.115)		(.099)		(.107)

NOTES: The entries are partially standardized regression coefficients for a dummy variable that is set to 1 if the respondent was a full-time homemaker at FU2, 0 if not. The coefficients are relative to the overall average across all of the following categories: full-time student, employed full-time, homemaker, unemployed, or other. Dummy variables for all of these categories were entered simultaneously in the regression models, including those for the rows somewhat misleadingly labelled "bivariate." The regression analyses are parallel to those in Table 8-1, and the Notes to that table apply to this one as well.

females (but not for males); however, substantial unemployment effects remain.

Analysis of change scores gives us a more complex picture of the effects of unemployment (rows 4 and 5 of Table 8-6): from this perspective, it appears that unemployment has some influence on the quality of life of men, but only a much smaller (and non-significant) influence on the quality of life of women. This is consistent with a finding reported elsewhere (Rodgers, 1977) from the 1971 Quality of Life study indicating that the subjective well-being reported by unemployed men was considerably below average, whereas unemployed women, although also below average, were not as dissatisfied as the men. Moreover, the relative dissatisfaction of

Table 8–6
Estimates of the Effects of Unemployment on
Life Satisfaction and Happiness
(Monitoring the Future Panel Data)

Model	Life Satisfaction		Happiness		Average
	Females	Males	Females	Males	
Static Scores:					
Bivariate	−.252	−.168	−.361	−.426	−.302
	(.077)	(.085)	(.072)	(.082)	(.079)
Include Y1	−.206	−.164	−.275	−.368	−.253
	(.075)	(.082)	(.068)	(.078)	(.076)
All predictors	−.146	−.214	−.187	−.354	−.225
	(.095)	(.105)	(.086)	(.100)	(.097)
Change Scores:					
Bivariate	−.038	−.218	−.075	−.241	−.143
	(.097)	(.113)	(.084)	(.110)	(.101)
All predictors	−.065	−.219	−.100	−.117	−.125
	(.097)	(.112)	(.083)	(.101)	(.098)

NOTES: The entries are partially standardized regression coefficients for a
dummy variable that is set to 1 if the respondent was
unemployed at FU2, 0 if not. The coefficients are relative to the
overall average across all of the following categories: full-time
student, employed full-time, homemaker, unemployed, or other.
Dummy variables for all of these categories were entered simultaneously in the regression models, including those for the rows
somewhat misleadingly labelled "bivariate." The regression
analyses are parallel to those in Table 8–1, and the Notes to that
table apply to this one as well.

unemployed women could almost all be explained by differences in economic
well-being, whereas such differences explained very little of the dissatisfaction of unemployed men.

Political Orientation

Young people, and young women in particular, who said that they
were politically liberal were somewhat less satisfied and happy with their

lives than those who said they were conservative (as shown in the first row of Table 8-7). Approximately half of this difference can be explained in terms of the other factors included in the multivariate analysis. Estimates based on change scores are much smaller than those based on static scores: the average value is $-.02$ without controls (row 4), and $-.01$ with controls (row 5). We conclude that political orientation has virtually no influence on subjective quality of life, and that the small differences observed at the static level are attributable to other characteristics that covary somewhat with the political variable (some of which we measured and included in the regression model, others of which we did not measure).

Table 8–7
Estimates of the Effects of Political Orientation
on Life Satisfaction and Happiness
(Monitoring the Future Panel Data)

Model	Life Satisfaction		Happiness		Average
	Females	Males	Females	Males	
Static Scores: Bivariate	−.077 (.030)	−.026 (.025)	−.120 (.028)	−.084 (.025)	−.077 (.027)
Include Y1	−.056 (.029)	−.017 (.025)	−.079 (.027)	−.076 (.023)	−.057 (.026)
All predictors	−.041 (.029)	−.007 (.025)	−.062 (.026)	−.063 (.023)	−.043 (.026)
Change Scores: Bivariate	−.001 (.033)	−.015 (.029)	−.024 (.029)	−.024 (.026)	−.016 (.029)
All predictors	.008 (.033)	−.016 (.029)	−.006 (.029)	−.026 (.026)	−.010 (.029)

NOTES: The entries are partially standardized regression coefficients for the political orientation variable (1 = "very conservative," 6 = "radical"). The regression analyses are parallel to those in Table 8–1, and the Notes to that table apply to this one as well.

Religion

There are two indicators of religiosity in the Monitoring the Future study: the frequency with which the respondents reported that they attended religious services, and the importance they attached to religion. We considered these two indicators jointly in the following regression analyses.

Attendance at Religious Services

Frequency of attendance at religious services, controlling only on the importance attached to religion, is associated with slightly higher levels on the subjective well-being measures, especially among women (first row in Table 8-8). These differences are cut in about half by controlling on the other variables (second and third rows). When we estimate the effects of this variable from change scores, however, we find no evidence of any positive effect on the subjective quality of life. As shown in the fourth and fifth rows of Table 8-8, none of the coefficients approach statistical significance, and those for satisfaction are actually negative.

Importance of Religion

The importance attached to religion by the respondents is associated with smaller (bivariate) differences than those associated with attendance at religious services, but the sex pattern is in the opposite direction: the differences are larger among men than among women (first row of Table 8-9). These differences change very little when we control on the other variables. Estimates based on change scores, while still small, average about twice as large as those based on static scores. Moreover, these estimates give little evidence of the sex interaction suggested by the estimates from static scores. They do, on the other hand, suggest a stronger influence on satisfaction than on happiness.

Dating Frequency

We observe from bivariate analyses (first row of Table 8-10) that the greater the number of dates per week reported by a respondent, the higher the average levels of happiness and life satisfaction. The entries in the second and third rows of this table show that controlling on the other variables has very little impact on these estimates. The estimates based on change scores (fourth and fifth rows) are somewhat smaller than those based on static scores, but lead us to the same conclusion, namely that the higher the frequency of dating, the higher the subjective quality of life of young people.

With respect to this variable, it is interesting to note that the transition from unmarried to married is accompanied by a *decrease* in the frequency of dating, even though the question about dating explicitly includes

Table 8–8
Estimates of the Effects of Attendance at Religious
Services on Life Satisfaction and Happiness
(Monitoring the Future Panel Data)

Model	Life Satisfaction		Happiness		Average
	Females	Males	Females	Males	
Static Scores:					
Bivariate	.056	.021	.123	.087	.072
	(.028)	(.030)	(.027)	(.029)	(.029)
Include Y1	.040	−.004	.091	.062	.047
	(.028)	(.029)	(.025)	(.028)	(.028)
All predictors	.036	−.012	.080	.039	.036
	(.027)	(.029)	(.025)	(.027)	(.027)
Change Scores:					
Bivariate	−.033	−.052	.003	.012	−.018
	(.036)	(.040)	(.032)	(.036)	(.036)
All predictors	−.031	−.054	.003	.009	−.018
	(.036)	(.040)	(.031)	(.036)	(.036)

NOTES: The entries are partially standardized regression coefficients for
self-reported frequency of attendance at religious services, with
importance of religion included in all of the regression equations
(including those for the rows somewhat misleadingly labelled as
"bivariate"). The regression analyses are parallel to those in
Table 8–1, and the Notes to that table apply to this one as well.

evenings out with one's spouse. It apparently is this pattern — positive effects of both dating and marriage, but a negative relationship between these
factors — which accounts for much of the enhancement in the estimated effect of marriage when the other variables are included in the prediction
model (Table 7–5).

It is possible, however, that a more proper causal model would specify
the frequency of dating as an intervening variable with respect to the relationship between marital status and subjective well-being. That is, one of
the effects of marriage may be a tendency to reduce the number of evenings
spent on "dates" with the person who has become one's spouse; and we have
just observed that the frequency of dating has an apparently positive effect
on the well-being. By controlling on dating frequency to obtain estimates of
the effects of marital status, we may be estimating a misspecified model. If

Table 8–9
Estimates of the Effects of the Importance of
Religion on Life Satisfaction and Happiness
(Monitoring the Future Panel Data)

Model	Life Satisfaction		Happiness		Average
	Females	Males	Females	Males	
Static Scores:					
Bivariate	.032	.066	−.018	.027	.027
	(.030)	(.029)	(.028)	(.029)	(.029)
Include Y1	.020	.057	−.010	.025	.023
	(.029)	(.028)	(.027)	(.027)	(.028)
All predictors	.019	.057	−.012	.029	.023
	(.029)	(.028)	(.026)	(.027)	(.028)
Change Scores:					
Bivariate	.083	.090	.037	.058	.067
	(.040)	(.040)	(.034)	(.036)	(.038)
All predictors	.081	.083	.035	.054	.063
	(.039)	(.040)	(.034)	(.036)	(.037)

NOTES: The entries are partially standardized regression coefficients for the importance
respondents said they placed on religion, with frequency of attendance at
religious services included in all of the regression equations (including those for
the rows somewhat misleadingly labelled as "bivariate"). The regression
analyses are parallel to those in Table 8–1, and the Notes to that table apply to
this one as well.

dating frequency is properly interpreted as an intervening variable, then an
estimate of the effect of marital status obtained from a regression analysis
which includes dating frequency as a predictor is really an estimate of the
direct effect of marital status — that is, the part of its effect that is *not*
mediated by frequency of dating. The effect of marital status as estimated
from a regression analysis which excludes dating frequency as a predictor is
an unbiased estimate of the *total* effect of marital status including both the
direct effect and an indirect effect that operates through the intervening
variable, frequency of dating. From the data we have just examined, we
conclude that if dating frequency is indeed an intervening variable between
marital status and well-being, its effect is to suppress the bivariate relationship; that is, if it were not for the fact that marriage seems to reduce the

Table 8–10
Estimates of the Effects of Dating Frequency
on Life Satisfaction and Happiness
(Monitoring the Future Panel Data)

Model	Life Satisfaction		Happiness		Average
	Females	Males	Females	Males	
Static Scores:					
Bivariate	.099	.094	.140	.112	.111
	(.015)	(.017)	(.014)	(.016)	(.016)
Include Y1	.091	.080	.123	.091	.096
	(.015)	(.016)	(.013)	(.015)	(.015)
All predictors	.092	.078	.124	.093	.097
	(.015)	(.016)	(.013)	(.015)	(.015)
Change Scores:					
Bivariate	.066	.061	.093	.062	.071
	(.016)	(.018)	(.014)	(.017)	(.016)
All predictors	.076	.067	.105	.067	.079
	(.017)	(.019)	(.014)	(.017)	(.017)

NOTES: The entries are partially standardized regression coefficients for self-reported frequency of dating. The regression analyses are parallel to those in Table 8–1, and the Notes to that table apply to this one as well.

frequency of dating, the well-being of married young people would be even higher relative to their unmarried peers.

This line of reasoning sheds new light on the relationship between engagement and subjective well-being. In Chapter 4 we observed that respondents who became engaged between successive data collections showed about as much of an improvement in their quality of life as did those who actually married, which made it appear that the important factor is the commitment to a marriage rather than marriage *per se*. Given the estimated positive effect of dating frequency, this interpretation is open to question. In contrast to marriage, engagement is accompanied by an *increase* in the frequency of dating, and if the proper causal model is one with dating frequency as an intervening variable, then dating frequency explains part of the positive effect of engagement on well-being. If we were to remove the effects of both engagement and marriage that are, according to this model, mediated by dating frequency, we would thereby enhance the residual effects of marriage and diminish those of engagement; and we would conclude that there are indeed positive effects of marriage that are not secured simply from the commitment to a marriage.

Background Characteristics

To this point we have not given much attention to the differences in subjective well-being of persons with different demographic characteristics except as control variables that might explain some of the differences observed between persons in various categories on status variables such as marriage. It is worth briefly documenting the relationships involving these background characteristics, both bivariate and multivariate, although we have not displayed them.

Race

The most important demographic characteristic with respect to subjective well-being is race; black respondents reported average levels of happiness and satisfaction almost half a standard deviation unit below the average for whites, and those in other races were about 0.2 units lower than whites. If we control on other background variables and the characteristics considered in this chapter (and listed in Table 5-1), the racial differences are reduced by about a third, but remain substantial.[1]

Region

Four regions were distinguished in this analysis: (1) South; (2) Northeast; (3) North Central; and (4) West. Only small regional differences in reported levels of subjective well-being were detected, with those living in the West reporting somewhat higher levels of happiness — but *not* of life satisfaction — than those in other areas. These differences were barely affected by controls on other variables.

Urbanicity

There were only very small differences associated with size of place of residence, which again were not affected by the other variables controlled in multivariate analyses.

---

[1]Recall, however, from our discussion of racial differences in the base year data in Chapter 2 that there are substantial differences in the use of the response scales which may account for much of these apparent differences.

Broken Home

Respondents were classified according to whether they were living, at the time of the base-year interview, with both, only one, or neither of their parents. There were moderate differences: children who lived in a broken home averaging about 0.1 standardized units below other children. Controlling on the background and other characteristics, however, all but eliminated this difference, so the apparent difference is confounded with racial and other differences associated with broken homes.

Parental Education

There was a slight trend for happiness to increase with the average education of the parents of the respondents, about half of which was eliminated in the multivariate analysis.

High School Grades

At the time of the base year interview the respondents reported their average grades received in high school. There was a moderately strong trend toward increasing levels of happiness and satisfaction for those reporting better grades (about .06 standardized units per third-unit grade, such as a B to a B+). This trend was cut almost in half by controlling on the other variables.

High School Truancy

The respondents were asked as high school seniors how often they skipped school for an entire day, or skipped classes during the day, without an excuse. There was no detectable relationship between these self-reports and levels of life satisfaction or happiness.

Summary

We have summarized the many regression analyses reported in this and the previous chapter in Table 8–11. In the first column are the bivariate coefficients based on the analysis of levels of subjective well-being and averaged across both men and women and both life satisfaction and happiness. In the second column are the average coefficients when we control on initial level of the dependent variable, and in the third column the average coefficients when in addition we control on all of the other variables in the table. The last two columns are averages from analyses based on change scores: the bivariate regression coefficients are in the fourth column, and the multivariate coefficients, controlling on all of the other variables in the table, are in the last column.

Table 8-11
Summary of Average Effects of Set of Variables on Life Satisfaction and Happiness
(Monitoring the Future Panel Data)

Predictor	Static Scores			Change Scores	
	Bivariate	Control Y1	Multivariate	Bivariate	Multivariate
Marital Status	.247* (.055)	.298* (.068)	.228* (.066)	.146* (.071)	.189* (.079)
Living Arrangements	-.208* (.046)	-.157* (.044)	-.083 (.048)	-.043 (.050)	-.005 (.053)
Parenthood	-.034 (.069)	-.048 (.066)	-.094 (.076)	-.004 (.091)	-.012 (.097)
Student Status	.103* (.031)	.086* (.030)	.126 (.069)	.070 (.067)	.078 (.068)
Employment Status	-.034 (.026)	-.026 (.025)	-.049 (.065)	-.001 (.064)	-.011 (.066)
Homemaker Status	.094 (.081)	.063 (.078)	.038 (.102)	.206 (.104)	.162 (.107)
Unemployment Status	-.302* (.079)	-.253* (.076)	-.225* (.097)	-.143 (.101)	-.125 (.098)
Political Orientation	-.077* (.027)	-.057* (.026)	-.043 (.026)	-.016 (.029)	-.010 (.029)
Religious Services	.072* (.029)	.047 (.028)	.036 (.027)	-.018 (.036)	-.018 (.036)
Importance of Religion	.027 (.029)	.023 (.028)	.023 (.028)	.067 (.038)	.063 (.037)
Dating Frequency	.111* (.016)	.096* (.015)	.097* (.015)	.071* (.016)	.079* (.017)

NOTES: The entries are taken from Tables 7-3 and 7-4 in Chapter 7 and from Tables 8-1 through 8-10 in this chapter. Each entry is the average of four bivariate or multivariate coefficients, across regressions with life satisfaction and happiness as the dependent variables and for men and women. The average standard errors of these coefficients are in parentheses.

Looking across all of these characteristics and factors we observe that the estimated effect of marriage on the quality of life of young people is among the largest no matter which column we examine, and based on the final column, which is the one in which we place the most confidence, it in fact has the largest average coefficient. This is somewhat misleading, since it is a dummy variable with a range of 0 to 1, whereas some of the other variables have multi-point scales; thus, respondents who differ by three points on the importance of religion or the frequency of dating scales would be expected to differ as much or more than married and unmarried respondents. It nevertheless seems clear that, relative to the set of variables we have examined in this chapter, marriage has a substantial positive effect on the quality of life of young people.

The relative importance of the variables we have examined changes considerably when other factors are controlled, as comparison of the first and last columns in Table 8–11 demonstrates. The estimated effect of marital status is somewhat diminished, but not nearly as much as the estimated effect of living arrangements or unemployment. The relevance of political orientation is markedly reduced when other variables are controlled, as is the effect of frequency of attendance at religious services. Occasionally, however, the estimated effect of a variable is enhanced by controlling on other variables, suggesting that one or more of those variables is suppressing its apparent influence on the quality of life. This is true for the indicator of the importance of religion, and also for the homemaker role although the small number of women who placed themselves in that category makes the estimated effect statistically non-significant. In the previous chapter, it will be recalled, we observed a suppression effect with respect to marriage when we compared the bivariate to the multivariate coefficients based on change scores (i.e., the last two columns of Table 8–11).

The analyses reported in this chapter are also interesting with respect to the methodological issue of how best to use panel data for the estimation of static causal models. Although the general pattern of the multivariate coefficients based on static scores (third column of Table 8–11) is similar to that of the multivariate coefficients based on change scores (last column), there are also some important differences. The estimated effect of living arrangements (with parents vs. any other situation) is reduced to practically zero if we derive the estimate from change scores rather than from static scores. The negative effect of parenthood also disappears if we use change scores, and the negative effect of unemployment is cut almost in half. In contrast, the estimated effect of being in the homemaker role is much larger if we derive it from change scores; and similarly for the effect of the importance of religion.

We cannot prove that the estimates based on change scores are more accurate than those based on static scores, but based on arguments described in Chapter 6 we expect the change score estimates are less likely to be biased and therefore place more confidence in them than in the static score estimates. Moreover, while the standard errors of the change score estimates are, as expected, higher than the static score estimates, the difference is not large. Averaged across the eleven variables shown in Table 8–11, the difference is only about ten percent.

CHAPTER 9

ESTIMATING THE EFFECTS OF MARRIAGE
COMMITMENT TRANSITIONS ON
SUBJECTIVE WELL-BEING

Introduction

A convincing case can be made that in order truly to understand the causal structure which explains virtually any relationship, it is necessary to specify and estimate dynamic models which explain the process whereby that relationship developed. Certainly this is true with respect to the relationship between marital status and subjective well-being. Marital status is not merely a characteristic which is useful in describing an individual; it tells us whether that individual has made the transition from single to married. For most young people in their early twenties, that transition, if it has indeed taken place, has happened fairly recently. We would very much like to know how any differences between those in different marital statuses developed. If, as we have observed, married respondents feel better about their lives than single respondents, why and when did this happen? Did they feel better before they married, or not until after the marital transition? Was the improvement immediate, or gradual? Permanent, or ephemeral? And to what extent is the difference due to other events or characteristics rather than the marital transition *per se*? During this age span, other events as well as marriage are befalling a large proportion of young people. As we have noted previously, they are finishing their education and starting careers; moving out of their parents' homes and making other living arrangements; and becoming parents themselves. We have tried to estimate the causal effects of marital status while taking into account status with respect to these other variables, but all within the context of what were basically static models, while the transitional nature of this age group begs the estimation of dynamic models.

We have tried to make the case in previous chapters that panel data offer important advantages over cross-sectional data with respect to the estimation of static models. The primary advantage of panel data over cross-sectional data, however, is the opportunity they provide to estimate dynamic as well as static models. In this and the following chapters, we exploit the panel data from the Monitoring the Future study to estimate the causal effects of marital transitions, and to a limited extent those of other transitions, on the subjective quality of life of young people. First, in this chapter, we illustrate the two approaches in the context of a simple, bivariate model in which we examine the effects of making a commitment to marriage on the subjective quality of life. In the next chapter we estimate the effects of marital transitions, and to a limited extent other variables

167

such as transitions into and out of the student and work roles, using multivariate models.

In Chapter 6 we specified a simple model to describe the relationship between marital status and the subjective quality of life. The model given by expression (6.2) in that chapter is a *static* model; that is, it explains differences in levels on the dependent variable as they exist at a particular point in time by differences on a predictor variable as they too exist at that time. No account is taken of the process by which individuals reached their present position on the dependent variable, nor of whether they are now in a steady state or in flux. With cross-sectional data lacking any information about durations, we cannot improve on static models; but with data that include a time dimension — panel data, time series data, and event history data are important examples — it may be possible to estimate the parameters in a dynamic model: that is, a model that purports to explain *changes* in the dependent variable as well as its level at any particular time.

An elementary example of a dynamic model is called for by the retrospective data summarized by Figure 4–1 in Chapter 4. As with the static models estimated in the previous chapters, the dependent variable is life satisfaction, but now we would like to understand variation over time — here, time since entry into a particular marital status — as well as variation over individuals. A causal model that might be hypothesized can be expressed as follows:

$$\frac{dY_{ti}}{dt} = \sum_{j=1}^{J} \nu_j D_{tji} + \epsilon_{ti} \tag{9.1}$$

where D_{tji} is a dummy variable that is equal to 1 if individual i is in marital status j at time t, 0 if not. Very simply (and not very realistically), this model postulates that level of subjective well-being changes at a constant rate, ν_j, for as long as a person is in status j. By integrating this expression over time, and by adding the assumption that level of well-being when a person first enters a particular marital status depends only on the new status, we obtain an expression which can be estimated using multiple regression:

$$Y_i = \sum_{j=1}^{J} \beta_j D_{ji} + \sum_{j=1}^{J} \nu_j T_{ji} D_{ji} + v_i \tag{9.2}$$

where T_{ji} is the time that individual i has been in marital status j. According to this formulation, each additional year in status j adds or subtracts a constant, ν_j, to one's satisfaction. Alternative hypotheses about the time course of the effects on satisfaction of remaining in a particular marital status could be tested by specifying variations on expression (9.1). For example, we might expect the rate of change in well-being to decrease the longer a person has been in a particular marital status. If the decline is linear, integration leads to an estimation expression that includes a quadratic term for time in status. We also might need to include terms to take account of the possibility of selectivity with respect to the type of persons who tend to remain in a particular status compared to those who exit that status.

The inference of a causal effect of one variable on another requires some degree of time priority for the predictor variable — variation on the independent variable must precede in time variation on the dependent variable for causality to be possible. With cross-sectional data it is often difficult to justify an assumption of temporal sequence in order to infer a causal relationship from an observed association. Retrospective data of the sort just considered are helpful, especially for fairly objective data such as marital status and timing of marital transitions, but we may question their validity with respect to evaluative and other subjective phenomena. Even with respect to retrospective reports about objective events, there is ample documentation in the literature (e.g., Andersen, et al., 1979; Cannell and Fowler, 1963; Cannell, Fisher, and Bakker, 1965; Neter and Waksberg, 1965) that the occurrence and timing of hospitalizations and other events frequently are misreported. For this reason there clearly is a great advantage to data collected over time, as with a panel design.

Not so clear, however, is the choice of how to analyze panel data in order to draw causal inferences. Two types of causal models, and the estimation procedures appropriate for each, were described in Chapter 6. The more conventional model includes current level of a variable as one cause of the rate at which that variable is changing, and the estimation procedure for this type of model involves the analysis of level of the dependent variable at one point in time and uses a prior level of that variable as a predictor variable. The alternative model that we described in Chapter 6 does not treat current level of a variable as a cause of its rate of change, and the estimation procedure for this type of model involves the analysis of changes in the dependent variable. Before we consider these alternatives in detail, it is informative to examine a particular relationship from a panel perspective.

The Effects of Marriage Commitment Transitions on Well-being

For this example, we return to the relationship between marital status and satisfaction, this time as observed in panel data from the Monitoring the Future study. Specifically, we consider the data summarized in Figure 4–2 in Chapter 4, which showed the patterns of happiness and life satisfaction reported by young people according to their commitment to marriage (married, engaged, or neither) at two successive data collections.

Predicting Level of Well-being

The first model that we estimate specifies that the level of the dependent variable at the end of an interval is influenced by marital commitment at both the beginning and end of that interval. The estimation model is expressed as:

$$Y_{2i} = \sum_{j=1}^{J} \sum_{j'=1}^{J} \beta_{jj'} D_{jj'i} + v_i \qquad (9.3)$$

where Y_{2i} is the level of life satisfaction (or happiness) reported by respondent i at time 2 (the *second* data collection); $D_{jj'i}$ is a dummy variable which is equal to 1 if the respondent was in marital status j at the first data collection (time 1) *and* in marital status j' at the second data collection, and equal to 0 otherwise; and $\beta_{jj'}$ is the regression coefficient corresponding to that pattern. That is, expression (9.3) specifies that life satisfaction at time 2 depends on the marital history from the previous to the current data collection. This model differs from the model given by expression (9.2) in that it allows for distinct effects of each type of transition between levels of commitment to a marriage, as well as for distinct effects of remaining at each level, and also in that it ignores the effects of remaining in a status longer than the interval between two data collections. The latter simplification reflects the nature of the data that we will use in this example, which are from the Monitoring the Future study, rather than a theoretically or empirically derived assumption; the respondents in that study were not old enough to permit the examination of the effects of longer durations in a particular marital status.

Estimates of the regression coefficients in model (9.3) are listed in Table 9–1. Each of these estimates is properly interpreted as the average level of satisfaction or happiness expressed by respondents who had a particular pattern with respect to their commitment to marriage across two data collections. These averages are expressed as deviations, in standardized units, from the overall average across all patterns, and are given separately for respondents in each of nine categories defined by their marriage commitment at the beginning and end of a one- or two-year interval between successive data collections (labelled times T1 and T2).[1] For example, the entries for the first pattern are for those who were single (and unengaged) at both T1 and T2. This group constituted a majority (61.4 percent) of the respondents, and their average satisfaction level at time T2 was one tenth of a standard deviation unit below the mean for all respondents.

---

[1]The entries in Table 9–1 are based on data combined from the base-year data collections and the first two follow-ups. In some cases T1 is the base-year and T2 is the first follow-up, and in the remaining cases T1 is the first follow-up and T2 is the second. Thus

The coefficients in Table 9–1 are consistent with the patterns that we observed in Figure 4–2: the respondents who married between data collections were more satisfied (and more happy) with their lives than were other respondents. Approximately equally satisfied were those who became engaged during this interval, so again the relevant transition appears to be the commitment to a marriage rather than marriage *per se*. Those who remained unmarried and unengaged, and those who broke such a commitment (i.e., those who went from engaged or married to unattached) were the least satisfied and happy with their lives, while those who were married at both times were intermediate between the two other groups.[1]

Controlling on Prior Level of Well-being

In sociological and psychological literature, dynamic causal models almost always include current level of a variable as a cause of its rate of change, and as pointed out in Chapter 6 this leads to an estimation expression that includes prior level of the dependent variable as a predictor of its current level. Although we are not convinced that this is a sensible model, and certainly not that it should be accepted unquestioningly as the "standard" dynamic model, it is the conventional one so it is useful to estimate the causal effects of marriage commitments using this procedure. After doing so, we will go on to estimate the type of dynamic model that we think should be given more serious consideration, one which does *not* treat current level as a cause of the rate of change of a variable, and which can be estimated by using change scores as the dependent variable in regression analysis. We conclude the chapter by comparing the estimates from these two procedures.

The first model that we will estimate may be written as follows:

$$Y_{2i} = \alpha + \sum_{j=1}^{J} \sum_{j'=1}^{J} \beta_{jj'} D_{jj'i} + \lambda Y_{1i} + v_i \tag{9.4}$$

This expression is identical to expression (9.3) except for the inclusion of prior level of the dependent variable, Y_{1i}, multiplied by parameter λ.

Table 9–2 displays the estimates of the parameters of the model given by expression (9.4) as applied to the present concern: predicting levels of

---

respondents who participated in all three data collections are represented twice in this table.

[1]As shown by the entries in the first column of Table 9–1, some of these estimated coefficients are based on small numbers of respondents and thus have large standard errors. In particular, less than one per cent of the respondents were engaged to be married at both follow-ups, and less than one tenth of a percent were married at the first follow-up but engaged at the second, so we do not put much confidence in the estimated coefficients for either of these groups.

Table 9-1
Average Levels of Life Satisfaction and Happiness
for Respondents Making Different Marital Commitment Transitions
(Monitoring the Future Panel Data)

Marital Status T1	T2	Proportion of Cases	Deviations from Overall Mean	
			Life Sat.	Happiness
Overall mean (St. dev.)			4.868 (1.463)	2.169 (O.600)
Unmarried	Unmarried	.614	-.102 (.011)	-.133 (.010)
Unmarried	Engaged	.075	.230 (.048)	.293 (.042)
Unmarried	Married	.099	.259 (.041)	.322 (.037)
Engaged	Unmarried	.025	-.102 (.085)	-.164 (.075)
Engaged	Engaged	.008	.311 (.155)	.425 (.138)
Engaged	Married	.055	.202 (.057)	.275 (.050)
Married	Unmarried	.017	-.046 (.104)	-.309 (.093)
Married	Engaged	.001	-1.318 (.559)	.202 (.497)
Married	Married	.107	.097 (.039)	.174 (.035)
Multiple R (adjusted)			.145	.194
Multiple R^2 (adjusted)			.021	.038

NOTE: The regression coefficients are deviations from the overall mean, divided by the overall standard deviation at T2. The entries in parentheses are the standard errors of these regression coefficients.

satisfaction at the end of a two-year interval from the pattern of marital commitment at the beginning and end of that interval *and* from level of satisfaction at the beginning of the interval.[1] The explanatory power of this model is considerably higher than that of the previous model (given by expression [9.3]): the proportion of variance has increased from two percent to over seven percent. Most of the estimated coefficients, however, are close to those observed in Table 9-1 for the previous model. In particular, the deviations from the overall mean in the satisfaction levels of those who made the transition from single to married or engaged during the interval are very similar in the two tables. The coefficients for those who remained engaged or married, and for those who made the transition from engaged to married, all become smaller when prior level of satisfaction is taken into account. Similar patterns are observed in the analysis of happiness, comparing the right-hand columns of Tables 9-1 and 9-2.

Predicting to Change in Well-being

In Chapter 6 we argued that the conventional assumption implicit in the model just estimated — that is, that one of the causes of the rate of change of a variable is its own current level — should not automatically be made, but only accepted if it is theoretically reasonable with respect to the particular variable under consideration. We developed an estimation procedure for a causal model which does *not* make this assumption, one in which the dependent variable is *change* rather than level. To illustrate this approach to the causal analysis of panel data, the change score model given by expression (6.13) was estimated for both life satisfaction and happiness, using the change from the first to the second follow-up data collections in the Monitoring the Future study as the dependent variables.

---

[1]The entries in Table 9-2 are all multiple regression coefficients. In order to obtain these regression coefficients and their standard errors, a modified version of the usual multiple regression procedure was used. It should be noted that coefficients are estimated for all nine categories of respondents classified according to their marital statuses at T1 and T2. The usual practice with categorical predictor variables of this type is to transform the categories into a set of dummy variables, omitting one such category in order to avoid redundancy (and thus a singular matrix). The coefficients obtained in this way estimate the difference between each of the remaining categories and the omitted category. These coefficients obviously depend on which category is omitted in the definition of the dummy variables, and thus are in a sense arbitrary and may have little direct meaning. An alternative procedure, known as effect coding, assigns those in the omitted Jth category a score of − 1 for all J-1 of the variables corresponding to the included categories; the coefficients derived using this procedure are estimates of the difference between those in each of the J-1 included categories and the overall mean. This removes the arbitrariness from the estimates. A problem remains, however: an additional calculation is necessary to obtain the estimate of the average deviation of those in the omitted category from the overall mean, and considerable computation is necessary to estimate the standard error of that deviation. The procedure we have used in obtaining the estimates shown in Table 9-2 and the tables in Chapter 10 involves the definition of a particular generalized inverse matrix, and provides direct estimates of the deviation coefficients for all categories and the standard errors of those coefficients (Rodgers and Hill, 1985).

173

Table 9-2
Average Levels of Life Satisfaction and Happiness
for Respondents Making Different Marriage Commitment Transitions
for Model which Includes Prior Level of the Dependent Variable as a Predictor
(Monitoring the Future Panel Data)

Marital Status T1	T2	Proportion of Cases	Adjusted Deviations from Mean	
			Life Sat.	Happiness
Overall mean (St. dev.)			4.868 (1.463)	2.169 (0.600)
Coefficient for prior level			.236 (.013)	.341 (.012)
Unmarried	Unmarried	.614	-.083 (.011)	-.099 (.009)
Unmarried	Engaged	.075	.222 (.046)	.300 (.040)
Unmarried	Married	.099	.254 (.040)	.321 (.035)
Engaged	Unmarried	.025	-.083 (.082)	-.189 (.071)
Engaged	Engaged	.008	.223 (.151)	.363 (.130)
Engaged	Married	.055	.129 (.055)	.139 (.048)
Married	Unmarried	.017	-.014 (.101)	-.265 (.087)
Married	Engaged	.001	-1.397 (.544)	-.038 (.469)
Married	Married	.107	.030 (.038)	.051 (.033)
Multiple R (adj.)			.275	.378
Multiple R^2 (adj.)			.076	.143

NOTE: The regression coefficients are deviations from the overall mean, divided by the overall standard deviation at T2. The entries in parentheses are the standard errors of these regression coefficients.

The estimates from these regression analyses are shown in Table 9-3. These regression coefficients reproduce the patterns of change observed in Figure 4-2. The largest average increase in satisfaction and happiness is found among those whose status changed from unmarried to *either* engaged or married. Those who made the transition from *engaged* to married, however, although above average in satisfaction and happiness at the time of the second follow-up, actually were *less* satisfied and *less* happy at the time of the second follow-up, when they were married, than they were at the time of the first follow-up, when engaged. This indicates in a manner more striking than could be observed in the analysis of static data that it is the *commitment* to marriage that has a positive effect on subjective well-being rather than the actual beginning of marriage.[1]

The analysis of change scores also highlights the decline in satisfaction which follows the continuation of a previous marriage: those who were married at the first as well as the second follow-up showed a decline in both satisfaction and happiness. Those who were unengaged and unmarried at both times, or who went from engaged to unengaged, showed almost no change in their average level of well-being; and even those who went from married to unmarried showed little change.

Comparison of Estimates from the Two Approaches

We have considered two types of dynamic causal models through the analysis of panel data: the more conventional model, which assumes that prior level of the dependent variable is one of the causes of its rate of change; and a model which assumes the *absence* of such a causal path. We have illustrated estimation procedures for both of these approaches with analysis of a particular relationship. The similarities and differences between the estimates derived from these two approaches to the analysis of the effects of marital status transitions on subjective well-being are shown in Figure 9-1, along with the simple mean levels at time T2 for those in each pattern. For most transitions, all three estimates are remarkably similar. There are also some differences, however, and these are interesting.

For those respondents who remained married, the average level of satisfaction and happiness at T2 is intermediate between that of those who went from unmarried to married and that of those who remained unmarried. This is consistent with the patterns observed in Figure 4-3, and again in the analysis of change scores, that the transition from unmarried to married is followed by an initial rise and then a decline in subjective well-being. It might be expected, then, that controlling on the initial level of satisfaction would change the coefficient for this group from positive to negative, but this is not quite what happens. Including initial satisfaction as a predictor of current level does reduce the magnitude of the coefficient for the married-

---

[1]As discussed in Chapter 8, however, this similarity in the apparent effects of engagement and marriage may be somewhat misleading.

Table 9-3
Average Changes in Life Satisfaction and Happiness
for Respondents Making Different Marriage Commitment Transitions
(Monitoring the Future Panel Data)

Marital Status FU1	FU2	Proportion of Cases	Deviations from Overall Mean	
			Life Sat.	Happiness
Overall mean (St. dev.)			0.043 (1.800)	0.026 (0.677)
Unmarried	Unmarried	.614	-.019 (.013)	-.034 (.011)
Unmarried	Engaged	.075	.197 (.059)	.314 (.048)
Unmarried	Married	.099	.235 (.051)	.319 (.042)
Engaged	Unmarried	.025	-.023 (.105)	-.238 (.086)
Engaged	Engaged	.008	-.063 (.192)	.244 (.157)
Engaged	Married	.055	-.110 (.070)	-.125 (.057)
Married	Unmarried	.017	.090 (.129)	-.179 (.106)
Married	Engaged	.001	-1.653 (.693)	-.503 (.567)
Married	Married	.107	-.186 (.049)	-.189 (.040)
Multiple R (adj.)			.091	.137
Multiple R^2 (adj.)			.008	.019

NOTE: The regression coefficients are deviations from the overall mean, divided by the overall standard deviation of the level at T2 (1.463 for life satisfaction, 0.600 for happiness), so that the units are the same in this table as in Tables 9-1 and 9-2. The entries in parentheses are the standard errors of these regression coefficients.

Figure 9-1
Level and Change in Measures of Subjective Well-being of
Respondents in Different Marriage Commitment Patterns
Monitoring the Future Panel Data

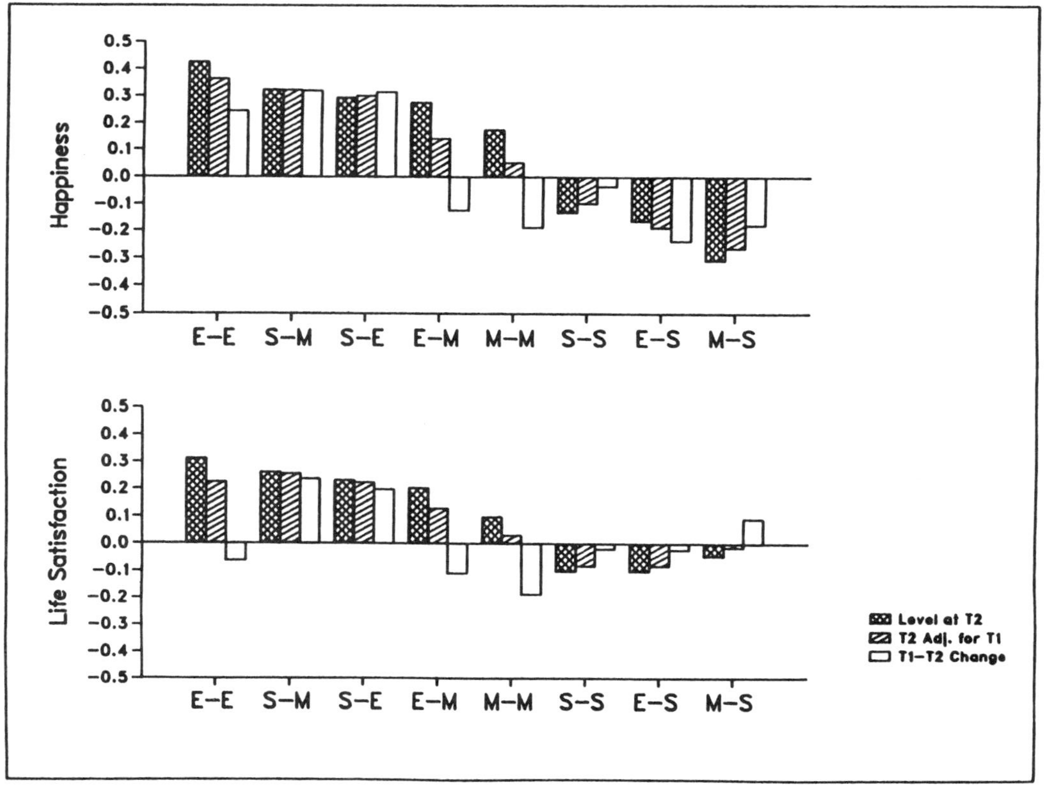

177

married group from about 0.1 to 0.03, and similarly the coefficient in predicting happiness for this group falls from .17 to .05; but the coefficients remain positive. In fact, the consistent pattern observed in Figure 9–1 is that the coefficients from the model which includes the initial level of the dependent variable are intermediate between the unadjusted T2 averages and the coefficients from the analysis of change scores.

The analysis of change scores also shows that there was a decline in the average satisfaction level of those who remained engaged, and in both the happiness and satisfaction of those who went from engaged to married. This pattern could not have been detected from simply examining the average levels of satisfaction and happiness of these groups at time 2; and, again, controlling on the initial level of the dependent variable produces estimates that are somewhat better than the unadjusted averages, but still considerably different from the estimates based on change scores.

Moreover, the transition from married to unmarried appears more benign when the dependent variable is change in level of well-being than when the dependent variable is level at time 2. The number of cases in this subgroup is small and, of course, limited to those who had both married and divorced at a young age; but with these qualifications as a caveat, it appears that, at least for some people, disappointment or disillusionment follows the initial commitment to a marital partner, and some of these people choose to end that relationship in rather short order.

Overall, the similarity of the findings from the analysis of static and change scores indicates that the model for static scores given by expression (9.1) is not seriously misspecified through the failure to include important predictor variables, at least relative to the model given by expression (6.7) for change scores. Moreover, the higher explanatory power of the former model (a consequence of the stability of the dependent variables) produces somewhat smaller standard errors for the estimated coefficients. On the other hand, there are enough differences in the estimates from the two approaches that the choice between them should be based on a decision about which best represents the causal processes, not on small differences in the precision of the estimates.

Summary

To illustrate the importance of the assumption about the causal influence of a variable on its own rate of change, we have estimated two regression models that were derived from dynamic models that, respectively, do and do not make that assumption. In both cases, we used panel data to estimate the effects of marital commitment transitions on indicators of subjective well-being. First we treated satisfaction level at a later data collection as the dependent variable, and its level at the previous data collection as a predictor along with dummy variables representing each possible pattern with respect to commitment to a marriage at both of those times. Then we used change in satisfaction from one data collection to the next as the dependent variable, with the same set of dummy variables as the predictors.

These two approaches yielded estimates of the effects of marital transitions that were often similar to one another. Both showed that the transition from unmarried to married is associated with higher levels of satisfaction and happiness. Both confirm that it is the commitment to marriage rather than just marriage that is critical: those who go from unmarried to engaged are just as satisfied as those who go from unmarried to married, and their increase in satisfaction is just as great.

Beyond these similarities, however, there were also some important differences in the estimates obtained from the two approaches: the analysis of change scores revealed effects that were not easily observed from the analysis of static scores. In particular, those who were married at the beginning as well as the end of the interval reported that they were less satisfied and less happy at the end than they did at the beginning of that interval. Similar declines in satisfaction and happiness were observed for those who were engaged at the beginning of the interval and married at the end. Moreover, the consequences of remaining single, or even of going from engaged or married to single, are assessed to be less negative if estimated from change scores than from static scores.

The comparisons we have made should be recognized as preliminary, based as they are on the analysis of a single relationship and with simple explanatory models. In the next chapter we will estimate more comprehensive models, again using both approaches to the analysis, to estimate the effects of marital status and other transitions on the subjective quality of life.

CHAPTER 10

ESTIMATING THE EFFECTS OF MARITAL STATUS AND OTHER TRANSITIONS ON CHANGES IN SUBJECTIVE WELL-BEING

Introduction

In this chapter we shall estimate the effects of marital status and other transitions on changes in subjective well-being, using both types of dynamic causal models which we introduced in Chapter 6 and exemplified in Chapter 9. Our first set of estimates are appropriate for a dynamic model of the general form given by expression (6.14) in Chapter 6, which specifies that the rate of change in the dependent variable is a function of its current level and of a set of predictor variables. To estimate the parameters of such a model from panel data, we use the following expression (derived through integration of a specific, linear version of the general model given by expression [6.14], and subsequent simplification of terms):

$$Y_{2i} = \alpha + \sum_{j=1}^{J} \sum_{j'=1}^{J} \beta_{jj'} D_{jj'i} + \underline{X}_{1i}\gamma + \underline{\Delta X}_{i}\mu + Y_{1i}\lambda + v_i \qquad (10.1)$$

where Y_{2i} is level of individual i on the dependent variable at time 2; $D_{jj'i}$ is a dummy variable that is equal to 1 if the respondent was in status j on a nominally scaled predictor variable at time 1 and in status j' at time 2; $\underline{X}_{1i}$ is a set of intervally scaled predictor variables at time 1; $\underline{\Delta X}_i$ is the vector changes on the X variables from time 1 to time 2; and Y_{1i} is level of the dependent variable as reported at time 1.

Our second set of estimates are appropriate for type of dynamic model that is given by expression (6.8) in Chapter 6, which differs from expression (6.14), on which the first approach is based, by the omission of the current level of the dependent variable as a cause of its rate of change. The parameters of such a model will be estimated by regression analyses based on expression (6.13), slightly rewritten as:

$$\Delta Y_i = \alpha + \sum_{j=1}^{J} \sum_{j'=1}^{J} \beta_{jj'} D_{jj'i} + \underline{X}_{1i}\gamma + \underline{\Delta X}_i\mu + v_i \qquad (10.2)$$

181

where ΔY_i is change in the dependent variable from time 1 to time 2 for individual i and the other elements are as in expression (10.1). In effect, the only practical difference between expressions (10.1) and (10.2) is that the latter places an added constraint, namely by requiring that the parameter λ in the former model (for the effect of the prior level of the dependent variable on its current level) be equal to 1. That is, the second model is somewhat more restricted than the first.

All of the analyses in this chapter were based on panel data from the Monitoring the Future study. We carried out four sets of regression analyses for each of the two approaches described above, using the two indicators of subjective well-being (life satisfaction and happiness) as dependent variables, and separately for men and women. In the interest of focusing on consistent effects, and with the loss of detail about differences between the sexes and between the two indicators, in the pages that follow we will comment primarily on the average estimates of parameters across these four sets of regressions. For the reader who is interested in the specific analyses, the coefficients from all of the regressions are shown in Tables 10-A1 through 10-A8 included as an appendix to this chapter.

Changes in Marital Status and Living Arrangements

Because marital status is confounded with living arrangements, and consistent with our multivariate analysis of levels of well-being in Chapter 7, we have combined transitions on these two variables into a single pattern variable in the analyses reported in this chapter. We have distinguished seven groups of respondents according to their marital status and living arrangements at the time of the first and second follow-up data collections (FU1 and FU2):

(1) Par-Par: living with parents at both FU1 and FU2;

(2) Par-Oth: living with parents at FU1, neither married nor living with parents at FU2;

(3) Par-Mar: living with parents at FU1, married at FU2;

(4) Oth-Oth: neither married nor living with parents at both FU1 and FU2;

(5) Oth-Mar: neither married nor living with parents at FU1, married at FU2;

(6) Mar-Mar: married at both FU1 and FU2; and

(7) Else: all who did not fit one of the first six patterns.

The average levels of life satisfaction and happiness at each data collection were shown in Figures 5-1 and 5-2 for each of the first six of these groups. We observed in our discussion of those figures that well-being increased from one data collection to the next whenever a particular group made the transition from unmarried ("Par" or "Oth") to married; that there were declines from FU1 to FU2 for the men and women who were married at both of those times; and that there was little systematic change for the remaining groups.

The first column of Table 10-1 gives the average regression coefficients for a model that includes only the set of variables which represent the pattern of marital status and living arrangements at FU1 and FU2 as predictors.[1] The first entry for each variable is based on the analyses in which the dependent variables are levels at FU2 (hereafter referred to as "method 1"), while the second entry is based on analyses in which the dependent variable is change from FU1 to FU2 ("method 2").

Looking first at the estimates from method 2, the coefficients are estimates of the deviation of those in each transition pattern from the overall mean change. For example, the entry for the first group in this column shows that those who continued to live with their parents at both FU1 and FU2 (the "Par-Par" group) showed very slightly less average change ($-.04$) than the total sample.[2] There was an increase of 0.1 units above the average for those who went from living with their parents to married ("Par-Mar"), and twice as much change among those who went from other living arrangements to married ("Oth-Mar"). On the other hand, those who remained in the married status at both times ("Mar-Mar") showed a *decline* in satisfaction of more than 0.2 units.

We now examine the estimates from method 1 in comparison to those from method 2. Both sets agree in showing an increase in well-being following marriage. The size of this effect depends on the estimation method, however; method 1 indicates larger positive effects than does method 2 both for those who went from living with their parents to married, and for those who went from other living arrangements to married. Method 1 also indicates a larger change than does method 2 among those who continued to live with their parents. The biggest difference in the estimates from the two methods, however, concerns those who were married at both FU1 and FU2; the average coefficient for this group derived from method 1 is very close to zero, whereas the average coefficient derived from method 2 has a rather substantial negative value. This is similar to the patterns observed in Chapter 9, where method 1 failed to indicate the decline in well-being

---

[1]The entries in Table 10-1 are all multiple regression coefficients, estimated using the procedure described in footnote 3 in Chapter 9.

[2]The units in which these and all other coefficients reported in this chapter are expressed are the standardized units described earlier: the dependent variables were divided by their standard deviations among all base-year respondents. This allows us to average across the two dependent variables; and since the same standardization was applied to the analyses reported in Chapters 7 and 8, the estimated effects reported there for static models can be compared to the estimated effects for dynamic models in this chapter.

Table 10-1
Estimated Effects of Marital Status Transition Patterns
(Monitoring the Future Panel Data)

Transition Pattern	Dependent Variable	Additional Predictor Sets			
		I	II	III	IV
Par-Par	Level, FU2	−0.118 (0.033)	−0.130 (0.033)	−0.103 (0.033)	−0.115 (0.034)
	Change	−0.043 (0.041)	−0.044 (0.041)	−0.038 (0.042)	−0.052 (0.042)
Par-Oth	Level, FU2	−0.014 (0.052)	−0.022 (0.052)	−0.031 (0.052)	−0.023 (0.052)
	Change	0.058 (0.064)	0.057 (0.064)	0.048 (0.065)	0.045 (0.065)
Par-Mar	Level, FU2	0.172 (0.070)	0.171 (0.072)	0.220 (0.072)	0.186 (0.074)
	Change	0.100 (0.087)	0.089 (0.089)	0.102 (0.090)	0.128 (0.093)
Oth-Oth	Level, FU2	0.046 (0.035)	0.032 (0.035)	−0.015 (0.039)	−0.005 (0.039)
	Change	0.021 (0.043)	0.019 (0.044)	0.012 (0.048)	0.006 (0.049)
Oth-Mar	Level, FU2	0.284 (0.091)	0.291 (0.093)	0.303 (0.092)	0.291 (0.093)
	Change	0.194 (0.113)	0.184 (0.116)	0.197 (0.114)	0.217 (0.117)
Mar-Mar	Level, FU2	0.005 (0.079)	0.091 (0.089)	0.091 (0.084)	0.128 (0.091)
	Change	−0.222 (0.098)	−0.208 (0.110)	−0.219 (0.104)	−0.190 (0.113)
Else	Level, FU2	−0.074 (0.071)	−0.073 (0.071)	−0.060 (0.071)	−0.061 (0.070)

Table 10–1 (continued)
Effects of Marital Status Transitions

Transition Pattern	Dependent Variable	Additional Predictor Sets			
		I	II	III	IV
	Change	0.006 (0.088)	0.006 (0.088)	0.029 (0.088)	0.018 (0.088)

NOTES: Each of the entries is the average of four partially standardized regression coefficients shown in Tables 10-A1 − 10-A8, across two dependent variables (life satisfaction and happiness) and for men and women. The parenthesized entries are the average of the standard errors of those four regression coefficients.

The first set of entries for each group is based on analyses in which the dependent variable is level at FU2, and level at FU1 was included as a predictor. The second set of entries for each group is based on analyses in which the dependent variable is change from FU1 to FU2. In each case, the regression coefficients for each marital status/living arrangements transition group are deviations of the average level (change) in the dependent variable for respondents in that group from the average level (change) for the entire sample, after controlling on the indicated variable(s).

The additional predictors included in the estimation models for each of the four columns, besides the seven dummy variables to represent the marital status transition groups (and the level of the dependent variable at FU1 in the case of the analyses of level at FU2), are as follows:

I. None.

II. Parenthood at FU1 and change in parenthood from FU1 to FU2.

III. Student and work status at FU1 and change in each of these statuses from FU1 to FU2.

IV. The variables in II and III plus level and change in political orientation; in frequency of attendance at religious services; in importance of religion; and in frequency of dating.

among those who were either engaged or married at each of two successive data collections.

Control on transition to parenthood

As with the estimation of static models, we must be concerned about the possibility that estimates of the effects of a variable on the rate of change in the dependent variable may be biased because of failure to include other important causal variables that are correlated with the variables which are included. We will consider the same sets of variables which were introduced in the multivariate analyses of static models in Chapter 7, except that now we will add both the initial levels and the changes of those variables to the regression analyses. We begin by considering the effects of introducing the transition to parenthood on the estimated effects of the marital status and living arrangements transitions.

The second column of Table 10-1 gives the average coefficients for each of the marital status/living arrangements groups when parenthood is added to the explanatory model. Other than an increase in the standard errors of the estimates, the only noticeable change is an increase in the average estimate for those in the "Mar-Mar" group, based on method 1. Note that the change is in the "wrong" direction: it indicates a *positive* trend in well-being for these respondents, whereas method 2 continues to indicate a substantial negative trend.

Control on Changes in Student and Work Status

The next series of regression analyses includes transitions into and out of student and work roles. The changes in satisfaction and happiness that accompany transitions in these roles were examined earlier (Figures 5–3 and 5–4). We now consider transitions in the work and student roles along with the marital and living arrangement transitions as predictors of satisfaction and happiness.

In the third column of Table 10-1 are displayed the findings when work and student transitions are included in the causal model. There are few differences from the first column. As with adding the control on parenthood, adding the controls on student and work transitions makes the estimated trend for those who remained married somewhat positive, based on method 1. The estimated trend for those who went from living with their parents to married is more strongly positive, according to method 1, when these controls are added; and the discrepancy between the two methods for this group is now larger than without the controls.

Changes in Larger Set of Predictors

In the last column of Table 10-1, we have controlled on both sets of variables that were controlled in either the second column (becoming a parent) or the third column (student and work transitions), plus changes in political orientation, religiosity, and dating frequency. Again, with the exception of the estimates for those who remained married based on method 1, the entries in this column are remarkably similar to those in the first column, indicating that the bivariate estimates are not substantially biased by the effects of these other variables.

The stability of the estimates in the face of introducing these additional variables implies that the discrepancies in some of the estimates from the two different methods are also not changed much by these controls; and comparison of the first and last columns in Table 10–1 confirms this inference. The major difference continues to be with respect to those respondents who were married at both FU1 and FU2: method 2 indicates a negative trend in the well-being of these young people, while method 1 indicates a positive trend. Additionally, method 1 suggests stronger positive trends than does method 2 among those who married between FU1 and FU2.

The Transition to Parenthood

Parental status was judged to have very little influence on the subjective quality of life of young people, based on our estimation of a static model in Chapter 8. Inspection of Table 10–2 suggests a more substantial effect of parental status on the rate at which well-being changes, at least in the bivariate sense before controlling on other variables. The first entry, $-.19$, is the coefficient for parental status at FU1 in estimating the dynamic model with method 1; and the next entry in the first column, $-.17$, is the same coefficient estimated with method 2. (For three of the four regression analyses summarized by the averages shown in Table 10–2, these coefficients are statistically significant, the exception being for predicting satisfaction among men; see Tables 10–A1 through 10–A2.) On the other hand, the transition to parenthood is assessed to have little influence on rate of change in well-being, based on both methods. The interpretation of this pattern is not clear, and analysis based on a longer interval would be helpful. Perhaps the initial effect of parenthood is mixed, inducing positive changes for some people, negative changes for others depending on whether the child was planned or not, impact of the child on the educational and occupational career of the parents, and so on; but the longer term effects (as the child gets older?) may be more consistently negative. With these data, another interpretation that must be considered is that the slight negative coefficient of parenthood at FU1 reflects not any general longer term effect of parenthood but only the negative effect of becoming a parent at a young age.

Any interpretation of the effects of parenthood must be informed by the estimates from multivariate as well as bivariate analyses, but again the estimates do not tell a consistent story. In the second column of Table 10–2 are shown the multivariate regression coefficients for parenthood when the dummy variables for the various patterns of marital status and living arrangements at FU1 and FU2 are also included as predictors. Based on method 1, the coefficient for initial parental status increases somewhat when these variables are controlled, but the estimates from method 2 become much smaller. The estimates for change in parental status remain small. In the third column, the whole set of variables considered earlier are included as predictors; the estimated effect of initial parenthood, based on method 1, becomes considerably smaller, and is not as discrepant from the estimate based on method 2 as is the case when only marital status and living arrangement transitions are controlled.

Control on Changes in Student and Work Status

We next consider the effects of transitions into and out of work, student, and homemaker roles, plus unemployment, as predictors of satisfaction and happiness. Each of these roles will be treated distinctly: for example, the "student transition" is simply the difference in dummy variables for student status at FU2 and FU1, so it has a value of -1 for a respondent who was a student at FU1 but not at FU2; $+1$ for the reverse pattern; and 0 for a respondent who was a student at both times and for one who was a student at neither time. We will speak of the effects in terms of the transitions most frequent for young people — out of the student role, into the work or homemaker role; but the estimates are of course based on data from respondents who made transitions in both directions.

Student Status

Initial student status is associated with positive trends in the quality of life, based on method 1; the average coefficient is .07. (This is an average of slightly larger, and statistically significant, effects when assessed with respect to happiness, and smaller, non-significant effects with respect to life satisfaction.) The estimate based on method 2 is considerably smaller. The estimates for change in student status are of about the same magnitude as those for initial status (though the standard errors for these estimates are larger, so they do not have the same level of statistical significance). Controls on other variables (second and third columns of the table) have little impact on these estimates, so the effects of student status, and of leaving that status, cannot be explained in terms of associated changes in marital status, living arrangements, or the other variables considered in this chapter.

Employment Status

The estimated effects of employment status, and of entering the work role, can be described very quickly: not much. As shown by Table 10–4, all of the average estimates are small; and inspection of the underlying regression coefficients in Tables 10-A1 to A8 fails to reveal any contrary evidence. This is true both for bivariate and multivariate regressions, and for both methods 1 and 2. This is perhaps a surprising finding: that we are unable to detect consistent effects on trends in the quality of life in consequence of transitions with respect to such a major role as employment. We suspect that the reason may be the breadth of the search; the analysis is based on a sample of a broad population of young people, with widely diverse jobs and

Table 10–2
Estimated Effects of Becoming a Parent
(Monitoring the Future Panel Data)

Dependent Variable	Predictor Variable	Additional Predictor Sets		
		I	II	III
Level, FU2	Status at FU1	−0.191 (0.097)	−0.241 (0.107)	−0.136 (0.109)
	Change to FU2	0.062 (0.079)	−0.057 (0.087)	0.024 (0.089)
Change	Status at FU1	−0.174 (0.120)	−0.076 (0.132)	−0.066 (0.137)
	Change to FU2	0.019 (0.098)	0.031 (0.108)	0.065 (0.111)

NOTES: Each of the entries is the average of four partially standardized regression coefficients shown in Tables 10-A1 − 10-A8, as described in the Notes to Table 10–1.

The additional predictors included in the estimation models for each of the three columns, besides the two variables to represent parenthood at FU1 and the transition to parenthood between FU1 and FU2 (and the level of the dependent variable at FU1 in the case of the analyses of level at FU2) are as follows:

I. None.

II. The marital status and living arrangements transition dummy variables listed in Table 10–1.

III. The variables in II plus level and change in work and student status; in political orientation; in frequency of attendance at religious services; in importance of religion; and in frequency of dating.

Table 10-3
Estimated Effects of Change in Student Status
(Monitoring the Future Panel Data)

Dependent Variable	Predictor Variable	Additional Predictor Sets		
		I	II	III
Level, FU2	Status at FU1	0.071 (0.027)	0.097 (0.030)	0.091 (0.031)
	Change to FU2	0.085 (0.070)	0.105 (0.072)	0.110 (0.071)
Change	Status at FU1	0.026 (0.033)	0.010 (0.038)	0.006 (0.039)
	Change to FU2	0.080 (0.087)	0.074 (0.090)	0.078 (0.089)

NOTES: Each of the entries is the average of four partially standardized regression coefficients shown in Tables 10-A1 − 10-A8, as described in the Notes to Table 10-1. The student *status* variable is scored as 1 if the respondent was a student at FU1, 0 if not. The student *change* variable is scored as +1 if the respondent was a student at FU2 but not at FU1; 0 if a student at both FU1 and FU2 *or* at neither time; and −1 if a student at FU1 but not at FU2.

The additional predictors included in the estimation models for each of the three columns, besides the dummy variables to represent status (as a student, employed, homemaker, unemployed, or other) at FU1 and the variables to represent transitions into or out of those statuses between FU1 and FU2 (and the level of the dependent variable at FU1 in the case of the analyses of level at FU2) are as follows:

    I. None.

    II. The marital status and living arrangements transition dummy variables listed in Table 10-1.

    III. The variables in II plus level and change in parental status; in political orientation; in frequency of attendance at religious services; in importance of religion; and in frequency of dating.

motivations for working. More detailed examination of particular groups of young people, more homogeneous with respect to such factors, might reveal that for some young people the work role has a positive impact on the quality of life, while for others it has a negative impact. Based on the present analyses, however, these must remain speculations.

Homemaker Status

The estimated effects of the homemaker role on the well-being of young women are somewhat complex. As shown in the first column of Table 10–5, those who were homemakers at FU1 had negative trends in their well-being over the interval from FU1 to FU2, whereas those who *became* homemakers during that interval had somewhat positive trends. An interpretation of this pattern might be that becoming a homemaker is often associated with the transition to marriage, which we have seen to have an initially positive effect on well-being, but later the trend becomes negative. This interpretation is only partially supported by the estimates in the second column, where marital status and living arrangement transitions are controlled. The estimate for effect of initial status as a homemaker that is based on method 2 (where the dependent variable is the change scores) becomes smaller when the marital transitions are controlled, dropping from $-.31$ to $-.10$, but the estimate for effect of change in homemaker status based on this method does not change much. On the other hand, the estimate for initial status based on method 1 (where the dependent variable is level at FU2 and level at FU1 is an additional predictor) actually becomes *larger*, going from $-.18$ to $-.33$, while the estimate for change in status drops from .17 to .03. The picture that emerges from these analyses, then, is not very clear. Depending on the method of analysis used, the longer term trend for women who are homemakers may be either negative or practically zero (but "longer term" here is only assessed with respect to young women for a three or four year period at most); and the shorter term effect is slightly positive.

Unemployment

Becoming unemployed is followed by declines in subjective well-being. This not very surprising finding is shown by the average estimates displayed in Table 10–6. A not so predictable finding that is lost in these averages is that the negative effect appears primarily among men: based on method 1, the average coefficient for men is $-.32$, while for women it is $-.19$; and based on method 2, the average coefficient for men is $-.30$, while for women it is $-.04$. Some cautions need to be noted here. The transition to unemployment is based on whether a person was unemployed at two particular times two years apart, and says nothing about how long the unemployment had lasted or, on the other hand, about spells of unemployment not overlapping those times. In addition, the number of persons

Table 10–4
Estimated Effects of Becoming Employed
(Monitoring the Future Panel Data)

Dependent Variable	Predictor Variable	Additional Predictor Sets		
		I	II	III
Level, FU2	Status at FU1	−0.019 (0.035)	−0.048 (0.038)	−0.055 (0.038)
	Change to FU2	−0.033 (0.068)	−0.044 (0.068)	−0.053 (0.067)
Change	Status at FU1	−0.014 (0.044)	−0.012 (0.047)	−0.013 (0.047)
	Change to FU2	−0.017 (0.084)	−0.026 (0.085)	−0.028 (0.084)

NOTES: Each of the entries is the average of four partially standardized regression coefficients shown in Tables 10-A1 − 10-A8, as described in the Notes to Table 10–1.

The additional predictors included in the estimation models for each of the three columns, besides the dummy variables to represent status (as a student, employed, homemaker, unemployed, or other) at FU1 and the variables to represent transitions into or out of those statuses between FU1 and FU2 (and the level of the dependent variable at FU1 in the case of the analyses of level at FU2) are as follows:

I. None.

II. The marital status and living arrangements transition dummy variables listed in Table 10–1.

III. The variables in II plus level and change in parental status; in political orientation; in frequency of attendance at religious services; in importance of religion; and in frequency of dating.

Table 10–5
Estimated Effects of Becoming a Homemaker
(Monitoring the Future Panel Data)

Dependent Variable	Predictor Variable	Additional Predictor Sets		
		I	II	III
Level, FU2	Status at FU1	−0.183 (0.117)	−0.325 (0.128)	−0.174 (0.136)
	Change to FU2	0.169 (0.100)	0.035 (0.102)	0.082 (0.104)
Change	Status at FU1	−0.306 (0.145)	−0.098 (0.160)	0.020 (0.170)
	Change to FU2	0.091 (0.123)	0.123 (0.127)	0.154 (0.131)

NOTES: Each of the entries is the average of two (for women only) partially standardized regression coefficients shown in Tables 10-A1 − 10-A8, as described in the Notes to Table 10–1.

The additional predictors included in the estimation models for each of the three columns, besides the dummy variables to represent status (as a student, employed, homemaker, unemployed, or other) at FU1 and the variables to represent transitions into or out of those statuses between FU1 and FU2 (and the level of the dependent variable at FU1 in the case of the analyses of level at FU2) are as follows:

I. None.

II. The marital status and living arrangements transition dummy variables listed in Table 10–1.

III. The variables in II plus level and change in parental status; in political orientation; in frequency of attendance at religious services; in importance of religion; and in frequency of dating.

unemployed at either time is small, so the standard errors of the estimates for this transition are large.

Whether a person was unemployed at FU1 has a negative effect on that person's subsequent quality of life, according to the estimates from method 1: the average bivariate coefficient, as shown in Table 10–6, is −.41, larger than the effect of becoming unemployed. This does not make a lot of sense, and it also is not found in the estimates based on method 2; the average value from this method is −.12 (−.31 for men, +.06 for women). It is clear that unemployment has negative effects on the quality of life, at least among men; but based on method 2, at least, those effects are transient and apparently dissipate upon return to the employed status.

Political and Religious Orientation

Whether a person considers him or herself liberal or conservative in political orientation, and whether this orientation changes, has no important effects on changes in his or her quality of life (Table 10–7). The estimates from method 1 indicate that those who were more liberal at FU1, and those who became more liberal, had somewhat negative trends, but this is not confirmed by the estimates from method 2. Similarly, the frequency with which one attends religious services, and the importance one attaches to religion, have little influence on trends in well-being (Tables 10–8 and 10–9). Those who reported at FU1 that they were attending religious services relatively often had more positive trends than those attending less often, according to the estimates from method 1, but again this difference is not confirmed by the estimates from method 2. The remaining average estimates shown in Table 10–7, 10–8, and 10–9 are small, whether based on method 1 or 2 and whether bivariate or controlling on the entire set of variables examined in this chapter. Inspection of the detailed estimates for each measure of well-being, and for men and women (Tables 10-A1 − 10-A8) reveals a few that are statistically significant, but none that are especially large and no obvious pattern.

Frequency of Dating

Those respondents who increased their frequency of dating between FU1 and FU2 tended to report improvements in their quality of life over that interval; the average coefficient based on method 1 is 0.10 (for a one unit change on the six-point response scale), and .09 if based on method 2. These estimates are changed very little when the remaining variables we have considered are controlled (Table 10–10). The average coefficients for dating frequency at FU1 are substantially different depending on the method used in estimating them. Based on method 1, the effect of initial frequency of dating (.09) is almost as large as that of change in frequency, but based on method 2 the effect of initial frequency is much smaller (.03). We conclude that change in the frequency of dating has a positive effect on

194

Table 10-6
Estimated Effects of Becoming Unemployed
(Monitoring the Future Panel Data)

Dependent Variable	Predictor Variable	Additional Predictor Sets		
		I	II	III
Level, FU2	Status at FU1	−0.410 (0.112)	−0.405 (0.113)	−0.366 (0.113)
	Change to FU2	−0.249 (0.101)	−0.257 (0.100)	−0.243 (0.100)
Change	Status at FU1	−0.124 (0.139)	−0.088 (0.141)	−0.080 (0.142)
	Change to FU2	−0.171 (0.125)	−0.162 (0.125)	−0.163 (0.125)

NOTES: Each of the entries is the average of four partially standardized regression coefficients shown in Tables 10-A1 − 10-A8, as described in the Notes to Table 10-1.

The additional predictors included in the estimation models for each of the three columns, besides the dummy variables to represent status (as a student, employed, homemaker, unemployed, or other) at FU1 and the variables to represent transitions into or out of those statuses between FU1 and FU2 (and the level of the dependent variable at FU1 in the case of the analyses of level at FU2) are as follows:

I. None.

II. The marital status and living arrangements transition dummy variables listed in Table 10-1.

III. The variables in II plus level and change in parental status; in political orientation; in frequency of attendance at religious services; in importance of religion; and in frequency of dating.

Table 10–7
Estimated Effects of Change in Political Orientation
(Monitoring the Future Panel Data)

Dependent Variable	Predictor Variable	Additional Predictor Sets	
		I	II
Level, FU2	Status at FU1	−0.059 (0.031)	−0.052 (0.031)
	Change to FU2	−0.050 (0.028)	−0.036 (0.028)
Change	Status at FU1	0.004 0.039)	−0.009 (0.039)
	Change to FU2	−0.014 (0.035)	−0.013 (0.035)

NOTES: Each of the entries is the average of four partially standardized regression coefficients shown in Tables 10-A1 − 10-A8, as described in the Notes to Table 10-1.

The additional predictors included in the estimation models for each of the columns, besides the variables to represent political orientation at FU1 and change from FU1 to FU2, are as follows:

I. None.

II. Variables representing level and change in parental status; in work and student status; in frequency of attendance at religious services; in importance of religion; and in frequency of dating.

Table 10–8
Estimated Effects of Change in Religious Attendance
(Monitoring the Future Panel Data)

Dependent Variable	Predictor Variable	Additional Predictor Sets	
		I	II
Level, FU2	Status at FU1	0.060 (0.031)	0.045 (0.031)
	Change to FU2	0.027 (0.034)	0.015 (0.033)
Change	Status at FU1	0.003 (0.038)	−0.005 (0.039)
	Change to FU2	−0.016 (0.042)	−0.018 (0.042)

NOTES: Each of the entries is the average of four partially standardized regression coefficients shown in Tables 10-A1 − 10-A8, as described in the Notes to Table 10-1.

The additional predictors included in the estimation models for each of the columns, besides the variables to represent political orientation at FU1 and change from FU1 to FU2, are as follows:

I. None.

II. Variables representing level and change in parental status; in work and student status; in political orientation; in importance of religion; and in frequency of dating.

Table 10–9
Estimated Effects of Change in Importance of Religion
(Monitoring the Future Panel Data)

Dependent Variable	Predictor Variable	Additional Predictor Sets	
		I	II
Level, FU2	Status at FU1	0.009 (0.032)	0.014 (0.032)
	Change to FU2	0.037 (0.034)	0.036 (0.034)
Change	Status at FU1	−0.025 (0.039)	−0.018 (0.040)
	Change to FU2	0.055 (0.042)	0.052 (0.042)

NOTES: Each of the entries is the average of four partially standardized regression coefficients shown in Tables 10-A1 − 10-A8, as described in the Notes to Table 10–1.

The additional predictors included in the estimation models for each of the columns, besides the variables to represent political orientation at FU1 and change from FU1 to FU2, are as follows:

I. None.

II. Variables representing level and change in parental status; in work and student status; in political orientation; frequency of attendance at religious services; and in frequency of dating.

the quality of life, but that it is questionable whether it matters if that change was from an initially high or low level.

Table 10–10
Estimated Effects of Change in Frequency of Dating
(Monitoring the Future Panel Data)

Dependent Variable	Predictor Variable	Additional Predictor Sets	
		I	II
Level, FU2	Status at FU1	0.093 (0.017)	0.086 (0.018)
	Change to FU2	0.100 (0.016)	0.104 (0.016)
Change	Status at FU1	0.026 (0.021)	0.016 (0.022)
	Change to FU2	0.085 (0.020)	0.085 (0.020)

NOTES: Each of the entries is the average of four partially standardized regression coefficients shown in Tables 10-A1 − 10-A8, as described in the Notes to Table 10-1.

The additional predictors included in the estimation models for each of the columns, besides the variables to represent political orientation at FU1 and change from FU1 to FU2, are as follows:

    I. None.

    II. Variables representing level and change in parental status; in work and student status; in political orientation; frequency of attendance at religious services; and in importance of religion.

Summary

The analyses reported in this chapter quantified the changes in happiness and satisfaction that accompany transitions in marital status and living arrangements. Although we first observed these changes in Chapter 5, the use of multiple regression analysis in the present chapter allowed us to examine the extent to which these changes could be explained by other characteristics of young adults and other transitions they were experiencing at about the same time.

The transition to parenthood is one that had been made by only a small proportion of the respondents for whom data were analyzed, and this factor was not relevant to the changes associated with marital status or living arrangements. The multiple coefficients for those in the various transition patterns were not affected to any marked extent by including parenthood as another predictor. This conclusion holds as well for changes in student and employment status. Indeed, even controlling on all of these changes, plus changes in political and religious attitudes and frequency of dating, does not reduce the estimates of the effects of the transition from unmarried to married. Whatever the extent to which these other transitions are associated with changes in marital status and living arrangement, they do not explain the effects of those changes.

The analyses reported in this chapter can be compared with those in Chapter 8 in which static models were specified and estimated. Those earlier analyses indicated that marriage has a positive effect on the subjective well-being of young people; the average difference after controls on other variables is about 0.2 standardized units, whether based on the analysis of change or static scores. This is consistent with the positive effect of the transition from unmarried to married on change in the quality of life as estimated in this chapter, again whether based on regressions to level or change in the dependent variables.

The analyses reported in this chapter add another insight into the effects of marital status on life quality that could not be detected from the estimation of static models in Chapter 8: the decline in well-being reported by those who were married at the beginning as well as the end of the two-year period between successive data collections. It is also of interest that this decline is reflected in the coefficients from a model in which the dependent variable is change in well-being from the beginning to the end of the interval, but *not* in the coefficients from a model in which the dependent variable is well-being reported at the end of the interval and that reported at the beginning of the interval is included as a predictor. Our perspective is that the former method is more reasonable on *a priori* grounds, for similar reasons to those for which we argued that change scores are preferable to level scores for the estimation of static models.

The estimated effects of transitions on the other variables considered in this chapter can be summarized more quickly. Becoming a parent has relatively little influence on the quality of life, at least in the following year or two. The transition out of the student role is followed by a trend toward lower life quality, but the transition into full-time employment has relatively little effect. Women who become homemakers report improved quality of life, but again there is evidence that this may be a short-lived trend. Becoming unemployed is accompanied by declines in well-being.

Estimates based on regressions with later reports of well-being as the dependent variable indicate that a conservative political orientation, and changes in that direction, may have a positive effect on the quality of life, but this is not shown when the analysis is based on regressions to change in well-being. In similar fashion, estimates from the first method, but not the second, indicate that quality of life is positively related to the frequency of attending religious services. Both methods agree, however, in indicating that quality of life improves when young people increase the frequency of their dating. Putting this finding together with the initially positive effects of marriage as reported in this chapter, and the equally positive effects of becoming engaged, as reported in Chapter 9, it seems clear that a meaningful relationship with someone who is at least potentially a mate is important to the subjective quality of life of young people. Dating does not always lead to marriage, but in our society, where a period of courtship almost always precedes engagement and marriage, dating can be regarded as a necessary but not sufficient condition for subsequent marriage. Moreover, dating as defined here does not end with marriage but includes evenings out with the spouse. It is reasonable to suppose that part of the initially positive effect of marriage is explained by the intervening variable of "dates" with an enjoyable partner, and that the subsequent decline as marriages continue may partially be explained by declines in the frequency of such "dates" as parental and other responsibilities interfere.

Table 10-A1
Multiple Regression Analyses to Satisfaction at FU2 among Women
(Monitoring the Future Panel Data)

Predictor					Regression #				
	I	II	III	IV	V	VI	VII	VIII	IX
Constant	0.034	0.046	0.058	0.042	0.049	0.223	-0.137	-0.323	-0.244
Satisfaction, FU1	0.241 (0.021)	0.249 (0.020)	0.239 (0.021)	0.243 (0.021)	0.233 (0.021)	0.245 (0.020)	0.244 (0.021)	0.240 (0.020)	0.223 (0.021)
Par-Par	-0.116 (0.034)		-0.129 (0.035)		-0.113 (0.035)				-0.122 (0.035)
Par-Oth	0.002 (0.055)		-0.009 (0.056)		-0.019 (0.056)				-0.019 (0.056)
Par-Mar	0.189 (0.065)		0.194 (0.065)		0.204 (0.067)				0.184 (0.068)
Oth-Oth	0.027 (0.037)		0.009 (0.038)		-0.011 (0.042)				0.000 (0.042)
Oth-Mar	0.280 (0.083)		0.298 (0.084)		0.286 (0.084)				0.296 (0.085)
Mar-Mar	-0.042 (0.058)		0.028 (0.065)		0.029 (0.067)				0.047 (0.069)
Else	-0.063 (0.071)		-0.066 (0.071)		-0.051 (0.071)				-0.061 (0.071)
Parent, FU1		-0.172 (0.083)	-0.194 (0.090)						-0.065 (0.097)
Became Parent		-0.004 (0.070)	-0.103 (0.077)						-0.029 (0.082)

Table 10-A1 (continued)
Satisfaction at FU2, Women

Predictor	Regression #								
	I	II	III	IV	V	VI	VII	VIII	IX
Student, FU1				0.047 (0.028)	0.067 (0.032)				0.059 (0.033)
Became Student				0.086 (0.071)	0.114 (0.073)				0.116 (0.072)
Employed, FU1				0.017 (0.038)	-0.001 (0.040)				-0.013 (0.040)
Became Employed				0.025 (0.067)	0.027 (0.067)				0.007 (0.066)
Homemaker, FU1				-0.125 (0.122)	-0.206 (0.135)				-0.084 (0.143)
Became Homemaker				0.161 (0.104)	0.063 (0.107)				0.100 (0.110)
Unemployed, FU1				-0.255 (0.106)	-0.253 (0.107)				-0.208 (0.108)
Became Unemployed				-0.144 (0.099)	-0.154 (0.098)				-0.136 (0.098)
Other status, FU1				-0.047 (0.070)	-0.053 (0.071)				-0.054 (0.070)

Table 10-A1 (continued)
Satisfaction at FU2, Women

Predictor	Regression #								
	I	II	III	IV	V	VI	VII	VIII	IX
Political, FU1						-0.062 (0.035)			-0.056 (0.035)
Political change						-0.048 (0.031)			-0.031 (0.031)
Rel. Att., FU1							0.066 (0.032)		0.059 (0.032)
Rel. Att. Change							0.015 (0.033)		0.014 (0.033)
Rel. Imp., FU1							-0.005 (0.033)		-0.004 (0.034)
Rel. Imp. Change							0.043 (0.036)		0.039 (0.035)
Dating Freq., FU1								0.098 (0.017)	0.088 (0.017)
Dating Freq. Change								0.090 (0.016)	0.095 (0.016)
R (adj)	0.267	0.251	0.270	0.255	0.272	0.250	0.253	0.280	0.302
R^2 (adj)	0.071	0.063	0.073	0.065	0.074	0.063	0.064	0.078	0.091

Table 10-A2
Multiple Regression Analyses to Change in Satisfaction from FU1 to FU2 among Women
(Monitoring the Future Panel Data)

Predictor	I	II	III	IV	V	VI	VII	VIII	IX
Constant	0.034	0.056	0.042	0.047	0.044	-0.026	0.169	-0.090	0.090
Par-Par	-0.016 (0.044)		-0.020 (0.044)		-0.017 (0.045)				-0.038 (0.045)
Par-Oth	0.103 (0.070)		0.101 (0.071)		0.098 (0.071)				0.086 (0.071)
Par-Mar	0.092 (0.082)		0.087 (0.083)		0.068 (0.086)				0.097 (0.087)
Oth-Oth	0.004 (0.047)		-0.002 (0.049)		0.034 (0.053)				0.017 (0.054)
Oth-Mar	0.194 (0.106)		0.190 (0.107)		0.197 (0.107)				0.241 (0.109)
Mar-Mar	-0.280 (0.073)		-0.250 (0.083)		-0.339 (0.084)				-0.276 (0.088)
Else	0.033 (0.090)		0.034 (0.090)		0.064 (0.091)				0.046 (0.091)
Parent, FU1		-0.250 (0.105)	-0.126 (0.114)						-0.181 (0.124)
Became Parent		-0.043 (0.089)	0.003 (0.097)						-0.008 (0.104)

Table 10-A2 (continued)
Change in Satisfaction, Women

Predictor	Regression #								
	I	II	III	IV	V	VI	VII	VIII	IX
Student, FU1				0.003 (0.035)	-0.039 (0.041)				-0.048 (0.042)
Became Student				0.149 (0.090)	0.129 (0.092)				0.126 (0.092)
Employed, FU1				-0.010 (0.048)	0.004 (0.051)				-0.003 (0.051)
Became Employed				0.054 (0.085)	0.040 (0.085)				0.018 (0.085)
Homemaker, FU1				-0.141 (0.156)	0.113 (0.171)				0.251 (0.183)
Became Homemaker				0.132 (0.132)	0.194 (0.136)				0.222 (0.140)
Unemployed, FU1				0.122 (0.134)	0.186 (0.136)				0.211 (0.138)
Became Unemployed				0.016 (0.125)	0.031 (0.125)				0.022 (0.126)
Other status, FU1				-0.002 (0.089)	0.008 (0.090)				0.005 (0.090)

Table 10-A2 (continued)
Change in Satisfaction, Women

Predictor	Regression #								
	I	II	III	IV	V	VI	VII	VIII	IX
Political, FU1						0.019 (0.044)			-0.001 (0.045)
Political change						0.008 (0.040)			0.008 (0.040)
Rel. Att., FU1							0.027 (0.040)		0.031 (0.041)
Rel. Att. Change							-0.016 (0.042)		-0.005 (0.043)
Rel. Imp., FU1							-0.072 (0.042)		-0.066 (0.043)
Rel. Imp. Change							0.046 (0.045)		0.038 (0.045)
Dating Freq., FU1								0.035 (0.022)	0.024 (0.022)
Dating Freq. Change								0.086 (0.020)	0.085 (0.020)
R (adj)	0.077	0.041	0.075	0.029	0.088	0.000	0.041	0.089	0.127
R^2 (adj)	0.006	0.002	0.006	0.001	0.008	0.000	0.002	0.008	0.016

Table 10-A3
Multiple Regression Analyses to Happiness at FU2 among Women
(Monitoring the Future Panel Data)

Predictor	Regression #								
	I	II	III	IV	V	VI	VII	VIII	IX
Constant	0.070	0.090	0.111	0.085	0.098	0.279	-0.149	-0.368	-0.254
Happiness, FU1	0.337 (0.018)	0.353 (0.018)	0.332 (0.018)	0.345 (0.018)	0.323 (0.018)	0.349 (0.018)	0.347 (0.018)	0.341 (0.018)	0.304 (0.018)
Par-Par	-0.170 (0.031)		-0.193 (0.032)		-0.167 (0.032)				-0.186 (0.032)
Par-Oth	-0.085 (0.051)		-0.103 (0.051)		-0.122 (0.051)				-0.121 (0.050)
Par-Mar	0.281 (0.059)		0.293 (0.059)		0.338 (0.061)				0.321 (0.061)
Oth-Oth	0.067 (0.034)		0.036 (0.035)		-0.025 (0.038)				-0.012 (0.038)
Oth-Mar	0.333 (0.076)		0.365 (0.077)		0.353 (0.076)				0.374 (0.076)
Mar-Mar	-0.018 (0.053)		0.100 (0.060)		0.147 (0.061)				0.180 (0.063)
Else	-0.051 (0.065)		-0.057 (0.065)		-0.046 (0.065)				-0.062 (0.064)
Parent, FU1		-0.250 (0.076)	-0.312 (0.082)						-0.109 (0.087)
Became Parent		-0.027 (0.064)	-0.182 (0.070)						-0.048 (0.073)

Table 10-A3 (continued)
Happiness at FU2, Women

Predictor	I	II	III	IV	V	VI	VII	VIII	IX
Student, FU1				0.106 (0.025)	0.153 (0.029)				0.140 (0.030)
Became Student				0.114 (0.065)	0.175 (0.066)				0.178 (0.065)
Employed, FU1				-0.033 (0.035)	-0.068 (0.036)				-0.083 (0.036)
Became Employed				0.011 (0.061)	0.021 (0.060)				-0.006 (0.060)
Homemaker, FU1				-0.241 (0.112)	-0.444 (0.122)				-0.265 (0.128)
Became Homemaker				0.177 (0.095)	0.007 (0.097)				0.064 (0.099)
Unemployed, FU1				-0.365 (0.097)	-0.395 (0.097)				-0.330 (0.097)
Became Unemployed				-0.216 (0.090)	-0.241 (0.089)				-0.210 (0.088)
Other status, FU1				-0.056 (0.064)	-0.068 (0.064)				-0.069 (0.063)

Regression #

Table 10-A3 (continued)
Happiness at FU2, Women

Predictor	Regression #								
	I	II	III	IV	V	VI	VII	VIII	IX
Political, FU1						-0.069 (0.032)			-0.067 (0.032)
Political change						-0.074 (0.029)			-0.055 (0.028)
Rel. Att., FU1							0.101 (0.029)		0.083 (0.029)
Rel. Att. Change							0.066 (0.031)		0.059 (0.030)
Rel. Imp., FU1							-0.020 (0.031)		-0.019 (0.030)
Rel. Imp. Change							0.000 (0.033)		-0.002 (0.032)
Dating Freq., FU1								0.121 (0.016)	0.110 (0.016)
Dating Freq. Change								0.122 (0.014)	0.128 (0.014)
R (adj)	0.366	0.344	0.372	0.355	0.383	0.343	0.346	0.375	0.419
R² (adj)	0.134	0.118	0.139	0.126	0.146	0.117	0.120	0.140	0.175

Table 10-A4

Multiple Regression Analyses to Change in Happiness from FU1 to FU2 among Women
(Monitoring the Future Panel Data)

Predictor	Regression #								
	I	II	III	IV	V	VI	VII	VIII	IX
Constant	0.070	0.098	0.085	0.082	0.085	-0.020	0.021	-0.089	-0.123
Par-Par	-0.034 (0.038)		-0.042 (0.038)		-0.041 (0.039)				-0.065 (0.039)
Par-Oth	0.034 (0.061)		0.028 (0.061)		0.016 (0.062)				0.012 (0.061)
Par-Mar	0.218 (0.071)		0.221 (0.072)		0.226 (0.074)				0.275 (0.075)
Oth-Oth	0.029 (0.041)		0.017 (0.042)		0.005 (0.046)				-0.009 (0.046)
Oth-Mar	0.238 (0.091)		0.249 (0.093)		0.242 (0.092)				0.299 (0.094)
Mar-Mar	-0.325 (0.063)		-0.280 (0.072)		-0.260 (0.072)				-0.224 (0.076)
Else	0.010 (0.078)		0.008 (0.078)		0.028 (0.079)				0.003 (0.078)
Parent, FU1		-0.265 (0.091)	-0.124 (0.099)						-0.046 (0.107)
Became Parent		-0.090 (0.077)	-0.066 (0.084)						-0.002 (0.090)

Table 10-A4 (continued)
Change in Happiness, Women

Predictor	Regression #								
	I	II	III	IV	V	VI	VII	VIII	IX
Student, FU1				0.056 (0.030)	0.042 (0.035)				0.035 (0.036)
Became Student				0.075 (0.078)	0.088 (0.080)				0.088 (0.080)
Employed, FU1				-0.045 (0.042)	-0.053 (0.044)				-0.052 (0.044)
Became Employed				-0.005 (0.074)	-0.012 (0.073)				-0.035 (0.073)
Homemaker, FU1				-0.472 (0.135)	-0.308 (0.148)				-0.211 (0.157)
Became Homemaker				0.051 (0.114)	0.053 (0.118)				0.085 (0.121)
Unemployed, FU1				0.000 (0.116)	0.040 (0.117)				0.053 (0.119)
Became Unemployed				-0.103 (0.108)	-0.096 (0.108)				-0.097 (0.108)
Other status, FU1				0.042 (0.077)	0.041 (0.078)				0.032 (0.078)

Table 10-A4 (continued)
Change in Happiness, Women

Predictor	Regression #								
	I	II	III	IV	V	VI	VII	VIII	IX
Political, FU1						0.029 (0.038)			0.019 (0.039)
Political change						-0.009 (0.035)			0.003 (0.035)
Rel. Att., FU1							0.035 (0.035)		0.018 (0.035)
Rel. Att. Change							0.022 (0.037)		0.022 (0.037)
Rel. Imp., FU1							-0.016 (0.037)		0.001 (0.037)
Rel. Imp. Change							0.029 (0.039)		0.030 (0.039)
Dating Freq., FU1								0.046 (0.019)	0.030 (0.019)
Dating Freq. Change								0.118 (0.017)	0.116 (0.018)
R (adj)	0.107	0.050	0.107	0.077	0.118	0.000	0.000	0.129	0.171
R^2 (adj)	0.012	0.003	0.011	0.006	0.014	0.000	0.000	0.017	0.029

Table 10-A5
Multiple Regression Analyses to Satisfaction at FU2 among Men
(Monitoring the Future Panel Data)

Predictor	Regression #								
	I	II	III	IV	V	VI	VII	VIII	IX
Constant	0.025	0.012	0.018	0.036	0.040	0.094	-0.104	-0.208	-0.249
Satisfaction, FU1	0.239 (0.023)	0.242 (0.023)	0.240 (0.023)	0.242 (0.023)	0.238 (0.023)	0.242 (0.023)	0.239 (0.023)	0.236 (0.023)	0.229 (0.023)
Par-Par	-0.061 (0.034)		-0.055 (0.034)		-0.043 (0.034)				-0.041 (0.035)
Par-Oth	-0.004 (0.052)		0.000 (0.052)		-0.006 (0.052)				0.010 (0.052)
Par-Mar	0.216 (0.080)		0.190 (0.083)		0.256 (0.083)				0.214 (0.087)
Oth-Oth	-0.001 (0.035)		0.005 (0.035)		-0.038 (0.038)				-0.027 (0.039)
Oth-Mar	0.206 (0.105)		0.178 (0.109)		0.220 (0.106)				0.174 (0.109)
Mar-Mar	-0.001 (0.105)		-0.025 (0.119)		0.032 (0.107)				-0.004 (0.119)
Else	-0.060 (0.075)		-0.059 (0.075)		-0.049 (0.076)				-0.048 (0.076)
Parent, FU1		-0.005 (0.118)	0.002 (0.131)						0.038 (0.130)
Became Parent		0.210 (0.093)	0.113 (0.104)						0.162 (0.103)

Table 10-A5 (continued)
Satisfaction at FU2, Men

Predictor	Regression #								
	I	II	III	IV	V	VI	VII	VIII	IX
Student, FU1				0.024 (0.028)	0.051 (0.031)				0.055 (0.032)
Became Student				-0.020 (0.075)	-0.013 (0.077)				-0.003 (0.076)
Employed, FU1				0.004 (0.035)	-0.035 (0.038)				-0.039 (0.039)
Became Employed				-0.089 (0.074)	-0.119 (0.074)				-0.110 (0.074)
Unemployed, FU1				-0.406 (0.126)	-0.400 (0.128)				-0.400 (0.127)
Became Unemployed				-0.254 (0.110)	-0.260 (0.110)				-0.259 (0.110)
Other status, FU1				0.041 (0.079)	0.045 (0.079)				0.044 (0.079)

Table 10-A5 (continued)
Satisfaction at FU2, Men

Predictor	Regression #								
	I	II	III	IV	V	VI	VII	VIII	IX
Political, FU1						-0.022 (0.030)			-0.012 (0.030)
Political change						-0.007 (0.027)			0.001 (0.027)
Rel. Att., FU1							0.009 (0.032)		-0.003 (0.032)
Rel. Att. Change							-0.028 (0.036)		-0.042 (0.036)
Rel. Imp., FU1							0.037 (0.032)		0.043 (0.032)
Rel. Imp. Change							0.081 (0.035)		0.078 (0.035)
Dating Freq., FU1								0.067 (0.019)	0.058 (0.019)
Dating Freq. Change								0.090 (0.018)	0.092 (0.018)
R (adj)	0.253	0.249	0.252	0.252	0.261	0.244	0.249	0.270	0.286
R^2 (adj)	0.064	0.062	0.064	0.064	0.068	0.059	0.062	0.073	0.082

Table 10-A6

Multiple Regression Analyses to Change in Satisfaction from FU1 to FU2 among Men
(Monitoring the Future Panel Data)

Predictor	Regression #								
	I	II	III	IV	V	VI	VII	VIII	IX
Constant	0.025	0.009	0.002	0.042	0.043	-0.079	0.223	0.017	0.182
Par-Par	-0.039 (0.043)		-0.022 (0.044)		-0.027 (0.044)				-0.014 (0.045)
Par-Oth	0.044 (0.066)		0.055 (0.066)		0.038 (0.066)				0.039 (0.066)
Par-Mar	0.134 (0.102)		0.090 (0.106)		0.156 (0.106)				0.177 (0.111)
Oth-Oth	-0.007 (0.044)		0.010 (0.045)		-0.030 (0.049)				-0.026 (0.050)
Oth-Mar	0.121 (0.135)		0.072 (0.138)		0.127 (0.136)				0.108 (0.139)
Mar-Mar	-0.218 (0.134)		-0.360 (0.151)		-0.208 (0.137)				-0.315 (0.152)
Else	0.019 (0.096)		0.013 (0.096)		0.037 (0.097)				0.025 (0.097)
Parent, FU1		0.112 (0.150)	0.273 (0.167)						0.278 (0.167)
Became Parent		0.188 (0.119)	0.211 (0.132)						0.249 (0.132)

Table 10-A6 (continued)
Change in Satisfaction, Men

Predictor	Regression #								
	I	II	III	IV	V	VI	VII	VIII	IX
Student, FU1				0.008 (0.035)	0.017 (0.040)				0.029 (0.040)
Became Student				-0.045 (0.096)	-0.038 (0.098)				-0.021 (0.098)
Employed, FU1				0.000 (0.045)	-0.011 (0.049)				-0.021 (0.049)
Became Employed				-0.153 (0.094)	-0.165 (0.095)				-0.144 (0.095)
Unemployed, FU1				-0.312 (0.161)	-0.313 (0.163)				-0.348 (0.163)
Became Unemployed				-0.380 (0.141)	-0.383 (0.141)				-0.385 (0.140)
Other status, FU1				0.079 (0.100)	0.076 (0.101)				0.071 (0.101)

Table 10-A6 (continued)
Change in Satisfaction, Men

Predictor	Regression #								
	I	II	III	IV	V	VI	VII	VIII	IX
Political, FU1						0.034 (0.038)			0.017 (0.038)
Political change						0.002 (0.035)			-0.006 (0.035)
Rel. Att., FU1							-0.072 (0.041)		-0.077 (0.041)
Rel. Att. Change							-0.093 (0.046)		-0.100 (0.046)
Rel. Imp., FU1							-0.007 (0.041)		0.001 (0.041)
Rel. Imp. Change							0.089 (0.045)		0.086 (0.045)
Dating Freq., FU1								0.002 (0.024)	-0.008 (0.024)
Dating Freq. Change								0.062 (0.023)	0.065 (0.023)
R (adj)	0.000	0.023	0.038	0.044	0.045	0.000	0.067	0.072	0.117
R^2 (adj)	0.000	0.001	0.001	0.002	0.002	0.000	0.005	0.005	0.014

Table 10-A7

Multiple Regression Analyses to Happiness at FU2 among Men
(Monitoring the Future Panel Data)

Predictor	Regression #								
	I	II	III	IV	V	VI	VII	VIII	IX
Constant	0.047	0.055	0.067	0.080	0.080	0.302	-0.183	-0.250	-0.188
Happiness, FU1	0.325 (0.021)	0.331 (0.021)	0.322 (0.021)	0.317 (0.021)	0.309 (0.021)	0.331 (0.021)	0.326 (0.021)	0.323 (0.021)	0.292 (0.021)
Par-Par	-0.126 (0.032)		-0.141 (0.033)		-0.091 (0.033)				-0.111 (0.033)
Par-Oth	0.032 (0.049)		0.023 (0.049)		0.023 (0.049)				0.038 (0.049)
Par-Mar	0.002 (0.076)		0.008 (0.079)		0.081 (0.078)				0.023 (0.082)
Oth-Oth	0.090 (0.033)		0.077 (0.033)		0.014 (0.036)				0.020 (0.037)
Oth-Mar	0.315 (0.100)		0.322 (0.103)		0.353 (0.101)				0.320 (0.102)
Mar-Mar	0.083 (0.100)		0.262 (0.112)		0.155 (0.102)				0.292 (0.112)
Else	-0.124 (0.072)		-0.110 (0.072)		-0.093 (0.072)				-0.071 (0.071)
Parent, FU1		-0.339 (0.113)	-0.463 (0.124)						-0.409 (0.122)
Became Parent		0.067 (0.089)	-0.054 (0.098)						0.011 (0.097)

Table 10-A7 (continued)
Happiness at FU2, Men

Predictor	Regression #								
	I	II	III	IV	V	VI	VII	VIII	IX
Student, FU1				0.108 (0.026)	0.116 (0.030)				0.110 (0.030)
Became Student				0.160 (0.071)	0.142 (0.073)				0.148 (0.072)
Employed, FU1				-0.064 (0.033)	-0.088 (0.036)				-0.087 (0.036)
Became Employed				-0.079 (0.070)	-0.107 (0.070)				-0.104 (0.070)
Unemployed, FU1				-0.615 (0.120)	-0.572 (0.121)				-0.524 (0.120)
Became Unemployed				-0.383 (0.105)	-0.373 (0.104)				-0.366 (0.103)
Other status, FU1				-0.012 (0.074)	0.012 (0.075)				0.012 (0.074)

Table 10-A7 (continued)
Happiness at FU2, Men

Predictor	Regression #								
	I	II	III	IV	V	VI	VII	VIII	IX
Political, FU1						-0.085 (0.028)			-0.073 (0.028)
Political change						-0.070 (0.026)			-0.058 (0.025)
Rel. Att., FU1							0.065 (0.031)		0.039 (0.030)
Rel. Att. Change							0.054 (0.035)		0.028 (0.034)
Rel. Imp., FU1							0.023 (0.031)		0.034 (0.030)
Rel. Imp. Change							0.025 (0.034)		0.027 (0.033)
Dating Freq., FU1								0.085 (0.018)	0.090 (0.018)
Dating Freq. Change								0.097 (0.017)	0.100 (0.017)
R (adj)	0.326	0.317	0.333	0.338	0.347	0.318	0.318	0.333	0.379
R^2 (adj)	0.106	0.101	0.111	0.114	0.120	0.101	0.101	0.111	0.144

Table 10-A8
Multiple Regression Analyses to Change in Happiness from FU1 to FU2 among Men
(Monitoring the Future Panel Data)

Predictor	Regression #								
	I	II	III	IV	V	VI	VII	VIII	IX
Constant	0.047	0.056	0.060	0.064	0.061	0.239	0.010	-0.031	0.209
Par-Par	-0.082 (0.039)		-0.091 (0.039)		-0.067 (0.039)				-0.089 (0.040)
Par-Oth	0.049 (0.059)		0.044 (0.060)		0.039 (0.060)				0.040 (0.060)
Par-Mar	-0.045 (0.091)		-0.044 (0.095)		-0.041 (0.095)				-0.039 (0.100)
Oth-Oth	0.058 (0.040)		0.049 (0.040)		0.041 (0.044)				0.042 (0.045)
Oth-Mar	0.223 (0.121)		0.225 (0.124)		0.222 (0.122)				0.218 (0.125)
Mar-Mar	-0.066 (0.120)		0.057 (0.135)		-0.068 (0.123)				0.054 (0.137)
Else	-0.039 (0.086)		-0.028 (0.086)		-0.013 (0.087)				-0.003 (0.087)
Parent, FU1		-0.295 (0.135)	-0.326 (0.150)						-0.314 (0.150)
Became Parent		0.022 (0.107)	-0.023 (0.119)						0.022 (0.119)

Table 10-A8 (continued)
Change in Happiness, Men

Predictor	Regression #								
	I	II	III	IV	V	VI	VII	VIII	IX
Student, FU1				0.038 (0.032)	0.021 (0.036)				0.009 (0.036)
Became Student				0.139 (0.086)	0.118 (0.088)				0.120 (0.088)
Employed, FU1				0.000 (0.040)	0.010 (0.044)				0.022 (0.044)
Became Employed				0.037 (0.085)	0.032 (0.085)				0.049 (0.085)
Unemployed, FU1				-0.306 (0.145)	-0.264 (0.146)				-0.234 (0.147)
Became Unemployed				-0.216 (0.126)	-0.200 (0.126)				-0.191 (0.126)
Other status, FU1				-0.034 (0.090)	-0.015 (0.091)				-0.013 (0.091)

Table 10-A8 (continued)
Change in Happiness, Men

Predictor	Regression #								
	I	II	III	IV	V	VI	VII	VIII	IX
Political, FU1						-0.064 (0.034)			-0.069 (0.034)
Political change						-0.056 (0.031)			-0.059 (0.031)
Rel. Att., FU1							0.019 (0.037)		0.007 (0.037)
Rel. Att. Change							0.023 (0.042)		0.009 (0.042)
Rel. Imp., FU1							-0.005 (0.037)		-0.005 (0.037)
Rel. Imp. Change							0.055 (0.040)		0.056 (0.040)
Dating Freq., FU1								0.022 (0.021)	0.018 (0.022)
Dating Freq. Change								0.074 (0.020)	0.074 (0.020)
R (adj)	0.037	0.036	0.051	0.045	0.048	0.033	0.000	0.076	0.103
R^2 (adj)	0.001	0.001	0.003	0.002	0.002	0.001	0.000	0.006	0.011

REFERENCES

Allison, P. D. (1982). "Discrete-time methods for the analysis of event histories." Pp. 61–98 in K. F. Schuessler (ed.), *Sociological Methodology 1982*. San Francisco: Jossey-Bass.

Allison, P. D. (1984). *Event History Analysis: Regression for Longitudinal Event Data*. Beverly Hills, CA: Sage Publications.

Althauser, R. P. and T. A. Heberlein. (1970). "Validity and the multitrait-multimethod matrix." Pp. 151–169 in E. F. Borgatta and G. W. Bohrnstedt (eds.), *Sociological Methodology 1970*. San Francisco: Jossey-Bass.

Andersen, R., J. Kasper, M. R. Frankel, and associates. (1979). *Total Survey Error*. San Francisco: Jossey-Bass.

Andrews, F. M. (1984). "Construct validity and error components of survey measures: A structural modeling approach." *Public Opinion Quarterly*, **48**, 409–442.

Andrews, F. M. and S. B. Withey. (1976). *Social Indicators of Well-being: Americans' Perceptions of Life Quality*. New York: Plenum Press.

Ashenfelter, O., A. Deaton, and G. Solon (1986). "Collecting panel data in developing countries: Does it make sense?" Living Standards Measurement Study, Working Paper No. 23, Washington, D.C.: The World Bank.

Bachman, J. G. and L. D. Johnston. (1978). *The Monitoring the Future Project: Design and Procedures* (Monitoring the Future Occasional Paper 1). Ann Arbor: Institute for Social Research.

Bachman, J. G., L. D. Johnston, and P. M. O'Malley. (1981). "Smoking, drinking and drug use among American high school students: Correlates and trends, 1975–1979." *American Journal of Public Health*, **71**, 59–69.

Bachman, J. G. and P. M. O'Malley. (1984a). "Black-white differences in self-esteem: Are they affected by response styles?" *American Journal of Sociology*, **90**, 624–639.

Bachman, J. G. and P. M. O'Malley. (1984b). "Yea-saying, nay-saying, and going to extremes: Are black-white differences in survey results due to response style?" *Public Opinion Quarterly*, **48**, 409–427.

Bachman, J. G., P. M. O'Malley, and L. D. Johnston. (1984). "Drug use among young adults: The impacts of role status and social environments." *Journal of Personality and Social Psychology*, **47**, 629–645.

Bradburn, N.M. (1969). *The Structure of Psychological Well-Being*. Chicago: Aldine.

Campbell, A., P. E. Converse, and W. L. Rodgers. (1976). *The Quality of American Life*. New York: Russell Sage.

Campbell, D. T. (1963). "From description to experimentation: Interpreting trends as quasi-experiments." Pp. 212–254 in C. W. Harris (ed.), *Problems in the measurement of change*. Madison: University of Wisconsin Press.

Campbell, D. T. and D. W. Fiske. (1959). "Convergent and discriminant validation by the multitrait-multimethod matrix." *Psychological Bulletin*, **56**: 81–105.

Cannell, C.F., G. Fisher, and T. Bakker. (1965). Reporting of Hospitalization in the Health Interview Survey. Washington, D.C.: PHS Vital and Health Statistics, Series 3, No. 6.

Cannell, C.F. and F.J. Fowler. (1973). A Study of the Reporting of Visits of Doctors in the National Health Survey. Research Report. Ann Arbor, MI: Survey Research Center.

Cantril, H. (1965). *The Pattern of Human Concerns*. New Brunswick, N.J.: Rutgers University Press.

Coleman, J. S. (1964). *Models of Change and Response Uncertainty*. Englewood Cliffs, NJ: Prentice Hall.

Coleman, J. S. (1968). "The mathematical study of change." Pp. 428–478 in H. M. Blalock, Jr. and A. Blalock (eds.), *Methodology in social research*. New York: McGraw-Hill.

Coleman, J. S. (1981). *Longitudinal Data Analysis*. New York: Basic Books.

Cronbach, L. J. and L. Furby. (1969). "How to measure change — or should we?" *Psychological Bulletin*, **74**, 68–80.

Drury, D. W. (1980). "Black self-esteem and desegregated schools." *Sociology of Education*, **53**, 88–103.

Duncan, G. J. and D. Hill. (1985). "An investigation of the extent and consequences of measurement error in labor economic survey data." *Journal of Labor Economics*, **3**, 508–522.

Duncan, O. D. (1969). "Some linear models for two-wave, two-variable panel analysis." *Psychological Bulletin*, **72**, 177–182.

Duncan, O. D. (1972). "Unmeasured variables in linear models for panel analysis." Pp. 36–82 in H. L. Costner (ed)., *Sociological Methodology 1972*. San Francisco: Jossey-Bass.

Harris, C. W. (ed.). (1963). *Problems in the measurement of change*. Madison: University of Wisconsin Press.

Heise, D. R. (1970). "Causal inference from panel data." Pp. 3–27 in E. F. Borgatta and G. W. Bohrnstedt (eds.), *Sociological Methodology 1970*. San Francisco: Jossey-Bass.

Herzog, A. R., F. M. Andrews, and W. L. Rodgers. (1981). Measurement effects in surveys: Age differences. Paper presented at the 34th Annual Convention of the Gerontological Society of America, Toronto, November 1981.

Herzog, A. R. and W. L. Rodgers. (1981). "Age and satisfaction: Data from several large surveys. *Research on Aging*, **3**, 142–165.

Herzog, A. R. and W. L. Rodgers. (1986). "Satisfaction among older adults." Pp. 235–251 in F. M. Andrews (ed.), *Research on the Quality of Life*. Ann Arbor, MI: Institute for Social Research, The University of Michigan.

Hoelter, Jon W. (1983). "The analysis of covariance structures: Goodness-of-fit indices." *Sociological Methods & Research*, **11**: 325–343.

228

Johnston, L. D., J. G. Bachman, and P. M. O'Malley. (1985). *Monitoring the Future: Questionnaire Responses from the Nation's High School Seniors, 1983.* Ann Arbor: Institute for Social Research.

Johnston, L. D., P. M. O'Malley, and J. G. Bachman. (1984). *Drugs and American High School Students: 1975-1984.* Washington, D.C.: National Institute on Drug Abuse.

Johnston, L. D., P. M. O'Malley, and J. G. Bachman. (1985). *Use of Licit and Illicit Drugs by America's High School Students: 1975-1984.* Washington, D.C.: National Institute on Drug Abuse.

Jöreskog, K. G. (1973). "A general method for estimating a linear structural equation system." Pp. 85-112 in A. S. Goldberger and O. D. Duncan (eds.), *Structural Equation Models in the Social Sciences.* New York: Seminar Press.

Jöreskog, K. G. and D. Sörbom. (1978). "LISREL IV: Analysis of Linear Structural Relationships by the method of maximum likelihood." Chicago: National Education Resources, Inc.

Jöreskog, K.G. and Sörbom, D. (1984), *LISREL VI: Analysis of Linear Structural Relationships by the Method of Maximum Likelihood,* Mooresville, IN: Scientific Software, Inc.

Kenny, D. A. (1973). "Cross-lagged and synchronous common factors in panel data." Pp. 153-165 in A. S. Goldberger and O. D. Duncan (eds.), *Structural Equation Models in the Social Sciences.* New York: Seminar Press.

Kessler, R. C. and D. F. Greenberg. (1981). *Linear Panel Analysis: Models of Quantitative Change.* New York: Academic Press.

Lazarsfeld, P. F. (1948). "The use of panels in social research." *Proceedings of the American Philosophy of Sociology,* **92,** 405-410.

Liker, J. K., S. Augustyniak, and G. D. Duncan. (1985). "Panel data and models of change: A comparison of first difference and conventional two-wave models." *Social Science Research,* **14,** 80-101.

Neter, J. and J. Waksberg. (1965). Response Errors in Collection of Expenditures Data by Household Interviews: An Experimental Study. Bureau of the Census, Technical Paper No. 11.

Novick, M.R. and Lewis, C. (1967), "Coefficient Alpha and the Reliability of Composite Measurements," *Psychometrika,* 32, 1-13.

O'Malley, P. M. and J. G. Bachman. (1979). "Self-esteem and education: Sex and cohort comparisons among high school seniors." *Journal of Personality and Social Psychology,* **37,** 1153-1159.

O'Malley, P. M., J. G. Bachman, and L. D. Johnston. (1983). "Reliability and consistency in self-reports of drug use." *International Journal of the Addictions,* **18,** 805-824.

O'Malley, P. M., J. G. Bachman, and L. D. Johnston. (1984). "Period, age, and cohort effects on substance use among American youth." *American Journal of Public Health,* **74,** 682-688.

Panel on Youth of the President's Science Advisory Committee. (1974). *Youth: Transition to Adulthood.* Chicago: The University of Chicago Press.

Pelz, D. C. and F. M. Andrews. (1964). "Detecting causal priorities in panel study data." *American Sociological Review,* **29,** 836-848.

229

Presser, S. and Traugott, M. W. (1983). "Correlated response errors in a panel study of voting." Paper presented at the Annual Meeting of the American Association for Public Opinion Research, Buck Hill Falls, Pennsylvania.

Rodgers, W. L. (1977). "Work status and the quality of life." *Social Indicators Research*, 4, 267–287.

Rodgers, W. L. (1981). "Density, crowding, and satisfaction with the residential environment." *Social Indicators Research*, 10, 75–102.

Rodgers, W. L. (1982). "Trends in reported happiness within demographically defined subgroups, 1957–1978." *Social Forces*, 60, 827–842.

Rodgers, W. L. and D. Hill. (1985). "MCA statistics from a regression program." Unpublished paper.

Rodgers, W. L. and A. R. Herzog. (1984). "Response style characteristics and their relationship to age and to item covariances." Unpublished paper.

Schuman, H. and S. Presser. (1981). *Questions and Answers in Attitude Surveys: Experiments on Question Form, Wording, and Context.* Orlando, FL: Academic Press.

Spenner, K. I. and D. L. Featherman. (1978). "Achievement ambitions." In R. H. Turner, J. Coleman, and R. C. Fox (eds.), *Annual Review of Sociology.* Palo Alto, CA: Annual Reviews.

Tuma, N. B. (1982). "Nonparametric and partially parametric approaches to event-history analysis." Pp. 1–60 in K. F. Schuessler (ed.), *Sociological Methodology 1982.* San Francisco: Jossey-Bass.

Tuma, N. B. and M. T. Hannan. (1984). *Social Dynamics: Models and Methods.* Orlando, FL: Academic Press.

Wilcox, A. R. (1978). "Dissatisfaction with satisfaction: Subjective social indicators and the quality of life." Paper read at 74th Annual Meeting of the American Sociological Association, August.

APPENDIX

DEFINITION OF VARIABLES FROM THE
MONITORING THE FUTURE PANEL STUDY

Each of the two measures of subjective quality of life used as dependent variables in the analyses described in this report (i.e., satisfaction with life and happiness) was measured at all three points in time (base year, first follow-up, second follow-up). For each variable, a respondent who failed to answer the question at any time point was assigned a missing data code for all three points. This missing data constraint excluded about 5% of the 3209 males and about 3% of the 3,807 females who were respondents from the high school classes of 1976 through 1980 and who returned both of the first two follow-up questionnaires. The following three transition or change scores were computed for each criterion dimension: the base year score subtracted from the first follow-up score, the base year score subtracted from the second follow-up score, and the first follow-up score subtracted from the second follow-up score.

Table A-1 presents, for each criterion dimension, the question text and percentage distributions by sex for each of the three time points. Note that the satisfaction question was asked in only four of the five questionnaire forms; thus, the number of cases is lower for this set of variables. Table A-2 lists item text and derivation information for each of the predictor variables that are used in the various analyses.

231